SPORT AND NATIONAL IDENTITY IN THE EUROPEAN MEDIA

Sports, Politics and Culture
A series of books from Leicester University Press

Series editors: **Stephen Wagg**
Department of Sociology, University of Leicester
John Williams
Sir Norman Chester Centre for Football Research,
University of Leicester

Published:

Rogan Taylor   *Football and its Fans*

John Sugden &   *Sport, Sectarianism and Society in a*
   Alan Bairner   *Divided Ireland*

Forthcoming titles:

John Bale   *The Landscape of Sport*

Grant Jarvie &   *Scottish Sport in the Making of a Nation*
   Graham Walker

Stephen Wagg   *Football and Society in Different*
                              Continents

Sport and National Identity in the European Media

Neil Blain, Raymond Boyle
and
Hugh O'Donnell

Leicester University Press
Leicester, London and New York

Distributed in the United States and Canada by St. Martin's Press

Leicester University Press
(a division of Pinter Publishers)

First published in Great Britain in 1993

© Neil Blain, Raymond Boyle and Hugh O'Donnell 1993

Editorial offices
Fielding Johnson Building, University of Leicester,
Leicester, LE1 7RH, England

Trade and other enquiries
25 Floral Street, London, WC2E 9DS *and*
Room 400, 175 Fifth Avenue, New York, NY 10010, USA

British Library Cataloguing in Publication Data
A CIP catalogue record for this book is available from the British Library

ISBN 0 7185 1451 3

Library of Congress Cataloging-in-Publication Data
Blain, Neil, 1951–
    Sport and national identity in the European media / Neil Blain,
Raymond Boyle, and Hugh O'Donnell.
        p.   cm. — (Sport, politics, and culture)
    Includes bibliographical references and index.
    ISBN 0–7185–1451–3
    1. Mass media and sports—Europe. 2. Sports—Social aspects
–Europe. 3. Sports—Political aspects—Europe. I. Boyle, Raymond,
1966– . II. O'Donnell, Hugh, 1949– . III. Title. IV. Series.
GV742.B53   1993
070.4'49796—dc20   93–3441
                                                                        CIP

Typeset by Florencetype Ltd, Kewstoke, Avon
Printed and bound in Great Britain by SRP Ltd, Exeter.

CONTENTS

ACKNOWLEDGEMENTS

Chapter 4, 'Games Across Frontiers' was originally presented as a paper to the Fifth International Conference on Public Communication at the University of Navarre (November 1990) and appeared in an earlier version as 'Italia'90 en la prensa europea: historias de la vida nacional' (N Blain/H O'Donnell) in *La información como relato*, ed C Barrera and M A Jimeno, Pamplona, 1991. Our thanks to the University of Navarre for their permission to produce this updated English version.

An earlier version of Chapter 2, 'Footprints in the field' (N Blain/R Boyle) was given to the Fourth International Television Studies Conference, London, July 1991.

Some of the material in Chapter 7, 'Centrality and peripherality at the Barcelona Olympics', first appeared in a paper entitled 'Centro y periferia' (N Blain/H O'Donnell) presented at the Sixth Conference of the Association for Contemporary Iberian Studies, Universidad Internacional Menéndez Pelayo, Santander, September 1992.

Some of the material in Chapters 1 and 6 appeared in papers to the first two *Screen Studies* conferences at the University of Strathclyde in Glasgow: 'Fashioning the contours of a continent: the outline of a postmodern Europe on British television' (N Blain 1991) and 'When Boris met Michael: Wimbledon as international hypersymbol' (N Blain/H O'Donnell, 1992).

We should like to express our thanks to the many colleagues in other countries who provided so much of the material analysed in this book: Lars Åhlander, Monique Bailleul, Heinz Bina, Ignacio Burrull, Lino Carballo, François-Xavier Denis, Roger Glass, Hans Hognestad, Beatriz de Oliveira Jost, Jaume Marín, Wolfgang Mertens, João Carlos Silva, Fernando León Solís, Sabrina Torri, François Vion, the editorial staffs of *Il Tennis Italiano*, *Matchball* and *Sovetskij Sport*, and the former Scotland-USSR Friendship Society.

Thanks also for help and support to Desmond Bell, Galina Bondarchuk, Tony Fahy (RTE), Brian McDermott, Martin McLoone, Bill Scott, Ken Ward, Garry Whannel and John Williams.

Finally, we should like to express our gratitude to the following authors and publications for their kind permission to reproduce the cartoons which appear on the following pages of the book: p.49, Castellazi and *La Gazzetta dello Sport*; p.60, Juan Ballesta and *Cambio 16*; p.61, Horst Haitzinger and *Bunte*; p.62, M. Diakov and *Sovetskij Sport*; p.72, Chenez and *L'Equipe*; p.121, Stefano Ferranti and *Il Tennis Italiano*; p.137, 150, and 176, Bill McArthur and *The Herald*; p.176, Luís Afonso and *A Bola*; p.183, Miquel Ferreres Durán and *El Mundo Deportivo*; p.185, Antonio Mesa Madero and *El Diario de Burgos*; p.190 Nicholas Garland and *The Spectator*. The former Soviet weekly newspaper *Sovetskaja Kul'tura*, from which the cartoon on p.78 is taken, is no longer in existence and could not therefore, despite numerous attempts, be reached in relation to reproducing this cartoon. The cartoon itself was not attributed by *Sovetskaja Kul'tura* to any specific author.

1

SPORT AND THE REINVENTION OF EUROPE IN THE MASS MEDIA

CONSTRUCTING THE NATIONAL DIMENSION IN THE MASS MEDIA

PROBLEMS IN THEORY

We look in this book at the relationship between mass media accounts of the national dimensions of sport, on the one hand, and developing patterns of self awareness in a rapidly changing Europe, on the other. In doing so we are closely concerned *both* with matters of discourse and ideology *and* with the political economy of the mass media. This means an equal interest in sport and politics.

We acknowledge the theoretical complexity of this task – a complexity which particularly attends questions;

   i) of the relationship between signs and objects;
  ii) of hegemony and the state;
 iii) of the structure of media institutions, output and audiences;
  iv) of identity, and especially collective identity;
   v) of media imperialism.

Of these, we deal directly with iv) and v) in our General Conclusion, although inevitably we touch on them throughout, and a note on our use of the terminology of the 'national dimension' is appended to section 6 of this chapter. Our approach to topics i) ii) and iii) we explain below.

SIGN/OBJECT RELATIONSHIPS

Within the study of the media it was possible, until the 1980s, to conduct a comparatively innocent debate about the adequacy of metaphors like 'the mirror' or 'the window', which acknowledged the existence of a reality beyond discourse. But, with the growing influence of poststructuralist and postmodernist ideas greater caution became necessary in the use of words such as 'invention' and 'construction' and, likewise, of realist alternatives such as 'representation' and 'mediation'.[1]

Postmodernist rethinking of the idea of 'representation' reached its high point, or its nadir, depending on your intellectual persuasion, with Jean Baudrillard's celebrated assertion, in *Libération*, that the Gulf War 'never happened'![2] Well before this, though, the work of Foucault, Lyotard and others had begun a trend toward 'textualising' what had previously been considered factual accounts of real events, such as general elections or wars. In this perspective, history itself could be read as a kind of fiction[3] and the notion that 'reality' lay beneath or behind representations was challenged. This challenge seemed to be mounted most strongly in French and, to a lesser extent, American academic circles.

A number of theoretical strands have converged. These derive from readings of the work of thinkers such as Kant and de Saussure. This convergence had led, by the 1980s, to a widespread acceptance that to talk of the media 'representing' or 'mediating' a 'real world' involved some sort of philosophical decision.

This decision has clear political implications: political positions and political action become pointless if we believe that there is no world beyond discourse. (How, for instance, could we respond politically to the situation in Bosnia if we believed that there were only 'constructions' of Bosnia?) Indeed, hostility toward postmodernist theory has been based as much on political reservation as on philosophical objection.[4]

In this book we are happy to talk both of 'representation' and 'mediation' and of 'construction' and 'invention'. This is because it seems to us legitimate to acknowledge, on the one hand, that the media fabricate versions of social and cultural reality, while, at the same time, insisting that, beyond discourse, there is a *real* set of historical circumstances – which, in this instance, comprise the latest stage in European political development. So, for example, it's a *fact* that the Yugoslavian national football team was excluded from the European Championship of June 1992 because of upheavals in the former Yugoslavia. But that does not prevent us from regarding media accounts of the Serbian or Croatian national character as constructions.

So we are sympathetic to some of the poststructuralist and postmodernist arguments here, and adopt them where we feel they are useful. For instance, our analysis of the coverage of Wimbledon in the European media, and of some aspects of the style of satellite TV, uses postmodernism theory – in particular, to account for the consciously ahistorical formulations of national character and behaviour by the media in their treatment of sports events.

So we accept that there is both 'construction' and 'mediation', and that the latter encompasses an element of the former. We turn now to another important aspect of this debate about renditions of the 'real world'.

IDEOLOGY AND HEGEMONY

Postmodern writers, such as Lyotard, challenge the notion that language can convey truth. In doing so Lyotard draws not only on the work of Kant but on

Nietzsche's argument that truth equals power – that, in other words, no discourse is disinterested. Theorists such as Baudrillard have, for many, carried this argument well beyond the point of philosophical and political acceptability. But it's important not to lose sight of the fact that much discourse *is* in the interest of one agency or another.

We argue in the following chapters that many of the versions of Europe propounded by sports journalists are motivated, much of the time, by considerations of interest and power. Again, this will not mean that there is no appeal beyond discourse, but it will be necessary to investigate the politics of media formulations of sport and nation. This means looking both at the world of media politics, including the political economy of the media, and at the broader world of national political cultures – because this sort of sports journalism is important in the production and reproduction of ideology within societies generally. We consider in Chapter 4 how the interests of media institutions will help to shape discursive practice.

But, inevitably, the discursive output of the media is bound up with the interests of the state and later in this chapter we look at how the coverage of sports events, in the popular and quality newspapers and on television, becomes an articulation of various kinds of ideological position at the level of state interests.

We refer in the following chapters to the 'symbolic' operation of mediated sports events and to the role they play in the 'production' and/or 'reproduction' of ideology. John B. Thompson (1990), suggests there are five modes in the operation of ideology: 'legitimation', 'dissimulation', 'unification', 'fragmentation' and 'reification'. Thompson uses these concepts to explore 'strategies of symbolic construction' and 'the ways in which symbolic forms interact with relations of power' We are often concerned with what Thompson calls 'critical conceptions of ideology', because much of our analysis of the discourse of sports journalism leads us to use negative concepts such as 'falseness' or 'partiality'. However, like most commentators, we also use what Thompson calls 'neutral conceptions' of ideology – as 'systems of belief', 'sets of values' and so on.[5] And when we refer to the 'symbolic value' of mediated sports events we do so in the knowledge that their symbolic operation is complex, and with multiple effects, in some of which the concept of ideology may be only marginally useful. We're aware, in other words, that sometimes mediated sport serves political and economic interests, but that sometimes it doesn't have very much to do with power relations at all.

We also deploy the concept of hegemony in the following chapters, using the more complex view of social structure developed recently within the Gramscian tradition.[6] Nevertheless, we assume that it still makes sense to speak of a 'ruling class', especially when we deal with the United Kingdom and the British media, although we accept that its symbolic domination is far from uncontested. So the terms 'ideology' and 'hegemony' are used in a contemporary way: in reference to a symbolic domain in which groups compete for power and where the determining influence of relations of production is now one of a number of background questions.

The term 'discourse', which we use very frequently, we likewise use in its flexible sense of talking about or constructing, televisually or photographi-

Lit review

cally, versions of reality that are ideological. The word 'ideological', in this context can be either neutrally or negatively conceived. The role of the state in this process is elaborated later in this chapter.

MEDIA INSTITUTIONS AND THE FRAMING OF EUROPE

Television and the press need a variety of Europes. French television requires a different Europe from German television, Italian likewise from British, each in order to sustain a dialogue with national viewerships whose idea of Europe varies. Non-EC European countries require a different Europe again. Relations of dominance at a national level exert influence also: Portugal's Spain is different from France's, Austria's Germany from the rest of Europe's. And we might find complications within each national television institution – with different needs among different stations – and, at a more investigable level, from department to department within television.

Channel Four News (taking British examples) needs a different Europe from more popular news broadcasts. And whereas a programme on regional cuisine creates an 'authentic' France, and an upmarket travel show finds a 'hidden' France, light entertainment needs a France of Breton shirts, berets and baguettes, accompanied by silly accents and blasts of garlic. No decent arts programme would recognise this France, but television must – because of its markets – produce what, overall, will be an incoherent, internally contradictory version of other cultures and societies. At the same historical moment we might find, for example, sympathetic news and current affairs reporting of the break-up of former states of Eastern Europe alongside jokes about Trabants on alternative comedy shows and crude caricatures of Russian culture in advertisments.

Explicitly postmodernist television (BBC2's *Reportage*, Channel Four's *Europe Express*) periodically superimposes style paradigms over cultural investigation but probably the postmodern cutting edge of constructions of Europe is in advertising (see Chapters 2 and 6 for more on television, and advertising specifically).

The determinants of the nature of each national press are the nation's social and political structure and its associated cultural characteristics, the foregoing viewed historically (see Chapter 4). We require, in order to understand why Britain has the kind of popular press it has, and why *Gazzetta dello Sport* or *L'Equipe* would not interest most British football fans, to provide a historico-cultural explanation. If British class experience is to an extent unique – a product of exceptional historical continuities in British social, cultural and political organization – we would be inclined to relate the apparent peculiarities of the British press to these same oddities in British social and cultural experience.[7]

Sometimes we speak about the United Kingdom as in some sense categorically distinct from countries such as France, Germany and Italy for whom bases of mutual comparison are more easily laid. This is not to overlook the fact that each country is materially distinct, but simply to acknowledge – putting this very carefully – that various factors in the social, political and cultural history of the United Kingdom necessitate the country's exclusion from certain assumptions about the commonality of (some) forms of European experience.

So when we talk about the segmentation of the British press into quality and popular newspapers, and when we further define the point on the spectrum which particular newspapers occupy, we have in mind not only some very extreme differences in the form and content of newspaper reports in Britain, but also the correspondingly wide range of social and cultural experience which still persists in Britain on the basis of social class. The reporting of sport must be seen in this light.

The notion that football in Britain remains an essentially proletarian sport is well-established in Europe as well as in the UK. For example, the *Hannoversche Allgemeine Zeitung* of 8 June 1990 remarks that 'From the start football in England was a game for the workers, the industrial masses, while rugby was reserved for the upper crust, for "gentlemen"'. And indeed in 1993, football in the United Kingdom, though it has adherents from across the social spectrum, is still much more of a working-class sport than rugby union football, cricket or tennis, despite a strong role in working-class culture in parts of England for cricket.

The very operability of such a statement about the demographics of the football audience is itself a consequence of the enduring class divisions which are inscribed within British experience. In addition, the size and spread of Britain's politically and culturally isolated underclass provides a further point of contrast with most of the rest of Europe.

The reciprocities of the relationship between sections of the British working class and underclass with the most downmarket of Britain's tabloid newspapers produce some especially disturbing discourses on race, nationality and gender, though these discourses are not class-specific, and are found, often in a more diluted fashion, right across British society.

The question, to put it at its bluntest, as to when the *Sun* is serving its own interests and when it is serving the interests of the state is about as difficult a question as one might seek to resolve, given the inevitably soggy ground on which such an inquiry has to be made (often it is serving both).

Semiological theory supplies an immediate comment, namely, that the utility value of any edition or campaign will depend much on how the newspaper is read and in which particular symbolic context: the stories selling the *Daily Mirror* and the *Sun*, in August and September 1992, on the adventures of the Duchess of York and the vicissitudes of the life of the Princess of Wales, sold newspapers by the hundreds of thousands. But the question as to how far the interests of whichever parts of the British state were advanced or depressed is very complicated indeed. On the other hand, the consequences for power relations in the world of *realpolitik* might not be so hard to determine.

The English popular press has several roles, to take another example, in the 'production' of the English football fan. A producer as well as a reproducer of the incivility and brutality of attitude and behaviour sometimes exhibited by some England fans, this section of the British press may seem to have an interest in sustaining the myth of the English fan as a Neanderthal far different from his (usually 'his') continental counterparts: but we will have to disentangle an economic motivation from a political one. Just as the insensitivity of tabloid discourses on gender could be argued to do a little to perpetuate the domination of women by men, the violence of its discourses on football position the English working class – and underclass – in an unenviable role as insensitive, aggressive and inarticulate: and apparently it also sells newspapers.

And it's more complicated than that. First, the degradation of British tabloid language is now on tap for any sport, and the *Sun's* influence has spread widely. It has arguably spread beyond the tabloids, but it has certainly spread throughout the tabloids. When distance runner Liz McColgan came a disappointing fifth in the Barcelona Olympics 10,000 metre final, she wasn't, according to the Scottish *Daily Record*, 'disappointed' or even 'shattered', she was 'GUTTED', much as when Tom McKean had a similar Olympic disaster he was an 'OLYMPIC CHUMP'. The language of the tabloids when directed at foreign sports competitors can be breathtakingly hostile. We look at this in a sustained way in Chapters 4 and 6.

The question of inarticulacy is of particular importance. Articulate conversation is a prerequisite of democratic participation in political and social affairs and there has been in the British popular press a trend increasingly to proscribe language of any subtlety or intelligence.

The literariness of, say, some French and Italian sports writing, to which we turn our attention in several following chapters, contrasts markedly with certain generic features of British sports journalism. Probably only cricket in England licenses on any significant scale sports journalism with aspirations toward literariness, despite one or two exceptions among sports journalists whose identity is strongly marked by literary writing (as exceptions, in other words, to a general rule). Bill McLaren's especially literate rugby commentaries on TV are another exception. In cricket journalism, John Arlott was probably the best recognised of stylists, though the radio commentaries of Henry Blofeld have extended this tradition, made more interesting by the element of self-parody which in England can be the necessary cost of such linguistic adventure.

Applying our model of the differential needs of television to what has been said so far about the requirements of British newspapers, we can see that different versions of Europe will be required according to the market position of newspapers and the nature of the sport concerned, these two factors themselves enjoying an inevitable structural relation.

In fact there are some quite complicated permutations in operation here. Football, for example, may be a predominantly working-class sport, in the sense here that media audiences for football will tend (with various qualifications) to be mainly working class. But there is a lot of middle class interest in football (we must leave unanswered some questions here about the differences between 'interest' and 'commitment' in this respect). Reporting in the British quality press will require some sort of discursive compromise between the conventions of journalistic style appropriate for newspapers like the *Guardian* and *Scotsman* with substantial socio-economic group A, B and C1 readers, and the symbolic resonances of the sport itself in British cultural life.

This requires considerably more of a compromise in the UK than in France or Italy, for example, where journalists can display without embarrassment an often very literary form of engagement with the game.

But it is necessary, before proceeding further, to be more explicit about the structural components in operation in the construction of other cultures attempted by the mass media. We wish now to consider more directly the question of broader ideological interests in sports journalism and to map as explicitly as we can the framework in which cultural production of this sort takes place.

MASS MEDIA, STATE AND POLITICAL CULTURE

Points of reference: the symbolic terrain of sport

The analyses in the following chapters concentrate chiefly upon media discourse and to a lesser extent in certain chapters also upon the political economy of TV terrestrial and satellite broadcasting.

However two more domains are often referred to, namely that of 'the state' and that of 'political culture' generally. In a book already as wide-ranging as this concepts such as these cannot be given any detailed attention, but nor do we wish attributed relationships connecting these four domains to appear to be taken for granted.

Neither can we offer any detailed analysis of relationships between media output, media institutions, states and political cultures in those many countries outside the UK whose sports journalism we analyse. Such a task would be implausibly ambitious, though periodically, for example in our discussions of Spanish/Catalan tensions over the Barcelona Olympics, and of the former Soviet press, we do provide complementary insights.

We none the less conceive of a quadripartite relationship linking MEDIA DISCOURSE with MEDIA INSTITUTIONS, THE STATE, and POLITICAL CULTURE which in this book is handled explicitly only in relation to the UK (and to an extent the former USSR) but which ought to provide some sort of template for speculation about the political and ideological ramifications of analyses of European and American sports discourse. This may at least offer the benefit of pointing up a number of very fruitful areas for future work. But it should also provide a productive set of terms in which to compare and contrast British media/cultural relationships with others.

We are aware of the dangers of generalising about the relationship between discourse and the other terms on our map and we recognise the need to refine any local discussion with an eye on the specificities of every instance. It is often initially attractive to make comparisons between phenomena of various kinds in different regions of Europe, yet most analysts will find that as their work progresses they become more conscious of the specific and local and less convinced by apparent similarities.

It is therefore desirable to keep in mind probable differences occurring in:

The relationship between, in particular, specific political cultures and their media institutions and outputs;

The kinds of media organization and practice which develop in different regions or states as a result of the previous relationships;

Television and press practice in mediating or constructing discourses linking sport with national dimensions;

Discursive practice in terrestrial and satellite television;

Discursive practice in the popular and quality press;

Discursive practice in the framing of different sports.

Our recognition of these differences underpins all the following chapters.

In the various analyses which follow, it would not be practicable continually to refer back to the various components of the complex theoretical background we have outlined. This means that the connections we adduce between different domains of social, cultural, and symbolic life may occasionally seem audacious. We make a number of assumptions about homologies and actual relationships between and among a number of widespread components of social, cultural, and explicitly economic or political life which we cannot invariably stop to justify. But, in simple terms, we believe that behaviour and discourse in sport and media coverage of sport can be used to inform our understanding of much broader political questions. For example, we assume, as do other commentators,[8] that sports fan behaviour tells us something about British or Russian or Swedish or Italian society and that discursive framing of the idea of 'the fan' is likewise diagnostically important.

A case study

An analysis of a short feature article on tennis personalities will illustrate how some of the theoretical approaches outlined above may be put into practice. We have chosen an example which extends the field of discussion beyond Europe, as we will periodically do in the following chapters, though the dominant motif of 'Latinity' in what follows operates transcontinentally.

The British tabloid newspaper *Today* (27 June 1990) carried a Wimbledon piece on Argentinian tennis player Gabriela Sabatini and a little-known English player called Sarah Loosemore. 'IN THE CLASH OF CULTURES THE A-LEVELS ALWAYS WIN' reads the odd and rather ambiguous headline, followed by the parenthesis 'How the priorities of genteel Sarah mean she will never be a match for devoted Sabatini'. 'Gabriela Sabatini has the Latin killer instinct. Her only aim is to win'. She was, we are informed, 'brought up in Argentina, where sport is seen as a passport to the better life'. 'Sarah Loosemore, on the other hand' (the piece continues) 'is a cool English rose, whose tennis ability surprised many when she beat No. 16 seed Barbara Paulus on the first day of Wimbledon'.

Two subordinate pieces on the contrasting lives of the two girls reveal a periodically utilised discourse of British common sense and instinctive amateurism as set against a foreign ethic of unfair and unbalanced competitiveness. Sarah and the other British girls, we learn, 'may not have the killer instinct of Gabriela Sabatini', but despite their tendency to lose all their tennis matches, they are in fact happier, Sarah being a prime example. 'Tennis, while remaining her first love, doesn't rule her life and she has remained remarkably unfazed by life on the international circuit'. She is also ranked world number 99, which though it makes her a fairly significant tennis player may also explain the difference between her attitude and that of Sabatini's. (In fact, although styled an 'English rose', she comes from Wales.)

On the other hand, 'winning is what really matters to tennis millionairess Gabriela Sabatini. She wants to be the best . . . success means everything to her. And when she doesn't achieve it quickly or decisively enough, Latin temperament takes its toll'. The two subordinate headlines sum it up. 'Game plan for balanced life', reads the headline over 'Sarah's story', while above Gabriela's tale is the daunting 'Bitter battle to be the best'. This piece demonstrates well enough the way in which sport and politics intersect. The political content of the piece implicates both questions of gender and of national character – here, also, transnational character in the notion of 'Latinity'.

The article assigns feminine values to Sarah Loosemore, through the hackneyed metaphor of the English rose, here 'cool' to contrast with the heat of Latinity. To assign contrasting masculine values to Sabatini ironically demonstrates the manipulativeness of the discourse. Generally, Sabatini's femininity is the focus of tabloid journalism, since she is held to be the most physically attractive of top-ranked female players. 'Gentility' as an aesthetic and moral attribute of Englishness has, again, seldom been part of the tabloids' vocabulary but in order to structure as marked a contrast as possible, the 'fair play' motif of the English symbolic structure of sport seems the most persuasive resource, along with more general devices such as the use of Loosemore's forename and Sabatini's second name.

To attribute 'killer instinct' to Latin culture seems puzzling in a number of ways.

The implied version of Sabatini's Argentine nature, which is a potent underlying force in the article, might not remind us only of the conflict which had taken place eight years before between Britain and Argentina. It could just as well remind us that the 'killer instinct' had been shown most effectively by the British forces. In general, 'killer instinct', as we demonstrate in several following chapters, is if anything supposedly a German characteristic. Latins from Brazil to Italy are generally accused of lack of 'character', here meaning 'grit'. To state that sport is seen as 'a passport to the better life' in Argentina ignores the utility value of sport in each and every society in which it appears and is of course thereby absurd. The point depends upon an available myth of Argentinian 'underdevelopment', here in contrast to the supposed achievement of British social and cultural aims.

We now discover that none of the British girls has the 'killer instinct', which confirms the apparent proposition that this is a national trait. Instead there is common sense and balance, partly explained by the fact that Sabatini is driven by desire for money – 'winning' is what matters to the 'millionairess'. This suggestion qualifies what is then said about Sabatini's desire 'to be the best' (she really just wants the money). The other component of the British sporting temperament – its quintessential amateurism – has now, in the age of

Linford Christie, Frank Bruno and Paul Gascoigne, been dusted down in the interests of rhetoric.

The mobility available in the marshalling of symbols of national traits is then demonstrated by the return to the 'weak' conception of the Latin personality – its 'temperament', the word itself in this context as it often does ('artistic temperament', 'female temperament') invoking a negative conception of personality. Here, the reference is to the 'weakness' of Latin character. This weakness endures despite having to cohabit with a 'killer instinct' and participation in an ongoing 'bitter battle'. This sort of internal discursive incoherence is something we discover again and again as journalists try to maintain the validity of fixed conceptions of national character against inescapable evidence of their inadequacy or inapplicability. We discuss a number of these moments of contradiction in later chapters, as we do the idealisation of history beneath this discursive conservatism. There is no space here for a comprehensive analysis of this piece that would trace all its symbolic and ideological connections and resonances. But it will be useful to note the kinds of questions it raises, and to do so in relation to the list of variables which we outlined above.

A full analysis of this piece would need to take into consideration a number of relevant factors in the social and cultural formation of the British popular press and its readership, as well as the economic context in which *Today* functions, both on its own terms and as a newspaper in the upper band of the British tabloid spectrum. This would be necessary in order to understand questions of why the newspaper speaks to its readership in this manner and what it is readers understand by this sort of piece, which is by no means clear. Considerations of specific discursive practice in different segments of the press and in relation to different forms of sport would need to be added. We could then begin to address questions of how meanings associated with gender and class are negotiated by the readership, what sorts of underlying views of foreignness, Latinity and Argentinianicity are present in English thought and specifically in the socio-economic groups primarily addressed by *Today*, how far this is a piece enabled by the specific parameters offered by tennis as a sport, and other similar questions.

A larger topic would be that of the relationship between, on the one hand, the types of cultural and social agreement achievable by parts of the readership over the various symbolic propositions of this article: and, on the other, the maintenance and/or development of existing sets of power relations characteristic of British society. The forms of operation of ideology suggested by Thompson (1990), which he stresses will in practice overlap, might operate here. Two of Weber's grounds for *legitimacy* (rationality, tradition) are visible: what is being legitimated may be seen as, to take just three examples, our relations with Argentinians, Latins or just foreigners: a social system in which the social dominance of the A-level gaining, tennis playing classes is naturalised: and a gendered account of behaviour in which it is seen as unnatural for women to want to compete in the way men do.

That *dissimulation* is present will be clear enough by now, not least the concealment of the economic drive in British sport as in all sport (not to mention the central fact of the perpetual ineffectiveness of British tennis).

Unification – 'a form of unity which embraces individuals in a collective identity, irrespective of the differences and divisions which may separate them' – is clearly present in the appeal to an idea of 'Sarah and the other British girls', but it operates even more significantly in the idea of a wider typicality ('English rose'), extending into the supposed consensus participation of the readership. This appeal to unification occurs again and again in sports journalism. We look at some especially striking examples in the chapter on Italia '90.

Fragmentation – 'orientating forces of potential opposition towards a target which is projected as evil, harmful or threatening' – is here in abundance, all the more pointed because that part of the discourse which is specifically about politics, about the relations between Britain and Argentina, may well be read by significant portions of the readership as the 'real' meaning of the piece.

Thompson's fifth category of *reification*, with its strategies of *naturalisation* and *eternalisation* can be observed quite specifically. The balanced, sensible calm of the English girl as 'cool rose' seems 'the inevitable outcome of natural characteristics', the maturation of a particular type of temperament in a particular moral climate.

What Thompson calls *eternalisation* – 'social-historical phenomena are deprived of their historical character by being portrayed as permanent, unchanging and ever-recurring' – is, though we would have reservations about the term itself, a feature which is again very important, in the following chapters, in the way nationalities are figured in relation to considerations of *character*, of national or sometimes (as in Celtic 'character') transnational, or regional, '*typical personality*'. Here, 'Latin temperament' is an ahistorical given, an attribution whose existence works to obliterate material conditions and material change.

The relationships between media institutions and the state are complex and certainly no less so in Britain than elsewhere. In Chapter 2, we speculate further about the reproduction of ideology in the context of development in delivery systems. But our assumption is that, to put it in simple terms, British media output is ideologically conservative on the whole and frequently quite remarkably consistent in its support for a number of existing relations of dominance in British society.

We shall seek in various examples to point out links between the operation of media sports discourse and the possible interests of states as they occur in practice. We do so against the background of a well-researched debate about clear links between state apparatuses and media organizations in Britain and elsewhere, so that examples of heavily interested discourse are simply some among a wide range of possible points of reference from which to construct a model of the ideological operation of the mass media.

MEDIATED SPORT AND POLITICS

Today many people engage with professional sport principally via media coverage of sporting events. The depth and range of audience reached by sports journalism is immense. Coverage of sport accounts for a large section of the television output of most European countries.[9] Television coverage of sport has transformed the relationship between sport and its vastly expanded audience (See Chapter 3). In part through its relationship with the medium, sport has become intertwined with advertising, marketing and corporate business (Whannel, 1992). In terms of political economy, quantity of output and international audience reach, sport and its relationship with the various media is a particularly rich field for investigation.

As we argue below, there are other equally valid reasons for examining media sport, and what we wish to do in this section is to explore further some of the issues and debates clustered around sport, the media and national identity, now focusing on the existing sports literature. We start by briefly reviewing some of the previous writing on sport and identity, specifically that relating to questions of nationhood and nationalism. For example we wish to look at the relationship that has always existed between politics and sport. This approach is then developed by reviewing the important role played by the media in disseminating ideas about what sport is and what it represents. A further step will be to look at the perceived impact of the 'new technologies' of satellite and cable, and of the globalisation of media sport on aspects of national cultural life.

For the purposes of this discussion the term sport will encompass not only the codified games, but also the institutional structures within which they are located. Until recently relatively little academic attention was focused on sport as a cultural form. However, recent work in social history, sociology and to a lesser extent cultural studies has done much to establish a body of work concerned with the cultural, economic and political significance of sport. As Jones argues: 'sport in industrial societies is an important economic, social and political activity in its own right, able to provide the specialist with vital evidence about labour markets, capital investments, class, gender and even international relations'. (Jones, 1992:2)

Due in part to the universality of sporting activity, sport has been an important cultural arena through which collective identities have been articulated. Writing as a social historian, Holt has documented how the political history and economic relationship of Scotland and Wales with England has been mediated through sporting occasions:

> Sport acted as a vitally important channel for this sense of collective resentment . . . Football gave the Scots a way of fighting the 'old enemy', whilst addiction to rugby came to be one of the major ways in which the English defined the Welsh and the Welsh came to see themselves. Cultural identity was a two way process. (Holt, 1990a: 237)

This viewing of cultural identity as a continual process which is subject to political, economic and cultural influences has already been stressed, and is a theme to which we return throughout the book.

While politically the United Kingdom is a single state, at many international sporting events, and within the domestic sport arena, it has four 'national' identities (though arguably, given the periodic Northern Ireland/ Republic distinction in team formation this is sometimes yet more complicated). Scotland, a nation without a state, can compete in the 1992 European Football Championships and exhibit to a wide international television audience a distinctive identity not wholly subsumed within a British discourse. This sense of distinctness was heightened, to choose one of many possible examples, by the treatment of the contrasting behaviour of the Scottish and English fans at the European Championships in Sweden in 1992. The Deputy Commissioner of the Stockholm police, commenting on the trouble caused by some English supporters at the Championships noted: 'I can't understand what makes these people act like this. The Scottish people have behaved extremely well and are very happy. It's strange that on an island two groups of people can behave so differently' (*Guardian* 19 June 92).

Other examples of similar comments are noted in Chapter 4. English newspapers do not seem averse to reporting such comments, though it is chiefly their coverage in Scotland which may be assumed to feed a sense of collective national identity. It also has other consequences. After the defeat by Switzerland in Scotland's first World Cup qualifying match in Autumn 1992, Scottish journalists were becoming weary of the Scottish fans' performance of endlessly durable good nature. The fans' rapturous response to defeat was widely considered pathological. It would appear that the reputation of English fans for anti-social behaviour has had an as yet insufficiently analysed effect on their Scottish counterparts, who may be performing in a consciously different way as a symbol of national difference. Other tensions can also be reproduced through sport, such as in Northern Ireland where specific games can carry with them connotations which link participants and followers (rightly or wrongly) with wider cultural and political configurations on either side of the sectarian divide. (Sugden and Bairner, 1993).

Organised sport has been viewed by governments of all political persuasions as an important sphere in the forging of 'national character', with the project often serving specific political ends. Shaw (1985), documents the politicisation of football in Francoist Spain during the period between 1939–75. Franco was not alone in attempting to align sport, and due to its universal popularity football in particular, with specific political regimes (Hoberman, 1984). This process takes place most notably at the level of international sport, and world-wide sporting competitions such as the Olympic Games or the football World Cup.

In the past, countries such as the former Soviet Union and the GDR (German Democratic Republic) directly linked the health of the state to its ability to perform successfully in the international sporting arena. Competing in international sporting events televised around the world can be an important element in the legitimation of political and cultural groupings. It can also provide examples of national disintegration. The Soviet Union qualified for the 1992 European Football Championships in Sweden, but had to compete (for one last time in international football) under the banner of the Commonwealth of Independent States (CIS), while fragmented and warring Yugoslavia were not allowed to take their place in Sweden by UEFA (Union of European Football Associations) despite the apparent willingness of the team to participate. The 'new' nations of Europe such as Lithuania, Latvia and Estonia, are all anxious to a secure a place in the international sporting arena, and thus compete as separate nations before the televisual audiences of the world.

This linkage of political discourse with sport is still evident throughout the developed and developing worlds. During the 1992 visit of the Brazilian football team to Britain, the team, in an effort to recapture past glories, decided to reject what they viewed as the 'Europeanisation' of their football and instead to revert to their 'original' playing style. The crisis in Brazilian football acquired a political dimension when the Brazilian President Fernando Collor suggested that the country's 'economic, social and political problems went hand in hand with the national team's crisis'. 'If our soccer is doing well, the country will do well', he suggested (*Herald*, 15 May 92). The image of football from the developing world is extensively discussed in Chapter 4.

Another recent example of the overt linking of sporting activity to political rhetoric was evident with the re-entry of South Africa into world cricket against a backdrop of political upheaval in that country. The relative success of the South African cricket team in the 1992 Cricket World Cup in Australia and New Zealand was used by President F. W. de Klerk as a political vindication of his reform programme and the need for these reforms to continue. As Matthew Engel commented:

> This was South Africa's first big post-boycott sporting success, just three weeks before the whites' only referendum on President F.W. de Klerk's negotiations over a democratic South Africa. A No vote would certainly lead to a return to sporting sanctions. The president was quick to make the connection. He sent a telegram to the team: 'The cabinet and I, together with the whole of South Africa confirm our Yes! for our cricket team.' (*Guardian*, 27 February 1992)

There is further coverage of explicit linking of sporting and political themes in the European press in the final section of Chapter 4.

To view this use of sport as some form of simple political manipulation by powerful interest groups in society is, as will be clear from what has been said above, both simplistic and patronising. It ignores the contradictions, tensions and struggles that exist within all national cultures.[10] Donnelly (1988), has argued that sport is a central area of cultural struggle, which has been used by various groups in society for their own particular ends, for instance the turning of that most imperial of English games, cricket, by the West Indies, into an expression of West Indian culture, and their using it as an international platform symbolically to contest the dominance of their former colonial rulers.

Sport was also used by the cultural nationalists of Ireland during the last century as a way both of reclaiming their cultural identity and of helping to forge a new Irish nation (Mandle, 1987). The setting up of the Gaelic Athletic Association in 1884 to promote Irish sport was part of a wider political programme to regenerate a cultural nation subject to colonial rule. As Holt comments, the founder of the GAA Michael Cusack stressed 'Irish ethnic distinctiveness through sport.' (Holt, 1990a: 239) Thus while sport, particularly international sport, has been used by governments and states as a form of political socialisation in an attempt to build or reinforce some homogeneous 'national collective', it is not an uncontested area.

Much of the placing of sport within a broader economic and political perspective has come from social historians. However, few have addressed the task of examining the role that various forms of media have played in any cultural process involving sport. That task has more often than not been taken on by academics working within the realms of sociology and the social sciences.[11]

An important strand in media coverage of sporting activity has always been keen to portray it as an apolitical arena, a space where people and countries come together in friendship (see Chapter 7 for further discussion). Whannel (1983) shows how much time is spent both in the media and within sport itself, decrying the intrusion of politics into sport. Yet it is this veneer of political (in the widest sense of the word) neutrality that gives media sport much of its ideological potency. Whannel notes how 'many people who laugh at the monarchy identify with their national football or cricket teams. Terms like English or British derive much of their significance from national sporting traditions. Sport provides us with a sense of belonging to a nation, however irrational that may be'. (Whannel, 1983: 27) Needless to say, given our later concerns, we are also conscious of tendencies in sports journalism which result in a much more overtly political handling of the topic.

The most fruitful academic and journalistic work into the area of sport and culture has emphasised the need both to historicise (in its purest sense) the development of sporting tradition and to place it within an explicit socio-economic framework which views sporting activity as an active constituent of the social process.[12] However, much of the sociological and historical writing on sport has not concerned itself directly with its relationship to collective identities.

In modern societies much cultural experience is gained through the mass media. Thompson talks of this process and tendency as the 'mediazation of modern culture' (Thompson, 1990: 3). While acknowledging that sport has played an important role in the process of identity formation – in the national aspect of identity as well as in class, race and gender formations – we are particularly concerned with the role of the media in this process.

Sport has its own dynamics and ideologies which develop in relationship with the societies in which it originates and is pursued. Increasingly however the expanding range of media is playing a central role in producing, reproducing and amplifying many of the discourses associated with sport in the modern world. It is that process and its ideological consequences which are of particular interest to us.

Thompson argues that:

Pop music, sports and other activities are largely sustained by the media industries, which are not merely involved in the transmission and financial support of pre-existing cultural forms, but also in the active transformation of these forms. (Thompson, 1990: 163)

It is this process of transformation which much of the recent writing on media sport has centred on (Goldlust, 1987, Whannel, 1992). As in other areas of media/communication studies the debates surrounding media sport and cultural production have tended to reflect the wider polarisation of research that exists within that academic field: between matters of political economy, on the one hand, and cultural representations on the other.

Barnett (1990), is a good example of an empirical strand of the former, providing us with an account of the economic relationship that has developed between sport and television both in Britain and the United States during the last 30 years. Whannel (1992) not only draws on aspects of political economy, but also addresses a range of key ideological questions clustered around the construction of sport through television coverage.

Both Goldlust (1987) and Whannel (1992) examine the role that mediated sport plays as a form of symbolic ritual in many modern industrialised societies (a concern dealt with in Chapter 3).

Hargreaves conceptualises the relationship between politics and sport in the context of the organisation of power in society:

> the sport – power relation is very firmly premised on the twin notions that sport is, above all, best categorised as a cultural formation, and that cultural elements constitute absolutely fundamental components of power networks. (Hargreaves, 1986: 8)

Much of his work addresses issues relating to sport and class, gender and ethnicity, as well as national identity. While our main focus is on the latter, we are aware that all these components are central to the constitution and reconstitution of a range of collective identities.

NOTE ON THE TERMINOLOGY OF THE 'NATIONAL DIMENSION'

In our General Conclusion, we address the question of 'identity' in its national and related dimensions on the basis of our analyses in the intervening chapters. However we must make some declaration about the use of terminology in advance, given the imprecise use and understanding in the communication and social science fields of terms like 'national identity' and 'nationalism'. We will not be much concerned with the phenomenon of *nationalism*, in its sense of political mobilisation, though we will have cause to note that some of the rhetoric of nationalism will be duplicated in discourses on other aspects of what we have called the 'national dimension'. By 'other aspects' we have in mind the way in which an awareness of or belief in aspects of national character, national difference or national identity become symbolic and/or ideological elements in processes of cultural production and exchange. We return to that element of collective identity termed 'national identity' in the conclusion.

In the following chapters we use separate terms such as 'nationality', 'national dimension', 'national feeling', 'national character' and 'national difference' for greater terminological precision. This will do two things. First, it will differentiate processes of typification, by clearly marking judgements applied to national cultures by others from beliefs nations have about themselves. Second, it should help focus on the specific nature of beliefs and attitudes – for example, the idea that the Germans or the English have a 'national character' which in fact amounts to a 'typical personality'.

NOTES

1 The most useful discussion of the earlier period was probably in Raymond Williams (1977) *Marxism and Literature*, Oxford, especially part II, 'Cultural Theory'.

2 'La guerre du Golfe n'a pas eu lieu', *Libération*, 29 March 1991. The sense in which Baudrillard was claiming that the war 'had not taken place' is a complex one. The phrase used is in fact an allusion to the title of the play 'La guerre de Troie n'aura pas lieu' by the French playwright Jean Giraudoux. In other words, the claim is arguably about 'theatricality' – that is to say the media rhetoric of the war – rather than its 'non-existence'.

3 For example, the nature of the 'history' of Auschwitz in Jean-François Lyotard (1988) *The Differend: Phrases in Dispute*, Manchester. See also Christopher Norris (1990) *What's Wrong with Postmodernism*, Hemel Hempstead. Also Mark Poster's (1988) *Jean Baudrillard: selected writings*, Cambridge.

4 Both kinds of concern are evidenced, for example, in Dick Hebdige (1988) *Hiding in the Light*, London, more polemically in Christopher Norris (1992) *Uncritical Theory: Postmodernism, Intellectuals and the Gulf War*, London.

5 John B Thompson (1990) *Ideology and Modern Culture*, Cambridge pp.59–73.

6 See E. Laclau and C. Mouffe (1985) *Hegemony and Socialist Strategy*, London.

7 See for example Jim White, 'Real footballers use the sink', *The Independent*, 12 January 1991, noting the almost complete absence of middle-class professionals from the British game, and claiming that boys at Harrow refer to the game as 'Kev-ball'. For a wider, albeit contentious discussion of the peculiarities of British class experience, see Tom Nairn's (1981) *The Break-up of Britain*, 2nd edition, London, and (1988) *The Enchanted Glass*, London.

8 See John Williams, Eric Dunning, and Patrick Murphy (1989) *Hooligans Abroad*, 2nd Edition, London.

9 For a breakdown of the amount of time devoted to sport throughout Europe see Special Report: Sports, *TV World*, April 1992.

10 An example from within football culture is the less than enthusiastic support given to the Scottish national team by a large section of the Celtic support due in part to the feeling of supporters being made unwelcome by the abuse certain sections of the crowd give to Celtic players who are representing their country. In part this merely reflects wider tensions within Scottish society, and in particular the west of Scotland, see R. Boyle, *Celtic F.C., Celtic supporters and Questions of Identity in Modern Scotland*, paper presented at International conference on Sport, Culture and Identity, University of Aberdeen, April 1992.

11 See Richard Holt (1990a) *Sport and the British*, Oxford, appendix on Some Observations on Social History and the Sociology of Sport. As an example of current social history writing on sport and also to emphasise how it increasingly pulls from academic areas outwith the field of history see *The International Journal of Sports History*, Frank Cass, Manchester.

12 From within academia see Hargreaves, (1986), Jarvie (1991) and Mason (1988), Williams and Wagg (1991), as examples. From journalistic encounters with sport, on snooker see Burns, (1986), on racism and English football see Hill (1989), and on the world of professional boxing see Hauser (1988).

2

FOOTPRINTS ON THE FIELD: TELEVISED SPORT, DELIVERY SYSTEMS AND NATIONAL CULTURE IN A CHANGING EUROPE

INTRODUCTION

We are still encountering contradictory views of the likely development of cable and satellite in the UK. From an industry view that the spread of cable is inexorable (however slow) to predictions of stasis in the cable industry and heavy losses on satellite broadcasting, the range of prognoses is wide.[1]

Much debate over the impact on audiences and cultures of new delivery systems and market deregulation has suffered from a tendency to accept partial and frequently only provisional aspects of broadcasting development as the whole and stable picture. Even before investigating some particularly exacting questions about the impact of a new broadcasting environment on audiences and cultures, we need to be clearer about just how greatly altered a broadcasting environment is in prospect.

There is a background to this chapter, then, of debate in two related domains. One is that of the political economy of the mass media and the other is that of the relationship between the mass media and the daily reconstitution of cultures. (For our purposes this latter will be most interesting where it impinges especially on questions of the culture of nationhood.)

It is hard to generalise about current directions in these debates, but some pattern is discernible even if it is uneven. Put simply, there has been a retrenchment in both areas. Where not so long ago a significant number of commentators assumed that the transformation in delivery systems would be certain and relatively swift, now,[2] the discussion is informed by an economic realism which recognises that technological possibilities are not necessarily translated, and certainly not immediately or even quickly, into widely sought commodities.

British comment has perhaps been rendered periodically more apocalyptic than it might have been because of the pervasiveness, even in the oddest circles, of some of the myths of Thatcherite radicalism. At the 1990 Edinburgh International Television Festival's closing session, for example, there was a feeling in the air that the duopoly were doomed and that Ted Turner and Rupert Murdoch were past the gate and on the way to the citadel. The fictive scenario under discussion was the battle to acquire rights to the televising of an important future Royal event. The point of debate centred around the removal from the public service sphere of this important national-symbolic occasion (we consider the significance of these events below).

It is not that we lack examples of actual developments to fuel such fears, either within a British or European context. We examine the 1992 BSkyB deal involving the FA English Premier League below, while elsewhere in Europe the case of the European television rights to the 1989 Wimbledon Tennis Championships serves to illustrate such fears.

The All-England Tennis Club employed Trans World International to sell the European television rights of the championship. BBC TV deals directly with the All-England club. The European public service consortium, the EBU, usually purchase these rights, however it was UFA, the television arm of the German publishing giant Bertelsmann, who outbid the EBU and secured the exclusive European rights. The consortium had offered between £15-20 million, higher than it had ever bid before, but was outbid by UFA. In turn the Germans then offered to sell the rights to certain public service stations at an inflated price, but they refused to do business. Having failed to reach agreement with this group UFA turned to the private sector and sold the rights to private TV companies and cable networks throughout Europe. Despite a public outcry and intense lobbying of politicians the five year contract remains intact.[3]

The apparent softening in the British context, however, of an ideological approach by government to PSB has required a revaluation of the position of the duopoly. The fears expressed by so many broadcasters over the last few years, while far from groundless, have possibly been exaggerated, a judgement strengthened by a growing financial realism affecting our conception of the relationship between terrestrial broadcasting and new forms. Therefore we propose a view governed by an awareness of the specificity of media industry cases, and the provisionality of present instances. This cautious approach holds good for politics, too. None the less our interest in sports broadcasting is partly conditioned by awareness of its innovative role in effecting actual change.

Caution will be extended to the second, much more theoretical, domain mentioned above. The retrenchment here has been, again unevenly but discernibly, from a position in which were exhibited various often gloomy concerns with the putative disappearance of national and regional and even supranational cultures (e.g. Europe's, among those who thought it had one): to an increasing awareness of the simplifications which might have been responsible for both an overestimation of the transformative power upon culture of the mass media and especially broadcasting, and a corresponding undervaluation of the importance of the various other components which give national and regional cultures their distinctness.[4] This trajectory has implications for another kind of discourse about homogenising influences on culture, one which prefers to welcome a presumed longer-term dissolution of national boundary marking influences in the realm of human relations, especially across major racial and world-economic divisions.

We adopt what may have to be seen as a conservative approach to prognostications about large-scale change to the national and regional dimensions of cultures brought about by changes in the delivery and content of broadcasting.

What follows is in two main sections. The first deals with the political economy of European satellite broadcasting and its interplay with the terrestrial companies. The second part addresses questions of sport and national culture, comparing aspects of terrestrial sports broadcasting with that by BSkyB. We have selected Sky Sports because of its domination of the British satellite sports market – such as it is.

1 EUROPEAN TRENDS IN SATELLITE SPORT: SOME OBSERVATIONS ON FINANCE AND CONTROL

Pan-European satellite broadcasting has been a financial disaster. Rupert Murdoch's Sky Channel closed its European offices in January 1989. By this time Murdoch had turned his attention towards the British broadcasting market which was in the process of being fundamentally restructured. It also marked a move towards a DTH (Direct to Home) system of delivery. By 1989, the then Chief Executive of Sky Television, Andrew Neil, could declare, 'We see Sky as a British popular entertainment channel' (cited in Collins, 1989: 367). It appeared that while the pan-European dimension in broadcasting held much appeal to advertisers, the publics of Europe responded with less enthusiasm.

Despite the programming schedules of the ITV-backed SuperChannel and other stations, language remained a key cultural barrier that hindered the creation of a homogeneous European viewing public. Sky TV, launched in 1982, had experienced the same resistance, as cultural and linguistic tastes varied from country to country.[5]

One area of pan-European television programming that seemed to offer the best possibility of transcending cultural differences between countries was that of sport. The major pan-European sports channel was Screensport, which was first transmitted in 1984. The parent company was initially W.H. Smith TV. Its footprint covered northern and western Europe and it was relayed along with Superchannel and Sky Channel via cable throughout Europe. Despite Screensport being the most popular of the new channels it was not initially a success story.

Now part of The European Sports Network (TESN) owned by Capital Cities/ABC (50 per cent, Capital Cities/ABC also own the American ESPN sports and entertainment channel), Canal Plus (25 per cent) and Compagnie Générale des Eaux (25 per cent), much of its programming is American in origin, while it has suffered in direct competition with the EBU-backed Eurosport. Recently Screensport has successfully taken Eurosport to the European Commission over unfair access to major EBU controlled events (*Satellite TV Finance*, 25 June 1992). The TESN channel is transmitted in four languages: in German it is Sport Kanal, in French TV Sport, in Dutch Sportnet, while Screensport is in English.

Eurosport, formerly owned by Rupert Murdoch, is now controlled by TF1 in France, and gets its programming through EBU members, including the BBC. It has successfully covered the World Cup, Rugby Union football and carried Spanish league football. In August 1992, it was available in 35.89 million homes throughout Europe, making it the European satellite channel with the largest network (*Satellite TV Finance*, 20 August 1992). However the recent (June 1992) EC Commission ruling which declared its cartel agreement with the EBU as impinging on free competition (the claim brought by Screensport), looks like leading to the station coming under increasing pressure in the future.[6]

Steven Barnett (1992), has argued that the problems facing pan-European sport channels arc two-fold. Firstly, European countries have different cultural attitudes to different sorts of sports, in other words what is popular in one country may not be in another. Secondly, within European broadcasting the centrality of public service broadcasting has resulted in a very national centred view and presentation of sport. The domestic sporting arena has usually been the most important for broadcasters, with international events being presented specifically for that domestic market (scc previous chapter). As TESN realise with their four language split, it is how the action is interpreted, and not just the pictures of the event, which are important. As Barnett comments:

> Despite, therefore, a single market of around 280 million television homes with the potential economies of scale well in excess of America's mere 220 million, it is a fractured and fragmented market for most television sport, possibly football and tennis being the main exceptions. (Barnett, 1992: 11)

As we will see below, within a British context, the tradition of universal access to sporting events is under threat: increasingly, to enjoy a major television sporting event you must have the financial ability to purchase a satellite receiver, or subscribe to a cable network. The cost of watching sport may not be complete even when receiver and decoder have been paid for. As we see later BSkyB have introduced a subscription charge to decode their Sports Channel, with plans to eventually make a number of its individual sporting events subscription based. In Europe subscription sport is already a reality. Canal Plus, one of the commercial French television stations whose development has been facilitated by a deregulated broadcasting system, has the exclusive rights to screen live French league football. While you can watch most of the channel's output on an ordinary TV set, the signal is scrambled as the match kicks off. A decoder and subscription fee are required to watch the game.

In America cable sports networks are geared towards a pay-per-view system of sports watching. It is not cheap for the armchair fan. W.J. Weatherby comments that:

> . . . you need roughly an extra $60 (about £40) a month to pay the cable fees plus

the occasional $20 or $30 for a ticket for exclusive coverage of a major event – usually boxing – by closed–circuit television. It makes sport an expensive hobby even if you never leave home. (*The Guardian*, 10 September 1986)

At the moment public service television offers the sport, and the sponsors, access to a potentially large audience. It also guarantees that the viewer can see major sporting events for the relatively minimal cost of a licence fee. As the costs of securing television rights to sport spiral, sport must address itself to examining the reasons why it wishes to secure a place in the 'sky revolution'. Can cricket and football truly claim to be Britain's national games when they are only available to a select television minority? More to the point for this chapter, how will they be reconstructed, if at all, in their national dimension, by satellite broadcasting, not least in the circumstances of increasing exclusivity? (We look at the ideological implications in section 2 below). The increased competition to secure sport for television is having a marked effect on the sports programming policies of all the terrestrial channels.

As noted above, ITV's sports programming policy is undergoing fundamental change as the network itself enters a period of uncertainty with the implementation of the Broadcasting Act (1990), resulting in the restructuring of the network into Channel 3 from 1993. (It has already suffered the blow of losing out on English Premier League football to both the BBC and BSkyB) The BBC appears in a stronger position. Traditionally noted for its superior sports coverage, it has secured a number of contracts, which while costing the Corporation more than it would have liked, guarantee a degree of stability in its sports programming. However the fallout from a 'freer' broadcasting market place is being felt everywhere.

No longer is sport guaranteed its place in the schedules. It has to produce the viewing figures to hold its position. This also leads to a curtailment in the sports television chooses to cover. British TV's coverage of athletics for example, tends to focus on the glamour events of the track (television having helped to create that aura of glamour). In contrast, other European countries tend to show an equal interest in the more technical field events, with television the ideal medium for transmitting and enhancing the viewers' understanding of the technical skills involved. However in Britain, athletics meetings staged for television in many cases do not have a field events programme, because sports producers do not feel that the audience is interested enough in the events. This is also the case with the European athletic Grand Prix which is staged purely for television.

Allied with the linking of news values to a channel's sporting output is the decrease in the already limited range of programmes on wider sporting issues.[7] Garry Whannel has noted that:

. . . for 30 years, television has presented sport very professionally, but its ability to report the affairs of sport has been abysmal. Issues such as drugs, apartheid, the growth of sponsorship, football hooliganism, the re-organisation of the Sports Council, and indeed the central role played by television itself, have invariably been reported poorly or neglected. (*Broadcast*, 17 February 1989)

Quality sports journalism costs money, while 'action' footage can be cheaply purchased from the Trans World International catalogue.

Economic pressures on the public service broadcasters dictate the programming policy of the sports departments, while the new satellite sports channels in search of an audience are going to be able to stray only so far from a path of tried and trusted sports presentation and programming. (We look also at this aspect of satellite output in section 2).

RELATIONSHIP BETWEEN TERRESTRIAL AND SATELLITE BROADCASTERS

The launch in February 1989 of the Astra satellite carrying Rupert Murdoch's Direct to Home (DTH) Sky channels supposedly heralded a new age in consumer choice for the television viewer. As the battle to entice people to buy an Amstrad-built dish receiver got under way (amid a chronic lack of dishes in the shops), it was first-run movies that were held up as the major enticement to the potential viewer. Sky's all sports channel, Eurosport, also featured prominently in Murdoch's promotional material.

British Satellite Broadcasting, which secured the British DBS franchise, began beaming down from its Marco Polo satellite in the spring of 1990. Included in its initial five channels was a sports channel which broadcast thirteen hours of sport a day. Unlike Eurosport which like Screensport beams across north west Europe, BSB was aimed (literally) at Britain and Ireland. The existing terrestrial channels provided 2,800 hours a year of sports coverage. When satellite channels were added, this figure rose to an astounding 16,500 hours per annum.

Suddenly the governing bodies of sport found themselves with a number of potential clients for their product. So large are the amounts of money which satellite companies were (and are) prepared to pay in order to secure exclusivity that many governing bodies of sport feel compelled, in the short term, to take the money and attempt to renegotiate with the terrestrial channels at a later date.

However the financial clout required to launch and develop satellite television was enormous. It soon became clear that two competing systems, launched during a recession and dogged by technical and manufacturing problems, would not be viable, and on 2 November 1990 BSB 'merged' with Sky. To all intents and purposes it was a Sky-driven take over, with BSB and Sky having spent a combined total of £1.25 billion in their attempts to establish a foothold in the British satellite market, with Sky losing up to £10 million a week (Chippindale and Franks, 1991). Out of the merger came the Sports Channel, and a commitment that the newly titled company BSkyB would be aggressively looking to build a powerful sports portfolio with which to attract new dish owners, which would in turn allow them to extend the subscription base of their audience.

This is the background to the 'Sky' revolution that has taken place within British sport during the last couple of years. However to view this as a straightforward fight between the traditional terrestrial channels on the ground and those in the air is to misunderstand the situation. There is no simple dichotomy of terrestrial and satellite sport, the picture is more complex, and predates the 1990 merger.

In 1988/9, Andrew Croker, then head of sports programming at BSB, and Adrian Metcalfe, former commissioning sports editor at Channel 4 and then head of Murdoch's Eurosport channel, both viewed their stations as not being in direct competition with the terrestrial channels. Adrian Metcalfe explained that:

> . . . terrestrial television has become much more concerned with ratings. [Sport] is being pushed to the margins. [Eurosport] will not be competing [with], but complementing the Beeb and ITV. (*The Independent*, 2 February 1989)

ITV had axed a number of sports from its portfolio, among them darts, which, while having good viewing figures, did not attract the type of viewer that advertisers were interested in. ITV Sport began to concentrate on providing boxing, football and athletics as the backbone of its sporting schedules. The securing for four years, at a cost of £11 million a season, of exclusive rights to cover the English Football League in 1988 was central to this policy.[8] Channel 4 had also trimmed its sporting coverage. It stopped covering snooker because it felt that it did not attract the viewer with the social profile that the station wished to sell to advertisers.

There were not only changes in programming. At ITV, their Head of Sport John Bromley left the network in 1989 after twenty five years to work in the independent sector. The network began to dismantle its sports department and move towards the Channel 4 policy of commissioning sports programming from individual companies. ITV also decided that it would not cover the 1992 Olympic Games in Barcelona as a result of its inability to capture a large enough section of the audience, despite the sizeable investment in its coverage of the 1988 Games in Seoul.

Section 14 of the Broadcasting Act (1990) lifted restrictions on the securing of exclusive rights to what have become known as the 'six sacred cows'. These national events were the boat race, the FA Cup Final, Wimbledon, Test matches, the Grand National and the Derby. For a number of reasons, most of these events have been covered almost solely by the BBC. However section 14 of the Act now lifts any restrictions on satellite companies buying the exclusive rights to any of these events and thus gaining a foothold in the market.

As a result of the new competition, terrestrial broadcasters also forged alliances with their satellite rivals. This was particularly true in the case of coverage of Scottish football within Scotland. There the take up of BSB squarials was not movie driven, but football driven.[9] As Bob Hunter, then M.D. of The Sports Channel noted,

> Scotland is a very important market to BSB in our development and distribution. Scots tend to watch more sport than people in other parts of the United Kingdom and everyone is aware of the passion Scots show towards football. We are making a major investment in Scotland and Scottish football. (cited in Forsyth, 1990:168)

BSB's weekend Scottish League and cup highlights were in fact those broad-cast earlier in the day by the Scottish terrestrial channels. For example on a Saturday night, BSB's programme carried extended highlights of the match shown earlier in the evening by BBC Scotland's *Sportscene*, while on a Sunday the same applied to the match carried by Scottish Television's early evening programme *Scotsport*.

Among Scottish supporters, especially in the west of Scotland, BSB became synonymous with football. Lower attendances at some of the tele-vised matches caused an outcry among some football observers. As a BSB spokesperson in Scotland commented:

> It was an astonishing turn around, in the space of eight or nine weeks, BSB went from being an irrelevance to something that was threatening the very future of Scottish football. (Dishing up a Healthy Diet, *The Scotsman*, 15 October 1990)

It appeared that despite the international age of the satellite, *domestic* coverage of Scottish football was viewed by broadcasters both inside and outside the country as being commercially very important for that particular market: something that is equally true in other European countries such as Germany (TV World's guide to Germany, *TV World*, September, 1992). However the complexities of the new sports broadcasting environment are best illustrated by briefly examining the fallout from the most expensive sports-television deal ever done in Britain: the securing in 1992 of the rights to show English Premier League football for the next five years by BSkyB and the BBC at a cost of £304 million.

TELEVISING PREMIER LEAGUE FOOTBALL

A protracted and controversial bidding auction between ITV, the BBC, BSkyB and the newly created FA Premier League, resulted in BSkyB secur-ing the exclusive rights to broadcast live Premier League matches, with the BBC carrying highlights on a Saturday night, at a total cost of £304 million over five years. Following the success in securing the exclusive live rights to the 1992 Cricket World Cup, on the back of which an additional 100,000 dishes a month were sold (*Independent on Sunday*, 24 May 1992), the securing of live English football was viewed as an audacious coup. The deal, which would pull top live English football from terrestrial television, raises a number of issues.

Firstly, it again highlights the strange alliances being struck between broad-casters. Many people viewed the development of satellite television in Britain as a major threat in the long term to the BBC, yet it appeared to be aiding BSkyB, at the expense of its terrestrial rival ITV.[10] The deal also raises the question of cross-media ownership and influence. Some of the most vocifer-ous supporters of the controversial contract were to be found in the Murdoch owned News International newspapers (ironically also some of sternest critics of the BBC).

However perhaps the most significant feature of the deal is the introduction of subscription sport in Britain at the expense of the traditional notion of the universality of British television sport. While increases in dish sales are important, it is the advent of a fee of around £5 a month to watch the Sports Channel that will make or break the deal (and BSkyB?). By June 1992 the number of homes with dishes was put at around 2.3 million, with a 45 per cent subscription take up on Sky Sports (*Satellite TV Finance*, 17 September 1992). By the end of the century it has been forecast that 10.2 million homes will receive Astra channels, 7.4 million with dishes, and 2.8 million through cable (*Satellite TV Finance*, 17 September 92). With the BBC's Charter up for renewal in 1996, what is clear is that the relationship between broadcasters and sporting organisations in Britain will never be quite the same again. For BSkyB, Premier League football looks like allowing the company to participate in the whole new ball game that is British broadcasting in the 1990s.

2 SPORT, DELIVERY SYSTEMS AND NATIONAL CULTURE

We wish to draw into relationship here the discourses, myths and ideologies of sport with those of the culture of national feeling and identity, examining both in the light of our discussion of developments in European satellite sports broadcasting above. We intend to examine specifically the interaction between satellite and terrestrial sports broadcasting in this domain. Negrine and Papathanassopoulos have argued that:

> . . . the internationalisation of television is a mosaic made up of many parts: politics, technology, business, diplomacy and industrial policy. (Negrine and Papathanassopoulos, 1991: 29)

This compound approach is welcome, as is the authors' relative caution in their formulation of what 'internationalisation' is likely to mean in practice. However we should prefer to add to that list, in order to bridge the gap between the domain of political economy and that of discourse, ideology and culture, a problematic concerning the further 'internationalisation' of discourse, myth, ideology and identity. For it is the implication that the latter is an imminent consequence of the former which gives a sharpened political edge to the debate, albeit that we may wish to retain scepticism about developments in both domains.

The discourses of sport and of national identity are interrelated in a structure whose complexities we look at in Chapters 1 and 4 and in the General Conclusion. What we want to do here is to point out that the relationship has a number of specific dimensions which need to be borne in mind when attempting to make generalisations. The relationship will be affected by the medium under discussion, by the sport, by the socio-economic group targeted by the producer, and by yet other factors. The specific role of various sports in specific countries has to be considered, as well as the nature and functioning of the mass media in specific countries. For example, the UK has a popular press whose equivalent cannot be found in Europe, and consequently produces idiosyncratic discursive forms, especially in relation to football, and football and national identity. (See Chapter 1)

As we've seen in the previous chapter, the political role of certain key sporting competitions gives them the status of political rituals, symbolic events important in the maintenance (reconstitution, reproduction) of a sense of national community and mythic and ideological communion (Chaney, 1986). However this political element is embedded with uneven visibility in much of the discourse generated in connection with all sport. In explicitly national or subnational/regional competition, such as the World Cup and European club competitions in football, or in the Home Countries annual rugby football competition, or in Northern English *vs* London club football matches, or a football match between Real Madrid and Barcelona, or Milan and Naples, there is a requirement that the event should be partly constructed in this discourse of national/regional identity: both, in a sense, in order that it can be consistently comprehended, and also because of the interest of the producers (or 'reproducers') of the discourse.

These producers may be variously conceptualised. They may be, say, the sport programming or marketing departments of broadcasting stations, or journalists on *The Sun*: or of course we may look, depending on our object of investigation, 'behind' these visible instances in discursive reproduction to the interests of 'the state' or of 'capital' or wherever we are inclined.

Suffice it to say here that in the instances both of sport events with a salient national dimension and of those in which this dimension is only intermittent or latent, our assumption is that we shall require to deconstruct the relationship between sport and national identity with an eye on the question of whose interests are being served by particular compound formulations.

SPORT AND NATIONAL CULTURE ON TERRESTRIAL TELEVISION

Terrestrial broadcasting has over a number of years evolved discursive habits and traditions in relation to the (broadly speaking) national-political dimensions of sport. A number of aspects have received attention elsewhere (Whannel, 1992, Goldlust, 1987)

It would appear that it is, in the sense implied above, in the interests of terrestrial broadcasting frequently to implicate sport in the politics of national culture. We might speculate that this would serve more than one purpose, and that some of these purposes are a consequence of forms of agency operative in superordinate spheres, rather than engendered within broadcasting. To approach the Home International rugby matches, for example, as 'national events', is not to be seen as a broadcasting initiative, for it is more complicated than that, and is a form of negotiation between and among broadcasters, the audience, the Royal Family, government, other sectors of the mass media, and sponsors. The very sort of debate which has recently taken place over the 'amateur' status of the Scottish, Welsh, Irish and English rugby union international game opens up in an intriguing manner questions about the symbolic utility and practical functions of their related events.

It is in the interests, then, of a number of parties that it should become a sort of national habit to listen to Bill McLaren commentating on Calcutta Cup matches and that, in a complex way, the availability of the match on public service broadcasting and specifically on the BBC, and in the presence of the

Princess Royal, and so on, should become a component of the British way of life. This example, for instance, is one of the many ways in which the potentially difficult relationship between England and Scotland is mediated on television, but also is thereby mediated by political culture. This involves, not least, controlled, harmless, therapeutic symbolic displays of English and Scottish nationalism. And the match, along with its present symbolic accoutrements, also serves the purposes of the Royal Family, the sponsor, the Scottish and English middle classes, the public school system, gendered accounts of power, idealist attributions of historical continuity, the matchless broadcasting skills of the BBC, and, in the occasional event of a Scottish Grand Slam, the Borders knitwear industry: and that list is far from exhaustive.

The role of the Boat Race, and of other sports évents serving analogous purposes, has been the subject of a degree of commentary. Beyond these most obvious instances, most sports commentary which we can encounter on terrestrial television will, like most discourse of any kind, support a distinct compound of interests. For example, if the attribution of stability is desirable with regard to British society, then the British football game will become comprehensible through a series of 'givens' which are ahistorical and understood in an essentialist manner, such as the 'flair', 'passion' and 'inconsistency' of the Scottish football game, or the 'grit' of sportsmen from Northern England. (This is as distinct from the sheer talent of Southerners: mythically, Scots and Northerners have qualities like 'flair' and 'grit', as compensations, while the Irish labour incessantly: and the Welsh remain enigmatic).

SATELLITE SPORTS BROADCASTING AND NATIONAL CULTURE: A SEPARATE ACCOUNT FROM THE SKY

Given the power of the interests vested in broadcasting conservatism, of which we have given examples from the sporting arena, it would have been surprising if the operations of ideology within British culture had failed to (co-)produce a discourse of fear and disapproval of the less controllable developments in satellite broadcasting. But the City has seldom been squeamish about such matters, and sees its interests clearly enough beyond the forms of the present (albeit usually not very far beyond). Since Thatcherism was so central an expression of both the opportunism and the limitations of City philosophy, the facilitation of satellite expansion by the British government under the conditions favoured was hardly surprising. The contrast of positive anticipation and fear of what satellite would bring which could be detected emanating from different components of the ruling metropolitan consciousness owed their particular admixture to the distinct structures of a British establishment which has to contain contrary interests.

A possible model for the contrast, if there is one, between satellite and terrestrial sporting accounts, is that satellite broadcasting will be formed, as a result of the differences in its mix of interests, in a different mould: it may not, or need not be encumbered with quite the same ideological responsibilities of terrestrial sports broadcasting in those areas where discourse about national culture and identity is most evident. We should qualify this statement by acknowledging (a) that ideology cannot necessarily just, as it were, be left behind with a change in broadcasting organisation and (b) both terrestrial and satellite broadcasters will carry forms of sports programming in which this set of arguments barely applies.

It might even be that satellite sports broadcasting style would consciously try to eschew the sort of reconstitution of the British self and state, and the corresponding construction of various Others, which seems in particular sports programming areas to recur on terrestrial television: not least because of marketing considerations, and not least if it wishes to market cosmopolitanism. And also, as we imply above, in the altered audience conditions whereby it is plain that 'the nation' is not watching the event but rather a small minority of its citizens.

Referring back to the trends among commentaries on mass media developments cited at the opening of this chapter, one might say that we could have been expected to approach the matter of satellite sport with certain preconceptions. Among the elements present in our thinking would be, as well as aspects of debates about media imperialism/cultural homogenisation, yet other debates about the ideological consequences of multinational media control: about European and American culture: about local needs in the face of globalising tendencies: and about the idea of 'Europeanisation'. And it would have harmonised well with earlier concerns about the effects of satellite broadcasting on national cultures to assume that the style of sports broadcasting emanating from above would somehow be less 'national' and more 'international' in style, whatever that would tend to mean in practice.

Of course, neither the programmes nor the ideologies are anything other than terrestrial. It is still worth stating this with a certain emphasis. But the very fact of producing, say, a major weekly programme of Italian league football for the (mainly) British viewer is an ideologically significant act in itself, although its fuller significance will lie in the choices made about how to construct a meeting of British and Italian culture, as Jock Brown, Martin Tyler, Graeme Souness or Trevor Francis mediate the Italian game. We return to this in detail, below.

We are going to restrict our textual examples to BSkyB (mainly in deference to the finite limits of this chapter). In doing so, we have in mind that its existence serves the interests of groups well beyond its investors, and that regarding it as an expression of British interests, as well as of American/ Australian ones, is legitimate. Yet precisely one of the considerations of satellite broadcasting uppermost in arguments about sovereignty in cultural production is the question of 'foreign' ownership. When placed beside the case of the British press, this may hardly seem to be an issue at all, but in comparison with the terrestrial duopoly, of course, a real contrast comes into play. So, in sports broadcasting, as in other areas of broadcasting, we will have in mind the possibility of 'neglect' of national culture.

ASPECTS OF PROGRAMMING AND TELEVISUAL STYLE ON SKY SPORTS

The most important general tendency to observe in BSkyB's sports coverage is its eclecticism, an eclecticism not only with regard to the provenance of its programmes in production terms, but a partly consequent heterogeneity of styles, modes of address, and discursive operation. We say 'partly consequent' because its heterogeneity is also a function of certain aspects of house style. (Incidentally, we would argue that this eclecticism is typical of satellite sports broadcasting in general.)

This is not to argue that terrestrial sports programme style is uniform, of course. For example, *Saint and Greavsie*, the football entertainment programme shown up to 1992 on ITV on Saturday afternoons, had been an attempt to compensate for an absence of hard sports coverage by substituting 'personality' values. The operation within sports broadcasting of values associated with showbiz or television personality formats can be detected variably in other areas of terrestrial output, and one might think of the very different styles of coverage typical of ITV and BBC athletics coverage.

Both BBC and ITV carry sports programmes produced by other companies, so that, say, aspects of both American and Australian broadcasting styles are familiar from duopoly programming and Channel 4.

However, we want to argue that sports programming on the duopoly channels occurs, however variably, within a perceived framework whose elements are built round a semi-stable core. This structure may be conceived in different ways, as a structure built in one sense of programming components, but which is also a structure of discourse, myth, ideology, and, very importantly, history.

For although sports such as snooker and darts have, in practice, made huge inroads into sports programming, terrestrial sports output is still understood and reproduced within the national memory as structured upon certain cornerstones, many of which have national significance: Wimbledon, rugby league and rugby union cup and international matches, the Grand National, key football fixtures, and the major international competitions such as football's World Cup and the Olympic Games.

That the traditional conception of terrestrial sports broadcasting lags behind actual developments may in itself be interesting: at any rate, the fact is, as we indicate above, that accessibility to certain, say, football events, has already been reduced because of satellite. Nonetheless, the context in which terrestrial sports programming has taken place has been one in which it is possible to speak of an overarching ideological framework which suggests stability and some degree of unity in shared national values.

A quiz show such as David Coleman's *A Question of Sport* acts, along with the recurrence of deeply familiar presenters such as Harry Carpenter or David Vine, as one of a number of conjunctive instances within the ideological syntax which makes sports programming a whole at some level of comprehension and enables thereby its consistent if highly complex ideological operation. Sportspersons from a number of fields come together largely to make sporting history coherent and to make a sense of sporting community plausible. An upstart, ideologically unassimilated sport like snooker can commune with a national game like cricket through the appearance of Steve Davis with Ian Botham.

It has already been suggested that satellite programming is unlikely to mark any sort of ideological severance from terrestrial programming, given its firmly terrestrial base, and, consequently, we do not argue that satellite sports programming is in any sense 'ahistorical'. The mere presence of a famous footballer like Ray Wilkins or Trevor Francis as commentator carries a sense of historical and ideological continuity with the discourses of terrestrial programmes.

However, we do wish to argue that the sense of an ideological design which also implicates the construction of a particular set of historical purposes is, to put it at its most cautious, a different matter when regarding satellite programming. That is to say, we would not wish to suggest that there is no ideological coherence to satellite programming, but if there is a coherence it is the coherence principally of the marketplace rather than that of the stability of the British nation.

We shall begin by looking briefly at the coverage of Italian football, which was carried on BSkyB up until the end of the 1991/2 season, and which is now being shown for at least one season on Channel 4. (Early season Channel 4 coverage of the top Italian league *Serie A* is notably 'Gazzacentric', preoccupied both with Paul Gasgcoine and his club Lazio at the expense of live coverage of some of the bigger Italian clubs such as Milan and Juventus.) On BSkyB, of note, first, was the fact that there was remarkably little reference at all to the presumed Italianicity of the matches. We have noted, for example, that the Scottish commentator Jock Brown would cover a whole game without any more reference to the nationality of the players than he would make if covering a Motherwell *vs* Dundee United game in Scotland.

In fact the interest was chiefly technical, and further characterised by an open admiration for the Italian game which was unqualified and wholehearted: 'wonderful skill, magnificent skill there from Berti' says Martin Tyler of an Inter Milan match and Trevor Francis adds 'what have we got, two foreigners on the pitch, Matthäus and Julio César, it's an Italian show'. This is not to say that there is never any qualification of any kind based on the strong foreign presence in *Serie A*, but the persistent references, say, to Milan's then Dutch trio or Inter Milan's Germans, which characterises some of the terrestrial output ('Chris Waddle's Marseilles', 'Gary Lineker's Barcelona', 'Jackie Charlton's Ireland', or now 'Gazza's Lazio' and 'David Platt's Juventus') seemed to be missing. (Indeed, it is generally only foreign (i.e. non-Italian) players in *Serie A* whom BSkyB's commentators seemed prone to identifying in national terms: Trevor Francis has Lothar Matthäus putting away a goal 'with an efficiency you can't credit really'.)

A discussion of how the emotional English player Paul Gascoigne may fare in the Italian league was completely free from any impingement from those discourses of British/English national interests which are never wholly absent from terrestrial coverage, suggesting in conclusion that in essence he may as yet lack the experience to co-exist with Italian referees: if anything it was an Italocentric conclusion from an English commentator.

We might say that it was the football that was being sold chiefly as a product, much as we would expect to be sold pasta or, to broaden the European perspective and avoid an uncomfortable comparison, German cars or French perfume. In fact, and in a rather refreshing way, the implication of the manner in which this Italian football programme was marketed, designed and presented is that it was uncomplicatedly evident that Italian football was a superior product. In other words, if a particular ethic dominated here, it was a consumerist one.

The title sequence could not be more different from the Pavarotti-drenched discursive paralysis of the BBC's Italia '90 sequences. There is no signifier anywhere to be found of Italian emotionalism or of any presumed character-istic of Latinity: instead, the suggestion was chiefly of exclusive access to the facts of the Italian game, with a montage of Italian football press reports acting as a visual backing for instances of skill and excitement from a selection of matches. The Italo-literacy suggested by this opening montage as well as by the commentators' very informed comments on events within the Italian football world confirm one's view of this element of BSkyB's coverage as technicist-consumerist, an intelligent connoisseur's selection from the European supermarket, from the delicatessen, as it were.

There could be no greater contrast than between this and Sky Sport's American-produced *Power Hour* of especially histrionic wrestling. The *Power Hour* is not mediated in any way for British audiences and therefore maintains a mode of address entirely suitable for a particular segment of the American audience. As conceded above, this is not without parallel on terrestrial broadcasting although (say) Channel 4's coverage of American Football is mediated for the UK audience. But the *Power Hour* is an extraordinarily American spectacle. Even by wrestling standards, this presen-tation is inordinately given over to showbiz values: in one bout, a glamorous 'personal assistant' of a rival promoter stalks the ringside while making an 'analysis' of the bout on the laptop computer which she carries with her. The camera and commentary are as interested in her as they are in the match. So the supermarket is a world supermarket and *Serie A* football and American wrestling are two selections.

The eclecticism of programming and the freedom of stylistic borrowing in the trailers and presentation frequently create some rather bizarre conjunctures.

A West Indies *vs* Australia cricket match is publicised by a trailer invoking a large range of clichés about West Indian life (for example heat, passion). A trailer for British rugby league football intercuts shots of the game with shots of a cheetah hunting and bringing down a gazelle, a rhinoceros charging at the camera, and two lionesses fighting: the voice over is particularly strident

> Go, go, go for it!! Go for rugby league on The Sports Channel! Every Sunday evening!! Only the fittest survive in the tough, mean, world of British rugby league! The best teams, the biggest clashes . . .

The same ideological/discursive structure is invoked in relation to the selling of Scottish Cup football where Scotland's football is full of 'flair and passion', and where, again, 'survival [is] solely for the fittest'.

What these instances indicate to us is that in no sense is BSkyB consistently eschewing the sorts of deployment of traditional discourses of national or regional character familiar from terrestrial broadcasting. In fact, in this marketing context, BSkyB is reproducing them in especially vigorous form, and outdoing even the Coleman-Motson-Hill conjuncture of BBC football coverage. It's all a question of what is appropriate for the selling of particular products. Italian football is known to be very good, and does not need this kind of marketing. Scottish football is known to need marketing. The overriding principle behind the televising of both, however, is to obtain viewers in economically restricted circumstances, and this project is (relatively) unclouded by other principles.

To complicate matters a little further, much of the actual coverage as distinct from the publicising of these cricket or rugby events does not in fact significantly differ stylistically or discursively from terrestrial TV at all. The tones of Ritchie Benaud, the Australian cricket commentator, are as pervasive in the sky as they are on the BBC's own coverage and that which they import from Australia's Channel 9. The view of the game of cricket or of British rugby league from BSkyB is not in fact radically or even very different from the views of these games available on terrestrial television. So part of BSkyB's discursive mix is a familiar part. (Though as it happens, and as a result of the commentator mix as much as anything, some of the occasionally rather contentious racial innuendos which periodically seep into BBC cricket coverage at lax moments on warm uneventful days do not seem as likely to be reproduced in this context. Echoes of Empire still reverberate around BBC's Test Match coverage: cricket as seen on terrestrial television is an ideology intensive sport.)[11]

The question of televisual style cannot be explored in any detail in this chapter, but it is worth noting that the forms of eclecticism we have identified have their parallels in, for example, the variable pace of cutting during links and between trailers and programme starts. BSkyB at times uses a fast-cutting style more reminiscent of the staccato continuity of US TV presentation than the carefully punctuated progress of terrestrial TV, but again this is not a uniform factor as it is on US television. Interestingly, while the BBC started using graphics depicting satellites around the time when that sort of technological competition was making itself felt, the BSkyB sets are less hi-tech in appearance than the one currently used, for example, in *Grandstand*, but that should require no explanation. Similarly, the approach to employing presenters and sports pundits has been a mixture of unknown faces and familiar personalities such as Sally Gunnell and Andy Gray.

That BSkyB will not fit into a pattern with regard to discursive formulations on national culture should not, of course, be surprising. That it may share certain of the discursive characteristics of duopoly sports culture is inevitable, in the sense that history and ideology are inescapable, and, furthermore, because there may in certain instances be some similarity of marketing requirements. But that BSkyB should not participate in aspects of the ideological project(s) of duopoly sports broadcasters was likely, given the relative purity of BSkyB's commercial drive, and appears to be confirmed by an examination of its products.

CONCLUSION: THE STATE OF PLAY

While satellite sport treats eclectically the construction of versions of national character and identity, the position on the ground, so to speak, is not entirely stable. In media coverage of sport generally, that is to say both in the press and on television and radio, often aggressive appeals to a chauvinistic sort of national sympathy are becoming more frequent and, in some quarters, more strident.[12] It is difficult to say how far this is a British characteristic, to what extent an English one. We have noted evidence of this in England and in Scotland, certainly. The apparent permissibility of an aggressively nationalistic tone in football journalism and other areas of sports coverage has been increasingly noticeable over a decade or so. It requires to be explained variously. It would be hard not to see some connection with certain prevailing ideologies of the Thatcher era: with developments in the popular press before and during that period, and in the spread of tabloid discourses: with general marketing considerations of competitiveness in sports broadcasting: and perhaps, as one among several audience considerations, with growing doubts and fears in the minds of sections of British society connected with the redefinition of their sense of national identity, these last consequent upon factors such as rejection of multiculturalism and the growing awareness of Europe.

The extent to which tabloid-engendered discourses have had their effect on broadcasting is of course, as indicated above, partly a matter of competitiveness. We might speculate, further, that as access to sporting events becomes more problematic for the duopoly, one of the ways in which they will have to compensate is by increasing the heat of nationalistic discourse, that is, in areas thought appropriate because of the nature of their audiences. We think, in fact, that this has already been happening. That this should additionally be a consequence of losing access to events with a particular sort of symbolic utility in the domain of national consciousness would be unsurprising: we would be witnessing a form of compensation, determined, by all means, in multiple fashion but significantly a response to deregulation. We might envisage this, then, partly as a sort of pathological warp set off by the obstruction of the public service brief in relation to the sacred national sports events. Put differently, it could be seen as an intensification of an already existing set of discourses of national identity, triggered not by elements in the 'public service' brief but by marketing requirements.

The promotion of the vernacular in, for example, certain areas of regional duopoly coverage is already notable, as signalled by increased emphasis on socio-regional accents: non-standard dialectal modes: local matters: and sharpened, more discriminatory reference to significant outgroups or Others. For example, fairly overt anti-Englishness has never been more sanctioned than in the last five years or so in the Scottish media: but just as it would always have been a mistake to overlook the market utility, in general, of this licence, it would be careless to fail to note the enhanced significance, in the satellite age, of terrestrial coverage of the local, and of a selective narrowing of vision accompanied by a wilful narrowing of imagination.

So if we were speculating on the effect of satellite/cable sports broadcasting on terrestrial output, we should not necessarily conclude that any new openness to Europe or elsewhere, any ideological adventurousness in the construction of the international world, would make itself attractive as an element of the riposte of terrestrial programmers to the delights of European football on BSkyB. The mixture in that circumstance of history and of present economic limitation would be a complex one. On the other hand, if this is the age of satellite, in terms of audience reach it is only beginning. What is chiefly of significance in the examination of current satellite output is not its programming or its styles in themselves.

What is important, first, is that the conception of deregulation and new technology as (either positively or negatively) internationalising in the domain of cultural production is one which requires to be constantly remodified by reference to the limitations of the rupture with the historical and ideological structures of terrestrial broadcasting: and by reference to the irregular and complex effects of the market. Secondly, of significance is the way in which the existence of satellite output and its relatively substantial impact on terrestrial broadcasting in the field of sport forces us to see the latter in a new light. Thirdly, it seems worth predicting that as the post Maastricht Europe of 1992 attempts (albeit with a degree of increasing uncertainty) to forge closer political and economic links between member states, television sport will continue to operate as an arena in which individual national identities retain important commercial and ideological functions, no matter what the future holds for satellite: and that the concept of a (post)modern satellite-borne sports geography will require further investigation.

NOTES

1 See, 'The Cable Revolution', *Scotsman*, 6 April 1990. 'Kink in the pipe dream', *Guardian*, 19 November 1990. 'Sky and BSB end the satellite war' *Observer*, 4 November 1990 and 'Glimmers in a grey Sky', *Guardian*, 18 February 1991.
2 See in particular, 'BSkyB to appeal against ruling', *Guardian*, 20 April 1991.
3 A similar outcry accompanied the exclusive deal in America that resulted in the national baseball matches becoming the property of cable companies, and thus disappearing from the national networks. The matter was raised at Senate level with pressure being brought to bear that would make illegal exclusive deals involving the national baseball and football authorities and individual TV stations. However this was viewed as a restriction on free trade.
4 See Schlesinger (1987), Robins (1989), Negrine and Papathanassopoulos (1991).
5 See Collins (1989) and Mulgan (1989).
6 As the commodification of sport by television continues, so the control exercised over it by a number of production companies increases. Despite the claims by advocates of 'free market' television that more de-regulation will help stimulate the independent production sector, in sport at least this has not been the case.
    Mark McCormack's television arm Trans World International ('TWI) secured the contract to supply BSB with all its sports programming. The deal was worth £31 million to TWI. The company not only sells the TV rights for sporting events, but also tenders out sports production work, while also having substantial in-house production facilities itself. If you want to purchase sport world-wide, you do business with TWI. This concentration has led to a number of discernible trends in sports production. There has been an significant increase in sponsor driven sports programmes. Many of TWI's programmes are backed by a large sponsor. Televised sport offers an advertising slot for multinational companies and, this leads to the sponsor having an increasing say in how the sport is organised and presented on television. Advertisers and sponsors use sport as a means of reaching a particular audience. American Football (Channel 4) has proven popular among males aged

between 16–24, traditionally a hard audience for TV advertisers to reach. As Keleher comments:

> It could be that this is attributable as much to their slick TV presentation, complete with popular music and trendy graphics, finding favour among younger viewers as to the games themselves which have yet to catch on in Britain's parks and playgrounds. (Keleher, 1989; 42)

Sports that fail to attract the right kind of viewer find a place in the schedules hard to acquire, or in the case of darts, hard to hold on to.

7   Recently it has become noticeable that the BBC's *Sportsnight* seems loathe to carry European football results, if one of the European matches has been carried exclusively on ITV.

8   The marriage between English football and television has always been an uneasy relationship. With the decline in the TV ratings for football on television that occurred during the late 1970's being accompanied by a feeling among football's governing body that television was getting football at too cheap a price, the two partners fell out completely in the early 1980's. When live football returned a new arrangement had been reached. BBC/ITV paid the disgruntled Football League £3.1 million a season for the rights to screen football. For the first time television would allow shirt advertising, and there would be a move away from showing recorded highlights to screening 'live' matches.

When the contract came up for renewal in 1988 the broadcasting environment had changed. BSB, under their chief of sport Bob Hunter, were interested in securing the rights to televise English football, and were prepared to offer more than the terrestrial channels. The summer of 1988 found football, not for the first time, making the front pages of the national press as each party tried to outbid the other. At this stage the BBC had joined forces with BSB in an attempt to secure exclusivity, this resulted in the final termination of the Corporation's uneasy arrangement with ITV.

By the end of the summer the Football League accepted the ITV offer of £44 million over four years. This gave the network exclusive rights to league and Littlewood Cup matches. The BBC and BSB had, at a cost of £30 million spread over five years, secured the rights to cover FA cup games and England's home internationals. This deal had been negotiated with the Football Association.

The coverage offered nothing new to the armchair supporter, but had ensured a screen monopoly for the five big first division clubs with little being seen of the rest of the league. However season 1988/89 saw ITV secure £22 million worth of advertising revenue for its *Match* slot, a profit of £11 million.

9   See 'How BSB is doing better in Scotland'. *New Media Markets*, 25 October 1990.

10 See in particular, Melvyn Bragg, A disastrous own goal for the BBC, *Observer*, 24 May 1992, and Michael Grade, Satellite TV: soccer's own goal, *The Guardian*, 23 May 1992.

11 Murdock (1989) has argued that 'More does not mean different. It means the same ideas and images in a variety of forms and packages . . . You can consume more of what you like (providing you can afford the equipment and the subscriptions) but you are less likely to come across something unfamiliar or challenging'.

12 Commenting on the exclusive live ITV coverage of a recent European Cup Winners Cup quarter-final between Manchester United and French club Montpellier, *Libero's Sporting Diary* noted that, 'the superior skills of the Montpellier team were overlooked, while there was much banging on about their "time wasting" tactics . . . let's hope that when ITV [show] the second leg live, we have rather less jingoism coming out of our screens' *Independent on Sunday*, 10 March 1991.

3

WE ARE THE BOYS IN GREEN: BRITISH AND IRISH TELEVISION COVERAGE OF THE 1988 EUROPEAN FOOTBALL CHAMPIONSHIP

INTRODUCTION

In this chapter we examine how television has transformed sport as a form of popular culture. In discussing the various aspects of this process there are a number of areas which we wish to explore in detail. These include sport as a form of political ritual and sport as an arena in which representations of nation and nationhood are continually being worked through.

We propose to elucidate these themes by focusing on a specific television event which will allow us to examine this process in more detail. By comparing the television coverage in two countries of a major international sporting event we can investigate not only the codes and conventions which television brings to bear in its treatment of sport, but also the differences in approach characteristic of different national concerns. It will be against this backdrop that the more general discussion on the relationship between television, sport and 'nation building' is formed. Before turning to our investigation of the European Championship, a brief introductory discussion of the influence of television on sport is required.

SPORT AS A TELEVISION INSTITUTION

It has already been pointed out that television does not simply reflect reality, or provide, as it were, a 'window on the world'. Television programmes involve the arranging of a complex set of visual and verbal codes which are refracted through a technical and institutional process of selection and organisation. In covering sport, television does not simply represent the event (although of course in a sense it does do this) but it also anchors and attempts to make sense of these events for the viewer. This account contradicts the view held by many television sports producers that the medium acts as a neutral channel through which the event is simply relayed.

To most people today spectator sport means televised sport. Such is the critical position that television has in the sporting 'world' that it is becoming increasingly difficult to separate and unravel the economic strands that bind them together.[1] Television is the primary medium disseminating ideas about sport as a form of popular culture today. The medium has brought its established codes and conventions to sport and superimposed them on the cultural form. It would be wrong to view this process as purely uni-directional. Sport has its own characteristics which are embedded in its rules and conventions: however television has amplified these indigenous traits and brought to sport on TV its own forms and contents. Television perceives sport as a form of light entertainment or drama which has the ability to attract large audiences outside peak viewing time, while at the same time being capable of holding a moderate viewership over an extended period. Thus television has to minimise what it sees as viewer boredom in its sports coverage. In short, sport on TV must offer entertainment, excitement and above all provide television producers with what they perceive as being 'good television'.

Televised sport is a hybrid of televisual codes and practices. Coverage of football comprises a mixture of studio based material, filmed reports and interviews, graphics, music, visual aids and the actual match itself, which may be live or consist of edited highlights. Televisual codes such as lighting, editing, camera placement, all act as filters through which the sporting event is structured and mediated (Whannel, 1992). What is of particular interest here is the verbal interpretation given by television to an event, in this case a major international football tournament: for television, despite being a visual medium, is also a medium of the spoken word.

Televised sport revolves around stars, stories and action. A narrative structure, both visual and verbal, is imposed on the sporting event in such a way as to allow television to make sense of it for the viewer. This process of selection and interpretation is portrayed as natural and unproblematic by television. In so doing it constantly underplays its mediating role in the process, and attempts to convince the viewer of the apolitical nature of the seemingly hermetically sealed 'world of sport' (Whannel, 1984).

Embedded in both the visual and verbal discourses of televised sport are assumptions and ideas which articulate particular ways of seeing and under-standing the society in which both sport and television operate. As we have pointed out above, the role of the individual within society, the 'natural' division of gender activities, the legitimation given to the dominant views on law and order, and the construction of national character and identity through sport, are all strands which run through television's treatment of sport (Har-greaves, 1986). These discourses are underpinned by the continual pseudo-separation of sport from the 'real' world. Thus the structural division of the 'news' and 'sport' is extended to frame, for example, debates about racism in football, or drugs in athletics, rather than attempting to place these issues within a wider social framework of reference. As Frank Keating has com-mented: 'Sport is either clean-limbed sport or schmaltzy showbiz. Current affairs it ain't'. (*The Guardian*, 7 October 1986) This trait of television will be discussed in more detail later in the chapter.

FOR MEN WHO PLAY TO WIN

A woman should be in the kitchen, the discotheque, or the boutique – not in football. Football is a man's game. There aren't any women managers and I can't see there being any. They'd be slaughtered. (Ron Atkinson, then Sheffield Wednesday and current Aston Villa manager and ITV Sport expert, *The Guardian*, 10 June 1989)

Another theme embedded in television's coverage of sport in general, and football in particular, is the construction and reproduction of masculine and feminine characteristics which are conducive to the continuance of a patriarchal society. Sport as portrayed on television is a male world where women's sport is treated as being of secondary importance. Women in sport are made sense of by continually attaching supposedly feminine connotations to their activity, or portraying them as crypto-men.

Both in production and content, football on television is a male dominated arena. The sexual division of labour is clearly articulated: men play, women watch. If women are accommodated into the discourses of televised football they are treated in both a marginal and trivial manner. Football as portrayed on television remains a bastion of male identity. Television's coverage of the Euro'88 tournament simply reproduced aspects of what supposedly constituted masculine characteristics such as competitiveness and aggression.

Speaking on the role (or lack of it) of women in the production side of televised football, John Bromley, then Controller of Sport on ITV commented:

I can't see a woman fronting *The Match* [ITV's 1988–92 live soccer programme] on a Sunday afternoon because the audience would be uncomfortable . . . women, with great respect do not play soccer at any level, in the park maybe, but not at any level and the audience would not accept it . . . [women] shouldn't be involved in a major [football] presentation on television. (*Fairplay*, Channel 4, 12 March 1989)

While noting that male values are reproduced in this area of television output, there has to be a realisation that many of these values are embedded in the sporting activities themselves, and in the sub-cultures which have evolved around them. However, television does not simply relay these themes but brings its own institutional codes and value systems to bear on the sports which it covers. These values have increasingly found themselves converging with those that exist in the sports coverage of the popular press both in Britain and more recently in Ireland.

SPORT AS LIGHT ENTERTAINMENT

Birrel and Loy (1979), highlight five areas in which television has transformed sport into a light entertainment spectacle. They highlight the reduction in the size of the image received by the spectator, the compression of time (edited highlights), the stopping and slowing of time (replays and freeze frames), the isolation of individual events (post match analysis) and the provision of additional information (commentary) as the core transformations that have occurred. Through the use of televisual technology the medium presents the world, through sport, within its own institutional framework and provides a fundamentally different experience to the viewer from that which the spectator has at the 'live' event. All the time television is legitimising and naturalising this process and blocking out alternative interpretations of the event.

Goldlust (1987), has noted that the two major types of sports presentation fall into either the more journalistically orientated coverage given by public service organisations such as the BBC, or the show-biz sensationalism of the commercial networks, specifically the American stations. In recent years however the distinction between the two systems has become less clear cut. The adoption of the American style treatment of sport, with its rapid cutting, overbearing commentary and show-business hype, has become increasingly evident as television stations attempt to maximise their share of a fragmenting audience. The economically driven desire to present sport in such a way as to attract the 'floating' viewer, and thus secure advertising revenue has resulted in an insatiable desire for television to show action sequences using a multiplicity of camera angles. (See Chapter 2 for further considerations of style in relation to satellite.)

In turn this has increased the differences which exist between spectating at a sporting event, and viewing the mediated spectacle on television where a visual and verbal narrative is continually being structured. The world-wide Americanisation of sports presentation on television seems to have accelerated in the wake of the coverage of the 1984 Olympic Games in Los Angeles and looks set to continue.[2]

By using Radio Telefis Eireann's (RTE Irish television) coverage of the competition we hope to provide a concrete illustration of the foregoing discussion, not only by highlighting the way in which television has transformed the representation of sport, but also by focussing on two interrelated aspects of this process in particular. They are *televised sport as a site of secular ritual*, and how this in turn plays a key role in the process of *constructing and reproducing a sense of communal and national identity within Ireland*.

In the following discussion of coverage of the Euro'88 tournament by RTE, it will become obvious, by comparing it with the treatment the tournament received on British television (BBC/ITV), that the Irish station has been heavily influenced by the British mode of sports presentation. However, examining the treatment given to the tournament on British television (BBC/ITV) allows us to compare and contrast the extent to which TV *coverage* of the same sporting event may vary from country to country. By using the Republic of Ireland *vs* England match as a case study, many of the themes mentioned above can be examined in concrete terms, while themes such as the portrayal of the Irish on British television can also be placed against this backdrop. Before turning to the coverage itself some background information about the tournament is required.

EURO'88

The European Football Championship is an international football competition played between the countries of the continent. The final stages of the tournament consist of competition among the eight countries who have qualified through their respective groups. In international European football terms the competition is second in importance only to the World Cup. The 1988 finals were held in the then Federal Republic of Germany between the 10–25 of June. The Republic of Ireland had qualified for the final stages for the first time and had been drawn in the same group as the Soviet Union, The Netherlands and the tournament's second favourites, England. It was the first time that the Irish Republic had played England in the latter stages of any international football competition.

It was also the first time that RTE Television had covered a major international football tournament in which the Irish Republic were actively involved. British television had long been used to covering tournaments in which at least one of the 'home countries' was involved.[3]

Previous scheduling problems between the BBC and ITV which had resulted in simultaneous broadcasts of the same matches had by the period of this competition been resolved, with England's games being screened alternatively between the channels. In part this agreement was in recognition of the then declining viewership for football on British television, further fragmentation of the audience being particularly harmful to the size of ITV's share of advertising revenue.

Sport is used by television as an important weapon in a station's armoury in the increasingly competitive battle to secure advertising revenue. While sport rarely features at the top end of the rating charts, it can attract respectable viewing figures outside peak viewing time. As was evident from the Tam ratings achieved by RTE's coverage of the European Championships, sport can get and hold large audiences for major events. (The TAM ratings up to May 1989 measured the percentage of television homes viewing. From 1989 it measures the percentage of individuals in those homes viewing). In Britain however the ratings for the competition were in general very disappointing for the television producers (see Table 3.1). However the subsequent success of England in the 1990 World Cup would culminate in a combined BBC/ITV audience of 24 million watching the semi-final between England and West Germany.

Both countries received identical pictures of the tournament from Germany. While BBC and ITV used their own crews at the England matches (these were used to insert shots of England players into the main transmission and carry out post match interviews), by and large the visual material was identical. RTE, not having the resources of the British channels, relayed a large number of the games from both BBC and ITV. So for matches not involving the Irish, and not covered by RTE's second commentator, the station simply transmitted the game carrying the British commentary. Let us now turn to the broadcasts of the Republic of Ireland *vs* England match.

FOOTBALL: DRAMA AND HISTORY IN THE MAKING

The technology now available to broadcast television both changes our experience of drama inherent in the live event and creates an entirely new dramatic event. (Morris and Nydahl, 1985: 101)

Table 3.1   Television viewing figures for the 1988 European Football Championships

RTE Television: Tam Ratings

	Position	Tam Rating	No. of homes in thousands
RTE 2 *v* England, week ending 12 June	1	42	391
RTE 2 *v* Soviet Union, week ending 19 June	1	51	477
RTE 1 *v* Holland, week ending 19 June	1	47	449

BBC/ITV Coverage of England Matches

National Top 100 Ratings	Position	Million	TVR
ITV *v* Rep. of Ireland, Fri/Sun, 12 June	43	6.5	13
BBC 1 *v* Holland, 15th June	58	5.1	10
BBC 1 *v* Soviet Union (Highlights) Rep. of Ireland *v* Holland (live) 18 June	83	3.7	7

Source: Analysis, *Broadcast*, 8 July 1988

> ITV attracted the largest football audience of the week, (12–19 June) with 7.9 million viewers turning in on Wednesday evening to see highlights of the England *v* Holland match. Although this was 1.3 million viewers more than the BBC 1 football achieved, it is still two million viewers fewer than ITV attracted with a 'normal' schedule . . . However given England's current prowess on the football field it is possibly not surprising the [sic] Emmerdale Farm and Coronation Street have greater appeal. (*Broadcast*, 8 July 1988)

The opening game of Group 2 between the Irish and the English teams was broadcast live on RTE and ITV on the afternoon of Sunday 12 June 1988. The BBC carried edited highlights later in the evening. The need for television to legitimise its presence at the tournament is of central concern in the pre-match build up. This need to justify the station's coverage of the event often results in a barrage of superlatives which describe the atmosphere, and amplify the grandiose nature of the spectacle the viewer is about to witness.

All the stations began their respective programmes with their own opening titles. In televised football these tend to consist of a montage of action shots of goals being scored, near misses and over exuberant tackles. This cavalcade of action is accompanied by fast rhythmic music giving the opening titles at times the feel of a promotional music video, in general investing the opening with show business values. Television has highlighted what it defines as being the important parts of football, and the viewer is promised excitement, drama, spectacle and the prospect of a 'good show'.

Both live broadcasts (RTE/ITV) opened with their respective anchormen (in British TV sport it tends still to be a man, although this is slowly changing whereas many other European countries find it unproblematic to have a woman front sport on television) setting the scene. The anchorman performs a vital multi-functional role in televised sport. He naturalises both the language used and the televisual techniques incorporated by the medium. He becomes not only a TV professional, but a sports fan, friend and supplier of facts, figures and information. He provides the avenue of access into the programme and continually works to keep these channels of contact open (Whannel, 1992). The use of 'we', meaning production team, is balanced with 'you', the recipient audience. He also crosses the spatial divide as he becomes, like 'us', a sports fan: 'We can now join our commentator'.

As kick-off approached, Bill O'Herlihy on RTE commented that the game was: 'The most important football international played by the Republic of Ireland'. (RTE 2 12 June). ITV devoted little time to a tactical analysis of the game. In keeping with television's desire to secure the largest possible audience, not just the committed sports fan, ITV promised an entertainment show. Stars, action, human drama and, it appeared, with the potential crowd trouble in Germany, the possibility of some violence thrown in for good measure. As ITV took a commercial break, Nick Owen told the viewers: 'The atmosphere is really building up at the Necker stadium, and we will be right amongst it – next'! (ITV 12 June). Television it seemed was going to bring the excitement into our living room. Having promised us action, drama and history in the making all we had to do was keep watching.

EXPERTLY SPEAKING

The expert is to lend us his framework, we are to see through his eyes. He is to tell the story and we are to listen. (Tudor 1975: 153)

A key element in television's transformation of sport into a televisual spectacle is that of narrative construction.[4] As in other areas of television production, televised sport tells stories and imposes a narrative order on events which, as in the case of live sport, are inherently unpredictable. Having looked at the initial framing of the event by the stations, we now turn to the match commentary itself.

Nick Owen was joined in the ITV studio by Brian Clough, the Nottingham Forest manager and experienced football TV pundit. Also present was Ian St John, ex-Liverpool player now turned TV football presenter. BBC TV also drew heavily on the established 'media culture' of footballing experts, with Tottenham Hotspur's then manager, Terry Venables, and former Manchester United and England player, Bobby Charlton, (brother of the Irish manager Jack) in the studio being quizzed by anchorman Des Lynam.

RTE's Bill O'Herlihy was joined by the former Irish international player and manager John Giles, accompanied by another former Irish international of more recent years, Don Givens. These respective line-ups emphasise the symbiotic ties between the 'world' of football and the 'world' of television (Wagg, 1984). We are presented with the seemingly unitary world of televised football, with its familiar faces, and agreed rules on what constitutes a football 'expert'.

At the match itself ITV deployed their senior commentator Brian Moore who was accompanied by football manager and ITV Sport regular, Ron Atkinson. RTE's coverage saw George Hamilton provide the verbal interpretation of the match in Stuttgart. With Hamilton the 'Irish day out' began as the teams came out onto the park. Although impossible to confirm from the coverage, Hamilton assured the viewers that the Irish fans gave a louder cheer to their team than their English counterparts gave to theirs. As the camera panned the crowd, he continued to discuss the fans and how they 'have come from all parts of Ireland . . . to be part of this historic occasion . . . it seems that nothing else matters in Ireland but this match'. (RTE 2 12 June)

Domestic football commentary both in Ireland and England tends to be impartial in nature, with the commentator occupying a neutral position, but this changes at coverage of international events. Both the Republic of Ireland and England became unproblematically described by their respective commentators as 'us' or 'we'. Pretensions of neutrality are dispensed with as the commentator becomes a fan along with the partisan viewer whom television attempts to encourage. This trait was particularly evident in Hamilton's commentary, yet unconsciously he managed to highlight some of the contradictions running through 'the Irish day out' when commenting on the Irish goal scored by Glasgow-born Ray Houghton whom he called: 'the little Scot', adding 'we are one-nil in front, can you believe it?'

Over on ITV Brian Moore described the goal as 'a shattering blow for Bobby Robson's men . . . a shock lead'. Throughout the opening half Atkinson had commented on the no-nonsense style of the Irish team, explaining the pattern of the game in the particular language of tactical analysis which television legitimises as both authoritative and accurate. The English players were referred to at times by their nicknames as used by other players and by the tabloid press in Britain. Again we witness television helping to construct the unitary world of football: a place with its own stars, nicknames and language.

By half-time Hamilton was ecstatic, Moore concerned. Back in their respective studios the 'experts' made sense of it all. ITV's Nick Owen simply asked: 'What's happening?' The half-time discussion centred on the non-performance of a number of English players. On RTE Giles gave an accomplished structural (tactical) appraisal of the half, noting the disciplined and technically competent nature of the overall team performance of the Irish.

During the second half George Hamilton became fully integrated into his role as the Irish fan 'we are concerned . . . we can thank our lucky stars . . . we come away with the ball'. With the final whistle, and an Irish victory, televised sport once again became the site of dreams and stories (in this case fairy stories) and 'we' could all celebrate. Hamilton continued 'Jack Charlton schemes [sic] the victory we all dreamed of, but few of us believed would happen . . . the whole of Ireland rejoices'. However on ITV a 'day of great sadness' was already being reworked as Brian Moore helped create the framework within which the English viewer could adopt the Irish, and thus keep watching the tournament. It was, we were reminded, an Englishman who had masterminded the victory with a team full of familiar Scottish and English league players. We return to this point below.

In the ITV studio the result was greeted with dismay and disbelief. A sporting superpower (in the eyes of the English media) had been humbled 'How can it be?' asked Owen. England, the viewer was assured, could still qualify and 'we' would just have to wait for the next match. On RTE Giles gave an even handed analysis of the result, putting it in context by noting that while it was nice to beat England it was more important that the Republic of Ireland had won their opening group match.

Televised sport helps to make sense of the event when it is over. In the case of major sporting events such as the World Cup which run over an extended period of time (in the case of the football World Cup this can be four weeks), the story reaches open-ended interim climaxes which will be resolved in subsequent broadcasts. While the Irish-English match was now over, the important effect that the result would have on each team's chances of reaching the semi-finals meant that the match would be continually referred back to as the tournament progressed.

What we wish to do now is to turn our attention to some of the general trends which were evident in television's treatment of the fifteen day tournament, while also expanding and developing some of the issues raised above.

SPORT AND NATION

The presenters of both British and Irish television displayed one of the central characteristics of television's treatment of sport: that of audience-building by forging points of identification with the viewer. Thus O'Herlihy described the match as 'a great historic moment for Irish football . . . [a] marvellous moment for the whole of Ireland'. (RTE 2 12 June) On ITV Nick Owen informed the viewer that 'the eyes of the nation are focused on events in Stuttgart'. (ITV 12 June). What televised sport achieves is the presentation of sport as a form of ritual which heightens the sense of communal links between individuals, and the collective identification of these individuals with the political and cultural community of the 'nation'. Political and cultural tensions in Ireland and Britain disappear as television helps build on the idea of a unitary culture through the ritual of a shared cultural experience.

What we witness is the ability of television to transform an international sporting event into a wider ideological process. It attempts to construct a sense of social stability by offering an experience with which individuals can relate in such a way as (here) to encourage them to mark out one country from another, or, depending on requirements, unite two countries conceptually. Televised sport can help on certain national and international occasions to 'establish a public consciousness of collective identification through the creation of secular public rituals celebrated by a set of ceremonial events that will symbolise the validity of the social order and reconfirm the collective identification of the populace to the principles upon which it is based'. (Goldlust, 1987: 130) The importance that television places on the ceremonial ritual of the national anthem is one such example.[5] This process of nation-building, however, is also an important element of the commentary.

This would-be national community exists not only in itself, but also in explicit contradistinction to other communities. The distancing of the Irish from the English, both as a team and as a country was a recurring theme in the RTE television coverage. Likewise, ITV's pre-match discussion of the Irish team consisted of a filmed report from Elton Welsby who had travelled with the Irish squad for ITV. His report included at times rather stereotypical formulations which informed the viewer that the Irish were relaxed, carefree and obviously here to enjoy themselves.

None the less, an emergent element of British coverage of the tournament was a discourse which also emphasised the would-be links between the two countries. On ITV, club teammates who would be opposing each other were highlighted. It appeared that what separated the Irish and English was minimal, when contrasted with what they had in common. ITV also attempted to personalise the game by focusing on the two managers, Jack Charlton of the Republic of Ireland, and England's Bobby Robson. It was during this part of the broadcast that this theme was to emerge most clearly: the Irish team was continually referred to, and made sense of, in terms that emphasised its English connection through its English born manager. 'Jack Charlton's Ireland' became in effect England's adopted team, consisting as it did of some players who had in fact been born in England, and with the majority playing their football in the Scottish and English Football Leagues.

This process of adoption had been in evidence in the pre-tournament build up. The *Radio Times* of 11 June began an article on the Irish as follows,

> From the upper reaches of the English and Scottish leagues, with scarcely an Irish born player among them, comes the Republic of Ireland squad. Tony Gubba looks at the pack to be shuffled by Jack Charlton . . . they do provide a wealth of self inflicted comic relief . . . Indeed the hardest thing to find is an Irish accent. (*Radio Times*, 11 June 1988)

As though to back this up, in the London studio the lack of Irish accents among the players interviewed was a subject for humour. British television tended to emphasise the links between the teams and place the Irish and English together opposite the rest of Europe. As if to emphasise this division, Ron Atkinson on ITV told the viewers that the continentals 'are going to get a typical British game played on their own soil'. (ITV 12 June)

Subsequently, with the ending of England's chances of qualifying for the semi-final stages, the adoption of the Irish as surrogate sons of England was pursued with even greater vigour by both ITV and BBC. When the Irish played the Dutch in their final group match, still with a chance of reaching the semi-finals, it was this match and not the English game that was carried live by BBC TV. Both British stations were unequivocal in their support of 'Jack Charlton's Ireland'. Once again the need for television to encourage the viewer to take up a partisan position, in the hope of securing and holding his or her attention, is revealed as a central component of the competitive ratings war.

PANIC ON THE STREETS

We now consider the treatment RTE and BBC/ITV gave to the civil disturbances involving English supporters occurring during the tournament, placing this within the wider constructions of national character and identity evident in all three stations' coverage.

Prior to the competition much space had been devoted by the press, both in Ireland and Britain, to speculating on the possibility of crowd trouble in Germany involving travelling English fans. Following the Heysel stadium disaster in 1985 in which thirty-nine Juventus supporters were killed when a wall collapsed as a result of crowd violence involving Liverpool fans, all English clubs had been banned from European competition. Supporters of the English national team had acquired a reputation as troublemakers following numerous incidents on mainland Europe.[6]

On ITV Nick Owen introduced a discourse which would enjoy varying degrees of prominence within the hierarchy of discourses evident in television's coverage of the tournament, that of the threat of potential crowd trouble in Germany and its possible consequences for the England team:

A big day for Irish football, a crucial one for the English. If our footballers fail to perform on the pitch it could be the end of our hopes in the European Championships. If our supporters fail to behave off the pitch we could become the outcasts of world football. (ITV 12 June)

ITV also gave prominence to the potential 'hooligan' problem involving travelling English supporters. Owen presented the issue as a clearly defined 'law and order' problem in football. Brian Clough varied this treatment by noting the social nature of the problem, claiming that '[any trouble that occurs] is no different to what is happening throughout the country'. (ITV 12 June) However, any possible discussion of the social nature of the problem was ignored by the framing of the debate by the (then) British Minister of Sport Colin Moynihan. He was himself at the tournament in Germany and his main concern seemed to be with the potential damage that any violence would have on Britain's image abroad. Back in the studio Ian St John, a Scot, was extricating himself and his compatriots from this English problem by telling Nick Owen 'If your fans don't behave, you could get kicked out of Europe'. (ITV 12 June)

As Nick Owen's opening comment had made clear, the possibility of English clubs being allowed back into European club competitions was clearly weakened by events. As is the pattern of most hooligan incidents at football today, and as was the case in Germany, the trouble has been displaced from inside the stadium to outside. Fighting involving English supporters occurred throughout the tournament in a number of German cities.

The coverage of the hooligan problem by British television was typical of TV's treatment of violence occurring in or around sporting venues. These incidents were defined as a problem inherently exclusive to football, and as a sporting problem. There was no attempt to place the problem within a wider social context. All that was heard was the political call for stiffer penalties for those involved. There was certainly no examination of the possible role played by the media in helping to amplify the problem, nor their ability to construct what is generally perceived as being the irrational behaviour of 'the football hooligan'.[7]

BBC TV also gave much prominence to Moynihan, who stressed that if the football authorities did not deal with the problem then the British government would have to step in. This was subsequently borne out by events.[8] The disturbances also made prime time national news in Britain and Ireland. The reporting was factual: however, the underlying position was one of incomprehension at the apparently irrational and violent behaviour of the English fans. The debates were framed by the government official who once again would call for the introduction of even more stringent powers to punish the offenders.

Televised sport seems incapable of treating any issue as a social problem. Such is the insular nature of television's 'world of sport' that much of the debate actually centred around the likelihood of the English national team being banned from international competition.

RTE, while perhaps feeling that the problem was not of their concern as no Irish supporters had been involved in the trouble, did provide a classic example of televised sport's tendency to separate the fictional 'world of sport' from reality.[9] Bill O'Herlihy presented this issue as an English footballing problem that the Irish did not have: it was clearly illogical, anti-social and not Irish:

> . . . for six hours there was no talk of football at the European Football Championships . . . [There followed an ITN report of fans involved in street fighting] . . . those are the images that will isolate British soccer even more . . . it is a terrible commentary on English football and the supporters they have. (RTE 2 15 June)

THE CONTINENTALS

> . . . the Soviet Union are always dark horses, disciplined and strong, and the Republic of Ireland will come here to enjoy themselves. (Bobby Robson, then England manager, *The Guardian*, 13 January 1988)

Throughout the competition all three channels attempted to find the ethnocentric hook which they hoped would keep the elusive 'floating' viewer watching. Wherever possible the other six European teams were placed within a framework of reference that connected them to the Irish or English teams. ITV employed ex-Italian league player Trevor Francis as their European expert, while BBC's Terry Venables, having once managed the Spanish club Barcelona, was portrayed as their 'Euroexpert'.

Both stations displayed televised sport's tendency to operate restricted and conservative discourses when dealing with international sporting teams. It appears that assumptions about the characteristics of European countries are deeply embedded in the 'cultural baggage' which British television carries with it to these sporting occasions (though naturally these assumptions run deeper – see Chapter 1). Thus the Danes are 'brittle', the West Germans 'methodical and organised', the Soviets 'dark and unsmiling' and the Italians and the Spanish are 'fiery and unpredictable' (for detailed discussion on the operation of such discourses in the European press, see, especially, Chapter 4). On one occasion during the Italy-Spain match, ITV's Ian St John suggested that the poor form of one of the Italian players was due to the fact that he must be eating too much pasta.

In the build up to the Irish Republic's second group match against the Soviet Union, ITV's Elton Welsby began his filmed report by stating 'We think we have found a Russian spy'. (ITV 15 June) What followed was an interview with Irish international Tony Galvin who has a degree in Russian Studies. RTE was also guilty, although not to the same extent, of simply reproducing accepted myths and prejudices about other countries. George Hamilton's reports before the Soviet Union match were riddled with 'cold war' rhetoric and references to the unsmiling and unfriendly Soviets. Admittedly the Soviets did little to enhance their image by refusing to conform to the demands of the western media for interviews, photo-opportunities and the like. The Dutch were also annoyed by the intrusive nature of the media. However, they did not receive the negative coverage given to the Soviet Union team.[10]

'Socialist realism' – an Italian view of Soviet football during the 1990 World Cup (*Gazzetta dello Sport*, 29 June 1990)

British metropolitan-produced television's tendency towards an Anglocentric view of the sporting world was also evident with regard to its analysis of the football played in Germany. It was only when it became obvious that the Netherlands would reach the final that it was admitted that Dutch football might be superior to that played in Britain. Little attention or analysis was paid to the variety of diverse footballing cultures existing throughout Europe. RTE's Giles and Givens did examine patterns of play, and the role of the individual within a collective structure. The emphasis on individualism, even in team sports, is one of the major discourses articulated in television's treatment of sport.

Television sport always attempts to justify its initial framing of the event even if, as is often the case, this proves to be wildly inaccurate. Individual players who have been highlighted before the event, and who then in the eyes of the experts fail to live up to their pre-match billing, are heavily criticised. The coverage given to the Dutch player Ruud Gullit was one such example. His overall contribution to the team was ignored, except by Giles and Venables, with the other experts claiming that he had not fulfilled his potential. It appears that by nominating and highlighting 'stars' television creates a story for itself even if the player 'fails': if the individual is outstanding then television has a success story. This nominating of players in the pre-match analysis becomes not simply a personalising of the game, but a central technique in providing televised sport with the opportunity to do what it likes most, which is to tell stories which it hopes will keep the viewer watching.

Sportspeople exist, or so television would have us believe, in a classless environment. This group is portrayed as individuals who have achieved success through hard work and dedication, they are the rule, not the elite exceptions. The idea that anyone can achieve or attain the level of success represented by this group is of course a fallacy, yet in this classless account of the 'world of sport' anyone, regardless of background, can reach the top: such ideas were especially in tune with the Thatcherite ideologies which took root in the UK in the eighties.

THE TABLOIDISATION OF TELEVISION

During television's coverage of the tournament there was evidence of an increasing trend towards the penetration of television by the tabloid press's style of treatment of sport. This section of the press has become a reservoir of language from which television can draw, and an agenda setter which defines the most important sporting issues of the day. The press have become the primary definers of television's sporting news values. Both ITV and BBC panels displayed this tendency in the importance they attached to the tabloid press's coverage of football. The assimilation of this 'tabloid talk' into the mainstream of television discourses plays a crucial role in limiting the agenda to that characteristic of the back pages of the popular press. While the interrelationship between the press and other broadcast media has always been evident, a developed analysis of the symbiotic ties between the sports coverage of the press and television would be very productive. (See Chapter 4, and Wagg, 1991)

In general terms RTE's panel discussions did manage to expand on the limited agenda which preoccupied British television. As the coverage of the competition finished on RTE TV, the panel congratulated itself for providing a 'cliché free environment'. However, as the tabloid section of the Irish newspaper market increases, and the competition from other sports programming stations on RTE intensifies, the station may find itself under increasing pressure to conform to the dominant TV sports values of British television in order to secure its share of a fragmenting audience.

CONCLUSION

A sense of unity conferred by the feeling of belonging to the nation, cutting across class, ethnic, gender and other loyalties is, perhaps, the very lynchpin of a hegemonic system, and the media are, arguably, the most important institution reproducing national unity today. (Hargreaves, 1986: 154)

As Chaney (1986: 116) has noted, there is a tendency for secular rituals to link the social order to notions of assumed social stability: 'the essence of ritual performance is to affirm the experience of a collectivity which would otherwise have only an ambiguous cultural location'. If, as Anderson (1983: 15) suggests, the nation 'is an imagined political community', then television sport, especially at an international level, is an element in that process, an arena in which individuals who have never met can feel part of a wider community.

The role of television in transforming specific sporting events into national spectacles and political (in its widest sense) ritual is of course not unique to Ireland. The American Superbowl Final has been described as a marriage between the electronic media and sport which:

. . . structurally reveal[s] specific cultural values proper to American institutions and ideology; and it is best explained as a contemporary form of mythic ritual. (Real, 1977: 92/93)

Ann Karpf, writing about the BBC coverage of the Wimbledon Tennis Championships, notes how the economic structures which underpin a major sporting event are ignored by television in order to preserve the mystique of the event. (See Chapter 6 on European media coverage of Wimbledon).

The BBC's Wimbledon is like part of the heritage industry, inducing a glow of cultural cosiness . . . it's an icon of unchanging continuity and social cohesion. For two weeks in summer . . . its the thirties again [with] . . . the BBC as cultural authority and keeper of the national social calendar. (*New Statesman and Society*, 8 July 1988)

What has become evident from our discussion is that the vast global communications network has not eroded television's ability to foster a particularly insular view of national importance, the key point being the ability of the country receiving the pictures of the event to control the *verbal interpretation* of these images. These images are increasingly being selected by American television as they use their economic power to secure television rights for sport around the world.

Televised sport is not the apolitical arena TV likes to portray. Embedded in it are values and ideas about the social organisation of society. Television has increasingly transformed our own perceptions of sport at both the domestic and international levels. Due to the nature of the medium, television appears to offer a representation of 'actuality'. As Whannel comments:

> These processes of transformation cannot be grasped through analysis of representation alone, but require also analysis of the alarmingly direct relation between economic relations and cultural production that have come to characterize this sphere. (Whannel, 1984: 107)

The quarter of a million or so people who took to the streets of Dublin to welcome the return of the Irish football team (who had failed to qualify for the semi-final stages) were not primarily motivated by an interest in football. These people had not been to Germany. They had witnessed the matches in various locations throughout Ireland via television and radio, yet the outpouring of national pride was as strong as if they had attended the matches in person. The demonstration of support would be even greater after the team's successful Italia '90 campaign, where they reached the quarter-final stage.

An important element in this support was the communal nature of much of the television viewing. In Dublin, a giant video screen was erected and crowds of up to ten thousand paid to watch the Irish matches. Journalist and writer Colm Toibin reporting on the Italia'90 tournament for an Irish newspaper noted how the supporters in Ireland gave the impression of having a better time than those actually experiencing the matches in Italy.

> Everybody told me I was insane to be in Cagliari with the fans. At home, it was one big party: little old ladies had learned the intricacies of offside; when Ireland drew with England it was like the Pope's visit in the confines of your local bar. And the commentaries afterwards were magic. Men, women and children watched wide-eyed as John Giles and Eamon Dunphy, two players turned journalists, went through the match [On RTE Television]. (Toibin, 1992: 43)

Political leaders have never been slow to tap the resurgence of national pride that accompanies individual or team success on an international stage. The then Irish Taoiseach (Prime Minister), Charles Haughey, was on hand to welcome the team at Dublin airport, as he had been at the finishing line of the Tour de France cycle race to congratulate Irishman Stephen Roche on his winning of that competition. The links between the political élite and sport have a long history that is not of direct concern here.[11] What is of interest is the way that television has taken aspects of sporting competition and reconstituted them into a wider cultural and ideological construction of national stability.

For example, within the domestic Irish sporting arena, the pinnacle of the Gaelic games season is the All-Ireland Hurling and Football finals which take place in Croke Park during September. It is an occasion that television portrays as the coming together of the Irish nation to participate in its national games. In the absence of royal patronage, as at the English Cup Final, there is the presence of an array of dignitaries including the President of Ireland, the Taoiseach (PM), leading members of the Catholic Church and members of the main political parties. The pageantry of the pre-match band and the playing of the national anthem all help to create a concrete image of a national community.

Television mediates, legitimises and amplifies aspects of this complex process which symbolically unites the rural and urban community, as well as pulling together the cultural nation around a focus of national stability. The All-Ireland finals have of course pre-dated television. Radio coverage has been available since the 1920's, with the finals only becoming regular fixtures with the formation of the State in 1922 (Boyle, 1992). Through the televised sporting ritual a feeling of history and unbroken tradition is invoked: a national way of life. As Chaney notes:

> Rituals are a representation of the collectivity, a collective performance in which certain significant aspects of social relationships are given symbolic form and force. (1986: 122)

In the Republic of Ireland televised national sporting events can provide an arena through which nationalistic feelings can be vented in an unproblematic manner. The political channelling of this nationalistic energy proves more problematic for the populace. Sport seems to provide an essentially 'safe' channel of national self expression: 'safe' in terms of political stability because it tends to mask the political and structural changes which need to occur within the whole of Ireland if subordinate groups are to exercise more power over their own lives. It is important to understand the role that the media play in constructing sport as part of a national psyche which may ultimately reinforce the dominant political system.

However, as sport is partly a symbolic representation of aspects of culture, this is not to say that oppositional forces may not also be at work. It could be argued that the national expression of cultural solidarity expressed by large sections of the Irish people that followed Euro'88 and Italia'90 for what was traditionally viewed as a 'foreign' game, could be one manifestation of the 'new Ireland': a country personified by a new generation of young educated Irish people who view themselves as Irish within a European context. That however remains a debate for another day.

NOTES

1 For a detailed account of this process see Whannel, (1992).

2 This has involved the demise of the 180 degree cutting line rule that was held to be of central importance when televising sport, see Buscombe (1975). The Americanisation of coverage is linked to the economic development of the sport/ television nexus which is examined in more detail in Barnett, (1990) and Whannel, (1992).

3 See Buscombe (1975), for a detailed account of how a predominantly English

audience is encouraged to identify with Scotland, the only British representative at the 1974 World Cup Finals.

4 For a detailed analysis of the narrative structure of televised sport see Whannel's 'Narrative and Television Sport: The Coe and Ovett Story', (1982) *Sporting Fictions*, University of Birmingham.

5 This also causes problems for television. The Hillsborough disaster of April 1989 resulted in the death of 95 Liverpool fans due to a crush caused by inadequate crowd control. The 1989 post Hillsborough disaster FA Cup Final between Liverpool and Everton saw the national anthem being booed and sung over, much to the disgust of the television presenters. Similarly at Scottish Cup Finals, the British national anthem is no longer played due to its unpopularity, with 'Scotland the Brave/Flower of Scotland' being played at both Scottish finals and international games involving the Scottish national team.

6 For an ethnographic account of English supporters travelling abroad see, Williams, J. Dunning, E. and Murphy, P. (1989) *Hooligans Abroad*, 2nd Edition, Routledge, London.

7 A detailed account of this process appears in Dunning, E. Murphy, P. and Williams, J. (1989) *The Roots Of Football Hooliganism: A Historical and Sociological Study*, Routledge, London. Also see Taylor, I., (1991) English football in the 1990's: taking Hillsborough seriously?, in Williams, J., and Wagg, S., (eds.) *British Football and Social Change: Getting into Europe*, Leicester University Press.

8 The 1989–90 English League season would have seen, despite strong opposition from the Football League, the clubs and the supporters, the introduction of a government approved full membership supporters card scheme. However, as a result of the strong condemnation of the scheme that appeared in Lord Justice Taylor's report into the Hillsborough disaster (published February 1990), this has been dropped.

9 Such is the insular nature of the televised 'world of sport' that disturbances such as those which occurred in Birmingham in 1987 at the England *v* Pakistan cricket Test match were described as 'football hooliganism at cricket'. The fact that the disturbances were racially motivated and symptomatic of the racial tensions that exist in multi-cultural Britain went unnoticed in television news reports.

10 In a discussion with George Hamilton, he admitted that there is always a danger that a commentator, under pressure, will slip into the 'easy, convenient' phrase or stereotype, however he observed that it was a temptation that all professionals should try to resist.

11 Examples include the presence of royalty at the FA Cup Final in England, the presidential phone call to the captain of the winning team in the American Superbowl Final (initiated by J.F. Kennedy), Harold Wilson's close association with the English national football team after their 1966 World Cup win and more recently the scramble among some of the current Conservative government to associate themselves with sport, particularly football, not the least of whom has been that well known Chelsea supporter, the Prime Minister John Major (to say nothing of other celebrated Chelsea-supporting Conservatives).

4

GAMES ACROSS FRONTIERS: THE NATIONAL DIMENSION IN EUROPEAN PRESS REPORTING OF ITALIA'90

INTRODUCTION

We should like to begin with some preliminary observations about comparing newspapers from different countries.[1] We might open with the uncontentious observation that the structure of each national press has some characteristics wholly specific to that country, but we wish to take this observation back one stage and note that among the prime determinants of the structure of each national press are the social and political structure of each country, and its associated cultural characteristics. Of relevance among such differences from one country to another are variations not only in the nature of present-day socio-economic class segmentation, but also in historical developments whose determining influences need to be understood in specifically cultural terms.

As well as having in mind matters of the social structure of readerships, corresponding press segmentation, the role of football socially and the traits of individual newspapers and, of course, of individual journalists, we shall also make consistent reference to the question of who, nationally, is writing about whom. To use an example very familiar to us: the lack of charity demonstrated by Scottish sports writers toward English football teams is legendary. Similar quirky networks of relationship can be traced across many national boundaries.[2]

At all times we are concerned to relate the story of Italia'90 to its wider discursive framework. Our assumption is that every text generated by Italia'90 and every discourse produced or reproduced by the event can be related to meta-texts and meta-discourses which are produced within, or operate within, domains other than the sporting: that is, that they can be related both to these as well as to other more local discursive formulations. The group of discourses with which we are most concerned, those relating to national feeling, enjoy a complex relationship with those operating in the sporting world. We are not especially concerned to assert that the discourses of politics are in some determinist sense hierarchically superior to those of sport, but we are keenly aware that their relationship is very close.

THE BRITISH ON THE PERIPHERY OF EUROPE

BRITISH FANS IN THE BRITISH PRESS

We have discussed the particularities of the British press and its readership extensively in Chapter 1. We noted exceptional aspects (within a European context) in British class society and in corresponding features of British newspaper market segmentation.

The British, and more specifically the English, are a sort of eternal puzzle on Europe's boundary, puzzling to themselves and to everyone else. We shall concentrate on England, which mobilises by far the greatest weight of symbolic significance, and besides which the Scots and the Irish are, at Italia'90, merely the court jesters.

Even when England fans don't do anything, they get into trouble in the British press. In the *Glasgow Herald* (27 June), speaking of England's win over Belgium, James Traynor says 'at least their win in the Stadio Dall'Ara helped the mood of their notorious supporters, who had been on edge all night. At one point the police closed in, but there was no major outbreak of violence on the terraces'. Since the journalist cites no minor outbreak of violence either, it remains conceivable that, to put it more clearly, nothing much happened at all.

But at Italia'90 journalists had seldom to invent English misbehaviour. The same edition of the *Herald* reports 'England's win marred by 246 fans'. A contrast is drawn by the Scottish journalist with the good behaviour of Scottish fans. The same incident is referred to in that day's English *Daily Star* 'Flight of Shame: 246 English soccer yobs are sent packing' The *Daily Mail* adds an extra hooligan 'GET OUT, YOU ANIMALS: Italy expels 247 England fans after riot wrecks resort'.

With a generosity toward Scottish fans which the Scottish newspapers do not reciprocate, the *Mail* finds bar-owners who speak of the contrast with English fans. 'We have never seen anything like this. When the Scots were here, they drank more than the English and were very friendly. But the English are mental'. A connection with a wider framework of statements about English fan behaviour abroad is revealed by the appearance of a story on the same page about the Heysel disaster, as yet the lowest point of this tradition. *Today* (27 June) adopts a similar approach 'WE ARE SENDING BACK YOUR ENGLISH RUBBISH: Rampaging fans again bring shame to World Cup', and likewise carries positive comment about the Scots, and also juxtaposes the story with one on the Heysel disaster.

Writer Dave Hill provided (in two pieces, for the *Guardian* on 12 May, and for the *Independent on Sunday* on 24 June) the most lucid, and the most depressing, account of the relationship between the English fans' behaviour in Italy and their social and cultural background. His central idea is that 'the depravity of English fans abroad symbolises a wider crisis of Englishness': this extract (*Guardian*, 12 May) looks back to the European Championships of 1988:

> In Dusseldorf, Stuttgart and Frankfurt, the fundamentals of the invading hooligan psyche were clearly exposed as a cocktail of national chauvinism, rank xenophobia and the worst aspects of working-class masculinity – the unacceptable face of rank and file Englishness, writ large . . . There will be trouble in Italy, and England supporters will be in the thick of it.

During the World Cup, his predictions validated, the same journalist proposes a similarly depressing account of the consequences of the political backwardness of English society. In a piece entitled 'Gods and Men' (*Independent on Sunday*, 24 June), he draws a stark contrast between the behaviour of English fans and their Scottish and Dutch counterparts. The Scots have faced a terrible absence of drink – 'maybe hard experience has taught them that no degree of inebriation can help avert an impending catastrophe or deaden its grim effects' – with fortitude, and have suffered defeat at the first hurdle. 'So, once more the tartan army had marched to the ground as warriors and returned as men in skirts. But few of them seemed bitter, or even surprised. In defeat, the Scots made you almost proud to be British. As for England – well, that's another country'.

The Dutch, 'cosmopolitan and confident', have come to Sardinia 'for a party'. But 'the English, insular and out of their depth, had come to sulk'. Hill describes a number of instances of what he sees as the utter failure of English culture to equip some of its football fans with the ability to know how to behave outside a restricted segment of English society. He finishes with these examples, and a gloomy conclusion:

> The singing consists of gormless chanting, Ruud Gullit, the urbane and elegant black Dutchman, is tonight's recipient of the customary racial abuse. No one seems able to offer a word of advice to players or referee that is not scatological, misogynistic or plain full of hate. A whole language is being debased. We all know that football thuggery is no longer uniquely English and that English football thugs are no longer uniquely foul. But no other nation produces supporters that are so sourly, so uniformly uncooperative. There is nothing very frightening about most of them. But what utterly depressing company they are. In Rome, I had watched the *Azzurri* through a sea of blue confetti, feeling welcome, safe and engaged in the pleasures of the game. *Viva Italia*, indeed. We have a lot to learn.

This is one of the most striking instances in which one finds the behaviour of footballers or football fans read as an index of the nature of national characteristics.

English fans take on especially important symbolic prominence. This is not only a question of the unfortunate visibility – in, as it were, the civic context – of England fans. It is also that commentators belonging to a political society in crisis find the symbolic potential of that society's representatives *en masse* especially appealing: the Scottish and Irish fans are likewise interesting for reasons beyond their putative colourfulness or good nature, drunkenness or (in the Irish case) religiosity. The analysis of the behaviour of these denizens of the British Isles, laid out for observation on a foreign field, becomes a form of ultimately political introspection. The mood is self-conscious and defensive, within the awareness of separation or exclusion from the cultural mores and amenities of Europe.

We wish to argue that this is probably a uniquely British sense: we cannot find its equivalent in the self-scrutiny of thoughtful sports journalists from elsewhere. The metatext within which this obsession with British fans is subsumed is a social, cultural and political debate about the nature of Britishness and its relationships with Europe. The only certainty within the debate seems to be the certainty of exclusion, of categorical difference.

EUROPEAN REACTIONS TO BRITISH FOOTBALL FANS

There were a number of negative and at times extremely alarmist articles on the English fans in the European press prior to or in the early stages of the World Cup: for example *Cambio 16*, 4 June, with an 8-page article on the subject; *Spiegel*, 11 June, which suggests that 80 per cent of the British journalists in Cagliari have come only to report on the hooligans; *Izvestija*, 11 June, in an article entitled 'English threat to Sardinia'; *Hannoversche Allgemeine Zeitung*, 11 June, whose article carries the title: 'Fear grows: British hooligans threaten Cagliari before the first game'; *L'Express*, 22 June, in an article entitled 'World Cup: hunting down the English'.

However, we may note that the European press is in the main generous about English football fans. The *Hannoversche Allgemeine Zeitung* (27 June) quotes the Italian *Repubblica* saying that the 'English are victims rather than causes of tensions'. The Spanish sporting daily *As* (1 July), says 'that section of the English support made up of hooligans was violent and noisy – fortunately they are a minority and in no way represent the fan from the islands'. *Le Nouvel Observateur* (5 July) observes that the Cameroonians 'provided the British fans with an opportunity to show that they are also human – imagine, the hooligans from Manchester and Liverpool stood to applaud the lap of honour of Milla and his gang!'

The Italian *Gazzetta dello Sport* (6 July) contrasts the behaviour of fans and players. Speaking admiringly of the sporting virtues of the English players, it talks about those 'fans' who are so different from the players: 'if there is a group who do not deserve the hooligans, it is precisely the English players'. Significantly, it can find civilised virtues in the England hero Paul Gascoigne which the English *Sun* would not wish to acknowledge: 'Gascoigne reaches out to anyone who holds out a hand and helps up the person reaching out' and describes his 'caresses like those of a gruff uncle' (6 July). By contrast, the English *Sun* is concerned to admire Gazza, as he is popularly known – perhaps his foreign-sounding name has to be democratised – in quite other terms.[3] It is particularly admiring of Gazza's account of how he called Ruud Gullitt 'a long-haired Yeti' (26 June).

Finally, on this subject of England, let us note that both the Soviet and the Spanish press are less well-inclined toward the England fan. Sectors of the Spanish press use the term 'hooligans' for any English fan turning up without a hotel reservation (e.g. *El País*, international edition, 18 June). The same edition refers to the English fans wearing 'those indescribable *working class shorts*' (with the phrase in italics written in English), and suggests that 'all beer drinkers over 18 from the UK were in Sardinia'.

We do not have to look far for an explanation of this Spanish attitude. The myth – in that neutral sense established by Barthes – of the English football fan has its meaning constantly redefined by that other English invader, the drunken holidaymaker (see for example 'Mi verano en Ibiza' – 'My summer in Ibiza' – by Juan Ballesta in *Cambio 16*, 20 August 1990, for further developments of this link). Two such consonant elements make for an irrefutable reading of mythology.

The Soviet case is to some extent a case apart. It is studied at length in the following chapter.

MUTUAL REPRESENTATIONS IN THE EUROPEAN PRESS

The English popular press, has, in its most downmarket manifestations, long appeared licensed to exhibit a particularly nasty approach to other nationalities. The *Sun's* history of abuse of other nationals is notorious – Italians are 'wops' and Germans are 'krauts'[4] and so on – but what is interesting about it are those features which are typical of certain myths and ideologies operative in English society, rather than their exaggeration within this one newspaper. Where necessary the English popular press does not hesitate to attack the Scots and the Irish, but the Germans and the French have, especially in the Thatcher era, been frequent targets, as well as other obvious candidates such as the Argentinians.

In the early days of November 1990 the *Sun's* xenophobia explored new forms with an astonishing campaign of vilification against Jacques Delors and the French in general. On 1 November, it ran four pages of insults against the French. A huge front page headline read 'Up Yours Delors', and the edition contained four pages of anti-French stories and jokes.[5] French responses to this were in general restrained, but an unpleasant question about British culture remains, and not merely about working-class culture. This point is not lost on European journalists. Commenting on the 'xenophobic' campaign of the *Sun* against Jacques Delors, the French weekly *Le Point* (12 November) described the English 'gutter press' ('journalisme dit 'du caniveau') as 'a speciality which is just as British as, if less elegant than, tweed, cricket or the rain'. The parallels between the *Sun's* xenophobia and concurrent arguments within British parliamentary and governmental circles are too obvious to be ignored.

There is nothing elsewhere in Europe to match the aggressiveness toward foreigners of the British popular press. The German daily *Bild*, while both sexist and chauvinistically German, is none the less rather restrained by comparison with the *Sun* or some of its slightly less controversial competitors. On the day of the England-Germany match, the *Sun's* headline was 'We beat them in '45, we beat them in '66, now the battle of '90'. *Bild* reproduced this headline (it was also picked up by other German dailies, for example *Neue Presse*, 4 July, *Hannoversche Allgemeine Zeitung*, 4 July), but its response was the relatively mild-mannered headline (in English) 'Goodbye England' (4

'My summer in Ibiza' 1. We come to Ibiza because we like to get drunk cheap and then break up Spanish hotel rooms. 2. Break up Spanish bars. 3. Beat up Spaniards. 4. They're only Spaniards. 5. So why are they complaining. 6. If they weren't so primitive they'd realise that, since they're foreigners, they have to suffer the consequences. (*Cambio 16*, 20 August 1990)

A German response to English views of Germaness Board: 'Under construction – the common European home'. Text: 'How nice, the English contribution is already ready as well'. (*Bunte*, 26 July 1990)

July). The mildness of continental responses to British insults was exemplified in *Le Parisien's* response (2 November) to the *Sun's* Delors campaign. Using the term 'rosbifs' (roast beefs), which fulfils the same colloquial function in French as the term 'frogs' in English, it announced. 'Rosbif, les grenouilles vous saluent bien' ('roast beefs, the frogs salute you'). Apparently, continentals have no grasp of invective at all.

The British popular press refers consistently to the Argentinians as 'Argies', a term adopted during the Falklands/Malvinas conflict. For example, a piece in the *Daily Star* (27 June) on the claimed drugging by Argentinians of Brazilian star Branco is headlined 'NOBBLED! Argies doped me says Brazilian ace Branco'. There is a subtext here implicating the Argentinians as cheats generally, instigated by a response to the defeat of England in the previous World Cup as a partial result of Maradona's infamous 'hand of God' goal. By comparison, the German tendency to refer to the Argentinians as 'gauchos' seems almost unexpectedly civil.

Xenophobia is certainly not an Irish tendency – the Irish press is relatively generous toward its opponents. The *Irish Times's* World Cup 90 souvenir refers gently to the no-scoring draw with Egypt with the headline 'Egypt frustrate Irish effort'. 'Ireland Entombed: Day of frustration as the Egyptians put up shutters', says the *Irish Press* (18 June), rather stereotypically but none the less quite intelligently. 'What a Dreadful Bore', says the same edition in another headline. 'Curse of the Pharaohs', says the *Irish Independent* of the same day. 'Irish in Egyptian Tomb', says the same paper elsewhere.

A Soviet view of Maradona's famous 'hand of God': 'Untie at least one of my hands so that I can score a goal . . !' (*Sovetskij Sport*, July 1990)

While the press throughout Europe referred to the Egyptians as 'the Pharoes', or even 'the descendants of the Pharoes' (*Dagens Nyheter*, 14 June), the English *Sun* is not willing to dally with the glorious days of Egyptian history. 'Charlton's Heroes Stymied by Camel Men', it says acidly. If *Dagens Nyheter* (14 June) described Egypt's surprise draw with Holland as 'as big a shock as if the sphinx had suddenly started to speak', the *Daily Mirror* dismissed both countries in a single phrase: 'Holland's superstar Gullit looked as sick as a camel' (quoted in the *Hannoversche Allgemeine Zeitung*, 14 June). Meanwhile German journalists can be found romantically referring to the United Arab Emirates (UAE) team as 'Sons of the Desert' ('Wüsten-söhne'). (As we observe in several places in this book, however, there are limits to Europe's tolerance when it comes to the challenge of sporting rivals from the Middle East, Africa and elsewhere.)

Elsewhere in Europe the English are referred to as 'the lions' ('los leones británicos' in Spain, 'i leoni' in Italy), a degree of respect barely conceivable even in the British quality papers, which operate within the assumption that sport requires rather harsher terms of reference. At extremes, compare the *Sun* talking about 'wops' and *Gazzetta dello Sport* talking about 'lions', and a depressing picture emerges of British, or at any rate English, cultural life.

BRITISH XENOPHOBIA SEEN FROM EUROPE

There is considerable awareness of this British tendency toward xenophobic utterance in the continental press. On many occasions this xenophobia takes the form of violent attacks by British newspapers against the British teams themselves when they allow themselves to be dominated by teams which the British press considers to be insignificant. For example *Sovetskij Sport* (21 June) tells us (mistakenly writing *Daily Start* instead of *Daily Star*):

> The war between the British journalists and the trainers of those teams carries on. Bobby Robson and Andy Roxburgh are constantly catching it. The English daily *Daily Start* commented on the results of the first matches with undisguised irony. 'This has been a great night for British football. First of all Scotland lost against a country we had never heard of before, and then England proved that there is an even weaker team in the competition than Scotland'. As you have already guessed, they are talking about the Scotland-Costa Rica and England-Ireland matches. Attacks of this kind grow more violent every day.

Kurier (8 July) mentions the 'sneering' ('Spott und Hohn') with which the *Daily Mail* treated the English team when it was 'outclassed' by Cameroon. The *Gazzetta dello Sport* is surprised that that 'bastion of chauvinism, the *Sun*' (9 July) should finally recognise the skill of the Italian players.

In the then English trainer Bobby Robson the European journalists find a living example of this tendency towards xenophobia which they do not hesitate to exploit. The *Hannoversche Allgemeine Zeitung* (4 July) tells how, on ushering out a group of Swedish journalists who wanted to observe the English team's training session before the match against Germany, Robson explained that 'Hitler didn't tell us what his plans were when he sent over the rockets'. *France-Soir* (5 July), discussing the subsequent German victory over England, quotes the England manager, before the match, making yet another reference to the Second World War. The Germans, he says, were thought unbeatable in 1940, but we (England, does he mean?) had the last word. There is such a thing as an English sense of humour, says the paper doubtfully, but Bobby Robson doesn't offer the best examples.[6]

France-Soir comments that the British are not alone in such references, and cites Italian remarks about 'German panzers'. With slight hypocrisy, having treated outbursts of chauvinism elsewhere as rather infantile, *France-Soir* sums up the Germany-England game by remarking that 'Le pudding ne l'emportait plus sur le bretzel' ('the plum pudding was no longer beating the pretzel').

THE CONSTRUCTION OF NATIONAL AND TRANSNATIONAL CHARACTER TYPES

'You have defended the honour of Africa, the entire continent is proud of you. You have shown that people must reckon with Africa . . . it can and must move forward . . . using its own style and its own talents. You have achieved success thanks to your team spirit, inventiveness and resolve, and have given an example to an entire nation.' *Cameroon President Paul Biya awarding medals to his country's players on their return from the 1990 football World Cup. (Sovetskij Sport, 8 July 1990)*

'A football team represents a way of being, a culture.' *Michel Platini, French football manager. (L'Equipe, 9 July 1990)*

THE INERTIA OF DISCOURSE ON NATIONAL CHARACTER

We shall be especially concerned in this section with the conservatism and idealist nature of discourses of national identification and identity. By this we mean, first, that the rootedness of the ideas which Europeans have about each other is something located very deeply in the soil of the history of myth: and, second, that ideas about other peoples' national identity are strongly resistant to considerations of material influence. By this latter phrase we have in mind the twin facts that national characteristics and national feeling are continuously reconstituted, rather than stabilised within some pre-historical or extra-historical realm, and that, consequently, national character, if it exists, must change and keep changing. Yet the reporting of Italia'90 is frequently locked into that form of discursive paralysis which we call stereotypification.

A MYTHICAL GEOPOLITICS

To start with, let us consider in the briefest of outline the mythical geopolitics of Italia'90. Europe's artistic storehouse is to suffer another invasion: actually several. The Germans (and their Austrian cousins), no longer swarming over the Alps as military invaders, now bring their Mercedes across the Brenner as some of Europe's most financially attractive tourists. Yet their true nature has already been showing. The *Frankfurter Rundschau* (11 June) describes how in

Rome 'towards midday a terrified priest bolted the church door and peered out suspiciously at the Northerners from Vienna through the open gap' – once more Christianity seeks refuge from the Hun.

The English have invaded from the South. This is the unregenerate Barbarian invasion of history. 'The English are the XIII Century Turks', says *L'Express* of 22 June, and Anthony Burgess, in an article published in *Paris Match* (14 June), describes the English hooligans as follows:

> . . . they recall the grim raids of the Vandals or the Visigoths, ready to disfigure the monuments of the mother of civilisation with illiterate graffiti, to piss in the sacred chalices, to stab, to punch and finally to snore in their drunken vomit.

The Italians, having had enough of this kind of thing in the past, have tried to confuse them by making them start in Sardinia and work North, hoping that the team is knocked out before they leave the island.

Meanwhile the crazy South Americans briefly import their carnival to enliven the show: but neither that nor the moments of cabaret provided by the fans of the Celtic countries of the British Isles can enliven the spectres at the feast from what used to be Eastern Europe. The Austrian *Kronen Zeitung* (25 June) entitles an article: 'Poor Rumanians! They think of home. Being eliminated would be a godsend'. Similar expressions of sympathy can be found in many other European publications (for example *Kurier*, also Austrian, of 26 June, the Irish *Evening Press World Cup Souvenir* of 3 July etc).

THE INVENTION OF BRITISHNESS

While the English fans were the main carriers of the idea of Englishness for the media during Italia'90, a secondary, and to some extent more traditional set of (British rather than uniquely English) discourses crystallised around the English team and its footballing style. This was seen as a style characterised essentially by a lack of skill and imagination, and dominated by a physical, athletic, even aggressive approach.

Such an approach was not universally admired in footballing terms. However, for some continental observers English football style represented the best of the British fighting tradition. The *Hannoversche Allgemeine Zeitung* (13 June) contrasts this positively with the activities of the fans: 'Healthy toughness instead of rioting, fair play instead of brawling – old British football virtues celebrated their World Cup triumph during the 1–1 draw between England and Ireland in Cagliari'. And when England eventually made it to the last eight, the same newspaper added (4 July): 'it was the so-called typically British virtues such as resolve and tireless commitment which dragged these athletes . . . into the quarter finals of the World Cup'. *Kurier* (4 July) agrees: 'the English style – physical, totally committed – brings with it the danger of a tireless fight'.

Even the *Gazzetta dello Sport* (6 July) would eventually warm somewhat to this approach. During the game against Germany, it writes in a front-page article, 'England lived up to its traditions, when the warrior spirit which inspires it (the same spirit which drives its hooligans, but with opposite results) allows it to make the best of its own qualities'. *L'Equipe* (9 July) continues the same idea: the English team, during its third-place play off with Italy, would show itself to be 'faithful to its old warrior tradition'.

An essential element of this discourse is a 'never-say-die' approach. Britons never give up until the final whistle. For the *Gazzetta dello Sport* (2 July), the England of the early part of the tournament had been 'a little England, which, however, never gave up fighting'. Talking of their match against Cameroon, *El Diario Vasco* (2 July) writes: 'while there is a Briton in the race nothing is ever decided until the winner breaks the winning tape . . . The English did what they always do, admirably, to be imitated by anyone who can: they fought to the end'. *Kurier* (6 July) suggests that 'it's part of their mentality that they never give a match up for lost'.

A further key element is the ability to take punishment. 'The English victory was based on no virtue other than their ability to soak up punishment', writes *El País* (2 July), speaking of their victory over Cameroon. In the same game the defender Mark Wright would become a living symbol of the supposed British ability to withstand pain: 'Typically British: despite a heavily bleeding cut defender Wright did not leave his team in the lurch. He held out "one-eyed" during extra time' writes *Kurier* (2 July). The next day the same newspaper added: 'Indians and British footballers know no pain. Mark Wright also held out bravely. For the heavily bleeding cut which the English sweeper suffered in the 85th minute in the match against Cameroon could not be treated until right after the final whistle. With eight stitches . . .'.

The longest eulogy of British fighting spirit is to be found, however, in the Basque daily *Deia* (3 July), commenting on England's victory over Cameroon. This article contrasts the English style of play with what it sees as the behaviour of the Spanish players:

> I can't let the chance go by to express my delight that the English team has made it to the semi-finals . . . Their football brings pleasure to anyone who see this sport as non-stop effort during 90 minutes, where technique is relegated to a secondary level and physical ability is the basis of the victory of the team. England had to expend twice as much energy to get to the semifinals.

> Messrs Waddle, Gascoigne, Platt, Barnes combine good technical quality with a great ability to soak up punishment on the field. They're not like their lordships Michel and Butragueño who only make use of their physical capabilities where they're near the branch of a bank.

Fair play, already mentioned above by the the *Hannoversche Allgemeine Zeitung* (13 June), is another important element. *Kurier* (6 July) adds, with a somewhat unusual sense of geography: 'the footballers from the island are experts when it comes to fairness. It's not for nothing that the three teams from the island (England, Scotland, Ireland) are in the top positions in the fair-play competition . . . Fair play is a point of honour in England'. Needless to say, the idea of qualities which harmonise Scottishness, Englishness and Irishness would be a controversial one in these countries.

This discourse of Englishness/Britishness is extremely well established in

Continental Europe. Its lack of clarity about internal 'British' distinctions is of course part of a larger pattern of Celtic political invisibility in Europe, which is especially striking here in the case of Ireland, given its political identity as a separate EC member.

As a number of the quotes above make clear, this is essentially an account of something seen by European journalists as Britishness rather than Englishness, though the English are undoubtedly its main focus. However, similar ideas can be found relating to Scotland. Thus *Dagens Nyheter* (16 June), describes the Scottish player Murdo MacLeod as representing 'the classic hard Scottish school', and quotes manager Andy Roxburgh as saying: 'We always play best when we have our backs to the wall'. Analysing Scotland's victory over Sweden, the same newspaper (17 June) speaks of 'Scotland's aggressive game', its 'stamina', and adds 'the Scottish defence played with a typical British touch, in other words extremely resolutely, to use a rather mild description'. Describing the same game, *Kicker* (21 June), in an article entitled 'Scotland gave 110 per cent', adds: 'As far as commitment is concerned the Scots gave their all . . . the extremely aggressive Scots pulled off a good performance in defence and fought till they dropped'. Indeed, as the same article makes clear, these characteristics can be acquired momentarily by other teams: speaking of Sweden's supposedly 'kick and rush' tactics during this game, *Kicker* adds: 'The North Europeans played in a typically British manner'.

(Similar approaches characterise accounts of Scotland in the 1992 European Championship. Talking of their warm-up game against Norway, the Norwegian daily *Aftenposten* (3 June 1992) described the Scots as follows: 'They know their technical limitations, but have enthusiasm and a British never-say-die approach'. Some days later, when Scotland lost its opening game against Holland, the same newspaper added (14 June) 'Of course, they went down with all possible honour – but fighting qualities and little else do not bring you gold in international football').

As we have noted, it is rather more surprising when these ideas of 'British-ness' become applied to the Republic of Ireland, though many of the Irish players *were* 'British': 'Trainer Jack Charlton's team had dominated for long periods and had shone with its typical virtues: fighting strength and an indomitable will to win', writes the *Hannoversche Allgemeine Zeitung* (26 June) of Ireland's game against Rumania. Commenting on the same match, *France-Soir* (26 June) – in an article in which it refers to the Irish as 'les Britanniques'! – suggests that 'their greatest strength is their ability to pres-surise without respite', adding: 'the British have one virtue: they neither sell the game short, nor refuse it, even in they frequently mistreat it'.

Of their game against Italy, *Kurier* (2 July) writes: 'The Irish showed how to beat Italy: don't stop for breath, don't let them build anything up, attack and attack again'. On the same day *El País* (international edition), combining a number of elements of the discourse, suggested that 'it doesn't matter that the Irish style takes us back to prehistory. On this occasion the character of the players rose above their shortcomings, their resolve to stand up to a team of patricians, on foreign soil, with none of the forecasts in their favour'. On July 3 *Kurier* added: 'The Irish . . . are not a class football team, but they played football with heart. They fought the Italians with that attitude we expected from them . . . A physical game isn't our thing, the Irish grow up with this virtue'.

It seems clear from a number of the quotes that the discourse of Britishness derives essentially from definitions of Britishness which arose in connection with the Second World War, and as we shall see shortly, it is matched by discourses of Germanness which also derive from the same period. 'Bravery' is an essential element not only of the Continental view of Britain, but also of Britain's own way of viewing its performance in international arenas, sporting and otherwise. Indeed, it would be central to the way the British media would present the British athletes during the 1992 Olympics.

THE GERMANS

It is the major players who become most heavily mythicised, both at the national and individual levels, as might be expected. In international football, there is no more major player than Germany, playing in Italia'90 still as West Germany.

The homologies relating sport to politics are never more obvious in Italia'90 than in the reporting of German matches, underscored, as of course such commentary is, by awareness of renascent German nationalism. Naturally, the British press, British football commentators and British politicians are active in this process of conceptual and discursive merger.

A headline in the *Guardian*, 26 June, reads: 'World Cup brings out German stormtroopers again', and the article continues: 'The ugly face of German nationalism showed itself early yesterday morning as hundreds of young West Berliners took to the streets to celebrate Germany's victory over Holland in the World Cup'. The piece goes on to refer to attacks on Polish tourists, the reappearance of Nazi salutes and slogans, anti-Dutch feelings, and the indulgence of these outbursts by the police, many of whom are said to support the far-right Republicans.

The idealist conception of history to which we have referred above makes itself felt here. German nationalism's 'ugly side' is assumed to be a historical constant. 'This is the real German arrogance you're seeing and I feel deeply ashamed', Manfred, an electrical engineer, is reported as saying to the reporter. Manfred is apparently a pessimist. He refers to an old mutual hatred between the Dutch and the Germans. 'It's Germany on the march again', he says gloomily. The article refers to 'the explosion of ancient enmity against the Poles'. This reveals, in some sense 'underneath' discourses about Europeanisation and the expansion of Europe geopolitically, another set of discourses about archetypal characteristics and oppositions. Their interplay, and their interaction with yet other discourses, is extremely complex.

According to tradition, these supposedly Teutonic qualities have remained unchanged since the time of the Romans. For example, the *Gazzetta dello Sport* (25 June) describes the German fans during the game against Holland as follows:

The Germans shout 'Deutschland! Deutschland!' A powerful, dull, hollow sound

. . . it bears the hereditary imprint of the roar which a thousand years ago brought fear to the hearts of Drusus and the legions when for the first time they ventured through forests without name.

Throughout Europe the German team is presented as the personification of discipline, dedication to work and reliability. The Spanish daily *ABC* (26 June) tells us that it displays a 'highly disciplined football and a champion's mentality'. It is described on some occasions as a 'machine team' (*Dagens Nyheter*, 16 June), on others as 'a machine which has been programmed to win by asphyxia' (*El País*, 9 June). *El País* (international edition, 11 June) assures us that, during their match against Yugoslavia, all the Germans 'clocked on at the beginning of the game and filled out an impeccable work sheet'. According to the Austrian *Kurier* (6 July) 'you can always rely on the Germans'.

The German press itself (*Hannoversche Allgemeine Zeitung*, 25 June) observes that the German style of play is characterised by 'German virtues, namely discipline, a fighting attitude and a fast game'. As Germany prepared for its game against the United Arab Emirates, the *Hannoversche Allgemeine Zeitung* (14 June) pointed out that 'the method which will guarantee success against the UAE is a fundamentally German recipe' ('ein urdeutsches Rezept'), and consists essentially of 'pressurising'. These supposedly German virtues can at times be attributed to other teams. The issue of *El País* mentioned above informs us that the Swedish team showed 'Prussian discipline', another reference to the old Germany of history.

Yet it is plain that football commentators face a difficulty with German play which Germany's category within the givens of national character cannot, in fact, accommodate. Put simply, there is far more flair and individual skill in the German team than can be accounted for by the sorts of Teutonic properties mentioned above. *El País* (8 July) reluctantly acknowledges this when it says that 'the [German] trainer has put together a compact group where discipline prevails along with a few drops of creativity'.

Therefore sports journalists, rather than simply throw overboard these ascriptions of national character, find bizarre and revealing metaphors whose inherent tensions are indices of the underlying dialectic which cannot be admitted.

L'Equipe (19 June) resolves this difficulty ingeniously by inventing a new category, referring to 'Une technique . . . saxo-latine', which preserves at least some – half, anyway – of the discursive integrity of previous formulations. Then this section of the report goes on to explain away the problem. Littbarski says of Häßler, his protégé ('Berlinois comme lui', as though this in itself may account for something), that he is undoubtedly one of the last players of his generation to have learned football in the streets, 'like a Brazilian or an African'. So that's at least part of the problem out of the way ('Ceci explique cela').

The Italian press creates an even odder compound definition: 'We saw Teutonic organisation and the fantasy of the gypsies' says *Tuttosport*, while *Il Messagero* adds that 'Germany speaks Italian' (both quoted in the *Hannoversche Allgemeine Zeitung* 12 June).[7]

However, perhaps the most curious example of this phenomenon is to be found in *El País* (international edition, 11 June), which tells us that the German team adds to its habitual discipline 'a visceral, almost Khomeini-esque side, which will have caused fear among its future rivals'.

THE LATINS

The South Americans, on the other hand, are approachable only along the most well-worn of paths. Austria's *Kronen Zeitung* (24 June) can see the Costa Ricans only as 'calypso-footballers', *Sovetskij Sport* (22 June) informs us that 'the whole of Costa Rica was dancing the lambada', Austria's *Kurier* (24 June) describes the Brazilians as 'samba kings', the *Glasgow Herald* (25 June) relates how 'Maradona silences the samba drums' of the Brazilians. This Latin passion contrasts (usually unfavourably) with the 'cool' of the Europeans, in particular the Northern/Germanic Europeans, a situation which *L'Equipe* (2 July) refers to as 'the clash of cultures' ('le choc des cultures'.)

As regards the fans, these unstable Latins are presented as unable to cope with the stresses of football, particularly in the case of defeat. *Kronen Zeitung* (4 July), in an article entitled 'Losing must be allowed', describes the treatment meted out to the Brazilian trainer ('his children don't dare go to school') and also to the Uruguayan trainer ('slapped down morally and obliged to resign') following the defeat of their teams. This is contrasted with the behaviour of the Irish, here representing an unusually 'Celtic' (joyous rather than cool, but still essentially reasonable) version of the Northern European reaction.

> Fortunately this World Cup shows us that there are outcomes other than those in Rio and Montevideo. An enormous reception was organised for the Irish team in Dublin after their 0–1 defeat by Italy. The fans had the impression that their team had given its all.

Izvestija (26 June) picks up and develops at great length the same theme of the temperamental and ultimately reckless Latin, highlighting the passionate nature of the South Americans relating to football in general. Talking of Brazil it says:

> Suffice it to say that on those days when there are matches in which the national team is taking part the number of heart attacks doubles . . . In the waiting room of a hospital in São Paulo a female patient died of a stroke – all the medical staff were enthusiastically watching the match between Scotland and Costa Rica. And while Maradona joyously waved the green-yellow strip of his defeated Brazilian opponent above his head, fourteen criminals managed to escape from the grounds of a prison also in São Paulo, taking advantage of the inconsolable grief of the guards. No-one was particularly surprised: it's football . . .

This passionate nature binds the South Americans with their European Latin cousins, in particular the Italians (the Spaniards having been eliminated from the competition). *L'Equipe* (2 July), previewing the forthcoming Italy-

Argentina game (which it describes as 'Les Latins en famille'), points in one article to 'an ancient cousinship, identical roots between the nations'. In another it shows how the same hot blood runs through their veins. This second article, entitled 'an exchange of blows', describes a quarrel which broke out between Argentinian journalists and Italian police during a press conference. *L'Equipe* distances itself from such behaviour commenting some-what disapprovingly:

> The fight started up again a few moments later between Argentinans and Italian journalists, this time over who would be the first to ask Giusti [an Argentinian player] a question. 'Come on now, calm down!' ('Un peu de calme, voyons!')

However the characteristic Northern European view of South Americans as talented but unstable and lacking in character is not shared by at least one Argentinian fan, who, after riots in Buenos Aires is reported in *El País* (5 July) as saying: 'we don't win because we play better than the others. We win because we've got balls, for shit's sake'. Little does he realise how he is hijacking a central descriptor of Britishness.

THE AFRICANS

The unexpected victory of the 'internationally inexperienced footballers from Cameroon' (*Der Spiegel*, 11 June) over the reigning World Champions Argentina in the opening match of Italia'90 not only 'threw the would-be established order into confusion' (*El Pais*, international edition, 11 June), it also brought African football to the fore amidst sensational news reports throughout Europe. Though this sudden newsworthiness was strengthened by the subsequent good performances of Egypt, in particular its draw with the European champions Holland, it was mainly Cameroon's passage to the quarter-finals which kept African football in the limelight for most of the tournament.

In terms of their football, there was, initially, a noticeable tendency to describe the Cameroon players by reference to European or South American stars, present or past. Thus the *Frankfurter Rundschau* (11 June) described the Cameroon centre forward Omam Biyik as 'a black van Basten', while the *Hannoversche Allgemeine Zeitung* of the same date referred to him as 'an African Gerd Müller, a black Horst Hrubesch . . . an African Pelé'. However, this approach changed quickly to one which highlighted what were seen as the main differences between African and above all European foot-ball. Their football was seen as 'cheeky, refreshing' (*Kronen Zeitung*, 3 July) 'refreshingly attacking' (*Hannoversche Allgemeine Zeitung*, 8 June), this 'tiny football nation . . . played joyously without any respect for the title holders' (*Hannoversche Allgemeine Zeitung* 9 June), they 'came out on to the pitch with a free-and-easy style, not at all inhibited by the presence of the world champions' (*El País*, international edition, 11 June). They are joyful, uninhi-bited, enthusiastic. In this sense they fill a gap which had once been occupied by the Brazilians, whose play is now considered to have become disappoint-ingly 'European', dominated by 'Nordic cool' (*Hannoversche Allgemeine Zeitung*, 11 June).

What the Cameroonians share with Brazil (or at least the Brazil of the past) is that they bring 'magic' to the game. This magic is closely connected for European commentators with the magic of childhood, but it is not simply the childhood of the individual – these discourses connect with well-established European discourses of the childhood of Man, set in some idealised pre-industrial non-European society where people were free of the constraints of modern living and able to act in accordance with their instincts.

A French expression of a common European view of Africa (here represented by the Egyptian footballers). Top caption: 'Africa thumbs its nose at Europe'. Text: 'Obviously, since football is just a game for them'. (*L'Equipe*, 14 June 1990)

'The Cameroonians are instinctive footballers' writes Dettmar Cramer in the *Hannoversche Allgemeine Zeitung* (25 June). Their play is variously described in many newspapers as 'temperamental', 'inventive', 'creative' and above all 'joyful'. In extreme versions of this discourse their style of play is presented not simply as 'imaginative' but as 'irrational', as befits children below the age of reason. According to *Sovetskij Sport* (20 June) their game is characterised by 'frenzy'. 'This team draws its strength from a fluid game characterised by improvisation. Cameroon's victory is in some sense the victory of the irrational' writes *L'Equipe* (25 June). Henry Kissinger agrees: 'We hope that football will develop along the lines of Cameroon. Less intellectual, but with more enthusiasm for the game. We need more Cameroons in world football!' (quoted in *Die Presse*, 9 July). Indeed, the Cameroonians are in more than one sense football's version of the 'savage infant' who makes European man more acutely aware of the artificiality of his own environment.

As befits such an infant, their football skills are inborn and honed to perfection in spontaneous play. 'They seem to have learned their feeling for the ball in the cradle' says the *Hannoversche Allgemeine Zeitung* on 18 June. 'The Cameroonians have football in their blood', adds Nepomniashchij in *Sovetskij Sport* (26 June). 'They are footballers by the grace of god' writes *Izvestija* (3 June) in an interesting departure from the official atheism of Soviet ideology. 'Cameroon's footballers must have acquired this [skill] as whippersnappers on the streets. Otherwise such perfection cannot be explained' writes Ernst Happel in *Kurier* (3 July).

But it is not simply instinctive, uncontrolled football. The fact that the Cameroonians were trained by a Russian, and that a number of their players played professionally in France led commentators everywhere to present them as a unique fusion of African spontaneity and European training. One of the earliest expressions of this view appeared in the Spanish national daily *El País* (13 June):

> The main challenge which Nepomniashchij faced . . . was to bring some order and organisation to the chaotic and improvised Cameroon football. It's not a problem of talent, an innate element which led them to victory in the last African Cup tournament. The deficiencies are in the system. 'The players learn in the street. There they achieve great ball control, but they know nothing about tactics. The Cameroonians are the Brazilians of Africa. They need to hear the applause of the public more than the instructions of the trainer,' he lamented.
>
> Nepomniashchij introduced some notes of Soviet discipline, but he was very careful not to impose foreign ideas which could cramp the particular style of African football.

For the Swedish daily *Dagens Nyheter* (14 June) Cameroonian football is a 'successful blend of earlier African football and modern European football'. The Cameroon team, writes Lev Filatov in *Izvestija* on 25 June, 'gives the impression of being fairly well versed in modern tactics . . . However, it plays its game without abandoning its indigenous style and habits'. Indeed, as the tournament continued, Cameroon would be presented more and more as a blend of African instinctiveness and European discipline. Nepomniashchij has 'combined the joyful play of the Africans with tactics, discipline, order and toughness in combat', writes *Kicker* on 9 July.

The most highly developed example of this discourse is to be found, however, in *Kicker* on 5 July. Though this is a lengthy article, it is worth quoting at length, since in it Karl-Heinz Heimann brings together all the main elements of the dominant discourse in relation to Cameroon:

> Why our Bundesliga stars cannot play as well as the 'Black Lions' from Africa.
>
> THE ARTIST FROM AFRICA: IT'S PURE NATURE
>
> It's a long, long time since any World Cup tournament has set standards and given examples which other sought to emulate . . . Could the Cameroonians, with their heartwarmingly natural and spontaneous style, constantly surprising both opponent and spectators, find imitators, particularly in Europe? Unfortunately, our heads tell us that the answer must be no. But all who love football as a game wish with all their heart that we could admire something like this on a weekly basis on our football fields, and take joy from it.
>
> Why is this the case? There are many reasons. The catlike suppleness of the Africans is innate, not achieved by training. They have grown up with the ball. They are sadly lacking in what can be learned by training, more or less what we here so unattractively call 'set pieces'. Free kicks land in the stands, corners somewhere in no man's land.
>
> The things which make them stand out, their surprising passes, moves which cannot be rehearsed, arise from the inspiration of the moment. Informally put, it is 'pure nature'. Most of the players come from small villages. They mostly play barefoot. Kicking a ball around gives them fun and pleasure. It is, in the proper sense of the term, 'child's play' for them to learn how to control the ball. If some club from one of the few larger towns takes them on, they have long since been perfect at controlling the ball.
>
> It is only when they are considerably older that they receive some of the 'blessings' of tactics. But by that time they are so mature that no trainer, no matter how ingenious the methods he uses, can take away their joy at playing with the ball.
>
> That is the decisive difference from our highly civilised West: in Cameroon, everywhere in Africa and Asia the ball is the favourite toy of millions of children, they know no other. Neither surf boards nor mountainbikes, neither tennis courts or even computers are at hand to distract them from playing with the ball.
>
> There is no longer any 'street football' here in our country. Should children join a club, usually when they are considerably older, the first thing the trainer has to do is to apply his efforts to teaching them ball control. In most cases it's already too late. And tactics are already given too much importance in the youth work of our clubs.
>
> This is not a complaint, just the description of a situation. We cannot play football like the Cameroonians. Shame. It would be too nice if we could admire their spontaneity, their way of controlling the ball in the Bundesliga. But fairness requires us not even to raise such a demand. It is unfulfillable.

Like Karl-Heinz Heimann other Europeans long for a return of natural football to European stadia: 'Tell me, is it possible to see such adventurous scenes in the pre-packaged football which they dish up to us?! The Cameroonians have not broken any strict rules, but they have also not let themselves by bound by them. And we thank them for showing us this!' writes Lev Filatov in *Izvestija* (25 June). 'Wouldn't it be nice if we could import a little of this to Austria?' adds Ernst Happel in *Kurier* (3 July).

Such discourses are, of course, profoundly contradictory, as Karl-Heinz

Heimann recognises. These contradictions were to reach their peak in the game between Cameroon and England, where, it was generally agreed, Cameroon played the best football of the entire tournament. This match was to become emblematic of a clash between two styles of football. Even before the game had started the Spanish sports daily *As* had announced it in the following terms: 'first of all this is a clash of diametrically opposing styles: rigid and according to plan on the English side, improvised and on the limits of the rules on the Cameroon side'. For Christian Montaignac writing in *L'Equipe* (2 July), this game was to go beyond a clash of footballing styles to represent a profound clash of cultures:

> The Cameroonians, lost amid fluttering flags and echoing songs, played the part of the Brazilians on entering. To the scenes of today they brought the fresh air of a Yaoundé [the capital of Cameroon] bathed by the Mediterranean. The English played the part of the English closely escorted by stern-faced policemen . . . To the scenes of today they brought the idea of a strange carnival hijacked by the urgency of one day . . . It was all about . . . the contrast between a joyous folklore and a venomous expression of sport.

> So much exoticism troubled the English, so much rigour disorientated the Cameroonians . . . The tone was set by two musics scarcely made to be in tune . . . [On the Cameroon side] there were even mingled sounds where you could recognise Italian voices and Brazilian songs.

This game was to see a reversal of traditional roles, with the 'savage infant' teaching its old master a lesson. 'Hampered by the liveliness of their opponents, by their extraordinary technical skills and their constant changes of wings, the English ended up unable to play their game', suggests *L'Equipe* (2 July). 'Seldom had a seasoned European defence, which up to that point had let in only one goal, been left so helplessly exposed by the imaginative play of its opponent', adds *Kronen Zeitung* (3 July). For a while the infant was to become the father: 'At times the Africans had played with the representatives of the mother land of football as a father plays with his son . . . the black Africans surprised everyone with their refreshingly direct game' (*Kurier*, 2 July); 'Grampa Milla played with the brawny representatives of the mother land of football as a father plays with his son' (*Kurier*, 3 July).

At this moment the contradictions of the discourse reached their peak. Are the Cameroonians leaders or savage infants, wise men or children in loin cloths? Nowhere is this contradiction more clearly expressed than in *Izvestija* (25 June), where the sports commentator writes of Roger Milla: 'I don't know what best to call him – leader, shaman, Tarzan, Mowgli'.

Despite their superiority, however, Cameroon were to lose 3–2. The general note was one of regret. 'Power football triumphs over Cameroon's inventiveness', wrote the *Hannoversche Allgemeine Zeitung* on 2 July, while *Kronen Zeitung* (3 July) added: 'All football connoisseurs bemoan the fact that Cameroon has been eliminated . . . For there has been no other team in this World Cup which has played with so little stolidness and so much enthusiasm'.

Their defeat was felt by some to be a moral victory, but it had to be accounted for, and the dominant explanation of this defeat brings the discursive circle to a close: the Cameroonians lost because of those very character-istics which made them so attractive in the first place – their ingenuousness, their lack of professionalism and polish, even their lack of cynicism, in short, a style of football which had not yet grown up: Cameroon 'missed the historic opportunity to be the first African team to reach the semi-final by erring on the side of excess' wrote *Gazzetta dello Sport* on 2 July, adding 4 days later that they 'paid (excessively) for some moments of ingenuousness and a game which is still in its student days'.

Similar sentiments are not difficult to find elsewhere: 'What the black continent lacks to become the Brazil of the twenty-first century is professiona-lism . . . Professionalism would eliminate those moments of ingenuousness which penalised Cameroon in its final [sic] against England when it continued to attack in a scatterbrained manner instead of managing its advantage. But long live Africa, even for this', was the view of *Gazzetta dello Sport* (3 July). *El País* (9 July) continued in the same vein:

> What Cameroon lacked was precisely the weight of a past record in order to reach the semi-finals which it deserved . . . They have neither the personality nor the track record of Brazil, of course, but their players are as athletic as they are good ball players.

In the end Roger Milla would agree: 'With a bit of experience we would have held on to our 2–1 lead, we weren't smart enough, but we'll be back' (*Kronen Zeitung* 3 July). Herbert Hufnagl, writing in the Austrian newspaper *Kurier*, would sum up the closing of this discursive cycle in an article entitled 'Adieu Cameroon': following their defeat by England, the Cameroon players had reverted to being, he points out, 'nice, but harmless wild men from Africa' (3 July).

However, although the discourse comes full circle, the contradictions are not, of course, resolved. Are the Cameroonians capable of becoming 'smart' enough to defeat the more experienced teams without losing their appeal for the pre-packaged European man whom these discourses construct by impli-cation? We can be confident that, paraphrasing Milla's remark, along with the Cameroonians such contradictory discourses will also be back.

THE CELTS

As well as the 'battling British' identity carried by their football teams, the Scots and the Irish enjoy a parallel identity, represented in particular by their fans, which we might term 'Celtic'. The key elements of this identity are large-scale drinking accompanied by high spirits, good humour and a sense of fun.

The Irish, appearing in the World Cup for the first time, and getting much further than Scotland have in their many appearances in the finals, upstage the Scots as Europe's lovable Celtic eccentrics (the Scottish fans would recover this position during the 1992 European championship). Thus Austria's *Kronen Zeitung* (10 July) refers to 'the Irish fans: 25000 [sic] crossed through Italy, friendly and fair – high spirits, songs, but sober. Fans like the ones you'd like to have'. For *El Diario Vasco* (2 July) 'The Irish fans were the best bit of the World Cup'; they showed that 'for them football is above all a party', and that 'good sporting humour is more important than the results'. For the *Gazzetta dello Sport* (2 July) 'the Irish fans [were] the nicest and best behaved group in the World Cup . . . The elimination of Eire has not changed the fans' behaviour in any way: they were civil and joyful before, and they have remained civil and joyful now', adding that 'Jackie Charlton's team broke the record for niceness'.

Though enjoying a much lower profile than the Irish, the Scots appear as reformed characters and maintain their role as World Cup clowns and benign drunkards. The *Frankfurter Rundschau* (20 June) describes them as 'the other fans from the island – once cursed, now welcome . . . Many of them soon got really drunk, but they remained peaceful. No trace of violence'. Scotland, however, copes less well with defeat. The Scottish press, recovered from a brief bout of hysteria after the win against Sweden, during which it roared 'Bring on Brazil', sank back into resignation, invoking that view of historical constants examined above. 'Scotland have the knack of doing nothing at inordinate length', bemoans *Scotland on Sunday* (24 June), while the *Glasgow Herald* has, in the period after the Sweden match, reflected upon the religious determinism which explains Scotland's bewilderingly eccentric World Cup record: 'maybe it is an integral part of the Calvinistic soul but the latest footballing sons of Scotland echoed their predecessors' demand for humiliation first, salvation second, with another display of World Cup defiance' (18 June).

THE NATIONAL DIMENSION: QUESTIONS OF JOURNALISTIC STYLE

THE MILITARY METAPHOR

The German army

Throughout European journalism on the World Cup there runs a subterranean current of football as a 'substitute war'. However, the military metaphors are applied above all to the German team.

The *Gazzetta dello Sport* (25 June), for example, describes the game between Germany and Holland as 'the metaphor of the war' and the *Kronen Zeitung* (24 June) entitles its report on the same game 'The Thirty Years War'. The headline in the *Sun* mentioned earlier also equates football with war: 'We beat them in 45 . . . Now the battle of 90'. We have also discovered so to speak covert references to this theme. The Austrian *Kurier* of 6 July entitles its report on the forthcoming final 'Dritter Streich der Deutschen' ('The Germans' Third Strike'), a phrase which has an obvious similarity, both orthographic and phonetic, with 'Drittes Reich der Deutschen' ('The Germans' Third Reich').

The Spanish sports paper *As Color* (8 July) describes Matthäus as 'the resurgence of the German Luftwaffe', his legs are like 'machine guns' and he combines 'Wagnerian musicality with his usual steamroller style'. Klinsmann is 'the man who literally blasted the Dutch defence' (*Izvestija*, 26 June). *El*

A Soviet newspaper depicts Lothar Matthäus as an (admittedly somewhat limp) German tank (*Sovetskaja Kul'tura*, 14 July 1990)

País (9 July) describes the Germans as 'moving with the heaviness of a tank' and as 'always looking to measure up to armies like their own'. 'The panzers crushed a hesitant Yugoslavia' says *Il Messagero* (quoted in the *Hannoversche Allgemeine Zeitung*, 12 June). *Gazzetta dello Sport* (2 July) describes the forthcoming semi-final between Germany and England as 'a panzer-like semi-final'. *As* (8 July) entitles its article on the final 'Panzers against Argentina'. *France-Soir* (5 July), while ridiculing Italian allusions to the 'German panzer', cannot resist the temptation to develop this same theme in the same article, describing Germany's poor performance against England in the following terms: 'We were far removed, however, from the devastating panzer. At most a little armoured car whose axles were creaking a smidgen'.[8]

Le Monde (quoted in *Gazzetta*, 2 July) sees German victory in the World Cup as part of a 'pan-Germanic' offensive. Henry Kissinger, former American Secretary of State and himself of German origin, does not hesitate to develop this theme in an article on the World Cup which he published in the *Los Angeles Times* and which also appeared in translation in a number of other countries (e.g. *El País*, international edition, 25 June, *Paris Match*, 21 June):

> . . . there is no doubt that the German team plans its games in the same way as the Army officers of that country, paying meticulous attention to detail. However both suffer, when, under the pressure of certain events, they are forced to deal with eventualities which upset their intricate planning.

In general, there is a tendency to equate German football with power and remorselessness, and to report Germany as 'killing off' opponents. The German press itself recognises that its team is internationally knows as a 'Teutonic panzer' (*Spiegel*, 11 June).

The Scottish army

If the military metaphor is used in all countries in relation to the German team, in Scotland (and to a lesser extent in England) we find a purely local application of the same image. In the Scottish press there is also much use of military metaphors to describe what is invariably the 'campaign'. These metaphors are not used in other countries in relation to Scotland. What we have here is an example of auto-typification as opposed to the hetero-typification of the German team.

The *Glasgow Herald* develops this idea in a fairly sustained manner. On 12 June there are references to 'the tartan army', a phrase which almost all journalists in Scotland always use to describe Scottish fans: 'the bedraggled footsoldiers'· the dismissed tartan hordes in Genoa: 'campaign medals'.

But the Scottish team is not a triumphant team like the German one. It faces constant dangers. A later edition (14 June) has a headline 'STEPPING OUT INTO A MINEFIELD: Murdo the man to steer troops through "war zone' " – and it finally has to accept defeat: 'FORLORN TARTAN ARMY SUFFER SOBERING DEFEAT'. The tartan army is the representative of a nation which lacks confidence in itself both inside and outside the stadium. As the *Independent on Sunday* tells us on 24 June echoing the words of Dave Hill reported earlier: 'And so once more the soldiers of the tartan army marched to the stadium as warriors and returned as men wearing skirts'.

THE ITALIAN VOLCANO

Whereas only the British think they have a monopoly on character, grit and determination, by comparison with which continental character is invariably 'suspect' (with certain Northern European exceptions), everybody, including British journalists, think the Italians are wonderful footballers. Everyone however thinks that the Italians are volcanic. During the game against

Czechoslovakia, *Pravda* (21 June) assures us that 'the Italian team . . . reflected the explosive nature of its people', and *Izvestija* adds (28 June) that the Italians 'are at times inspired by an inner fire'.

All over the European press, the description of the defeat of Italy requires the annexation of Mount Vesuvius. *Bild* (4 July) has the volcano following the progress of the match. '[Italy scores] . . . Vesuvius erupts . . . [Argentina scores] . . . Vesuvius grows cold . . . [Italy loses the match] . . . Vesuvius, Naples and all of Italy weeps'. Examples of the role of Vesuvius in the comprehension of Italianicity abound. 'Italy is snuffed out beneath Vesuvius' (*Kronen Zeitung*, 5 July). 'The Italians . . . went to Naples and at the edge of Vesuvius were burned by the molten lava' (*Deia* 4 July). 'Vesuvius rumbles like an old boiler' (*L'Equipe*, 5 July, in an article which offers at least forty heterogeneous images, each more surprising than the next, apparently used in the Italian press to express the disappointment of the Italians). 'If Vesuvius, which loomed on the horizon, had erupted at the end of the match in Naples . . . this would not have caused that feeling of oppression which the defeat of their beloved team brought to the Italians. That evening in Italy you could speak in a whisper. A sea of almost funereal silence spread over this country which had noisily celebrated every victory of its footballers' (*Sovetskij Sport*, 5 July).[9]

This last quote combines the two key elements of the metaphor: eruption and extinction, Vesuvius and the new Pompeii. 'The silence of the tomb [fell on Italy] and the trumpets which had been prepared to announce the glory fell silent' (unidentified Italian daily quoted in *El País*, 5 July). 'And suddenly the shock! The city [Rome] was literally plunged into the silence of the tomb. (*Izvestija*, 5 July)'. 'Rome . . . was a genuine tomb' (the Basque daily *Deia*, 5 July). 'The quiet of the cemetery reigns in Rome' (*Kicker*, 5 July). 'There were no football reports, only obituaries' (*Hannoversche Allgemeine Zeitung*, 5 July). 'The flags hang at half mast. It is almost like a state funeral' (*Kurier*, 5 July).

War, a state funeral, experiences in which the concept of the nation is frequently mobilised as a personification of all the inhabitants of the country: as *Pravda* (19 June) explains with some incredulity:

> At times such passions are aroused in the stadiums and around them as if it was not a sporting competition but almost a war. A victory in the game becomes a nationwide triumph, and a defeat is equated with national tragedy . . . But it's only a game.

A UBIQUITOUS METONYM: 'ONE TEAM, ONE NATION'

The most universal form of expression we have found is the notion of the nation as one sentient being.

Bild (25 June) provides the most outrageous example, reporting on the German victory over Holland. On the front page, 'All Germany leapt from its seat'; then, inside:

> Yesterday evening, 9 o'clock: all of Germany is a giant living room. All of

Germany is on the football sofa. All of Germany in front of the television. And all Holland . . . [the match proceeds] . . . All of Germany asks itself 'what are these tactics?' . . . [Germany scores] . . . All of Germany jumps from the sofa . . . [the match is nearly over] . . . All of Germany is on its feet in the living room.

This idea of the nation as one is the *leitmotiv par excellence* of World Cup reporting. 'All of Italy is speaking of Totó [Schillaci]' (*L'Equipe*, 25 June). 'A nation [Italy] rejoices', (*Kronen Zeitung*, 1 July). 'A nation is plunged into despair': the defeat 'has brought an entire nation to tears' (*Kronen Zeitung*, 4 July). 'An entire land is wakened rudely from a dream' (*Kicker*, 7 July). 'An entire nation has the blues' (*Kronen Zeitung*, 6 July). 'The whole of Costa Rica was dancing to the lambada' (*Sovetskij Sport*, 22 June). 'All of Italy, without exaggeration, is counting the days until the match against Ireland' (*Izvestija*, 28 June). 'All England had a night of madness after the victory over Cameroon' (*Gazzetta*, 3 July). 'It is amazing what a goal or two can do for the nations's psyche!' (*Scotland on Sunday*, 17 June). 'The man who killed 60 million Italians' (*France-Soir*, 5 July). 'Maradona stunned the whole of Italy' (*Dagens Nyheter*, 4 July). Cameroon's victory over Argentina 'plunged its 10 million inhabitants into ecstasy' (*Frankfurter Rundschau*, 11 June). Romania's defeat of the USSR 'brought joy to 23 million' (*Romania Libera*, quoted in *Izvestija* 11 June). And, in a statement which history was to prove tragically wrong, Yugoslavia's trainer Ivica Osim would claim: 'My team . . . the national team is the representative of Yugoslavia, not just of its football, but of the entire country' (*Hannoversche Allgemeine Zeitung*, 14 June).

On occasions this metonym can acquire a supranational, or even continental dimension. When Egypt drew with European champions Holland, the *Hannoversche Allgemeine Zeitung* (16 June) suggested that 'the unexpected victory against Holland had plunged Egypt and the entire Arab world into ecstasy'. Speaking of Cameroon, *El País* (international edition, 18 June) suggests that 'all Africans see Cameroon as their representative in Italy'. The *Hannoversche Allgemeine Zeitung* (25 June) agrees that 'not just Cameroon, but the whole of Africa is proud of the team'. *Deia* (3 July), expands on the same idea:

Cameroon's defeat by England last Sunday was taken as a victory by the players and all of Black Africa . . . the Cameroon footballers today became national heroes and the pride of an entire continent . . . Africa yesterday paid emotional homage to the Cameroon football team for succeeding in banishing the myth of European supremacy and taking an African team to the rank of champion.

Izvestija (26 June) tries to present this metonym in a more explicit, but not any less exaggerated manner. 'There is, however, no greater error than trying to divide the Brazilians into fans and those who are indifferent to football – you won't find any of the latter'. And in the *Hannoversche Allgemeine Zeitung* (5 June) we found the only article which treats this figure of speech with irony:

> If we win the World Cup . . . the personal pronoun (first person plural) 'we' will refer not only to the players, but also to our baker, our garage attendant, our postman – even our Granny (80) will be a World Champion. Possibly even our cats and our neighbour's canary.

But the truth is that the metonym is extremely robust and is preserved even when statistics plainly contradict it:

> All Italy was plunged into the deepest silence yesterday when Vialli, Zenga and the other home favourites beat USA 1–0. No fewer than 25 million people followed the match (*Dagens Nyheter*, 17 June).

Italy has around 60 million inhabitants. Previously we mentioned the diachronic immutability of discourse of national character: in other words this account maintains its integrity from one period in history to another. What we have here is in a certain sense the synchronic axis of the same function, in other words, at any precise moment in history the discourse of national character maintains its integrity across the boundaries of mutual recognition.

A TRANS-EUROPEAN HYPER-NARRATIVE

And we finish this section with a small trans-european hyper-narrative.

> Cameroon is 'insolent' (*El País*, 25 June, international edition, 2 July/ *Hannoversche Allgemeine Zeitung*, 9 June): they play 'impudent football' (*Kronen Zeitung*, 3 June); Costa Rica is 'a cheeky upstart from Central America' (*Frankfurter Rundschau*, 20 June); when it wins 'it's a victory for impudence' (*Hannoversche Allgemeine Zeitung*, 22 June).

> However, the USSR 'puts Cameroon in its place' (Spanish *ABC*, 20 June): the Germans, in turn, 'give the Yugoslavs a lesson in modern football' (*Politica*, Belgrade, quoted in *Hannoversche Allgemeine Zeitung*, 12 June); and they also 'teach the United Arab Emirates a lesson' (*Hannoversche Allgemeine Zeitung* 16 June); and 'simply put, this professional team [Germany] taught the semi-professional Czechs a lesson' (*Izvestija*, 3 July).

> Finally, although 'the schoolmasterish football of the English was made to look completely ordinary for a time' by Cameroon (*Hannoversche Allgemeine Zeitung*, 2 July), during this game the Africans received a 'harsh lesson in realism' (*L'Equipe*, 2 July), and they 'still have a few lessons to learn before they can pass their football exam' (*Dagens Nyheter*, 3 July).

This brief but pungent narrative has a clear logical and thematic continuity, but it is made up of quotes from nine different newspapers in six languages. As in the case of hypertext, the elements which make it up have a psychological and cultural continuity, not a spatial or temporal one. They are fragments of a European meta-discourse which materialise in independent accounts throughout the continent.

SPORT AND POLITICS IN JOURNALISM

Finally, in this section it is worth remarking on some of the fully conscious and often rather contrived parallels which are made between footballing events at Italia'90, and political circumstances.

After the bombing by the IRA of the London Carlton Club, a leader in *Today* (27 June, 1990, headed 'IRA scores an own goal') did what a number of journalists and politicians did, and drew connections between claimed British delight in Irish successes in the World Cup and the putatively misplaced desire of the IRA to undermine this close relationship.

Much of the English press (we have already seen an example) referred to Ireland invariably as 'Jack Charlton's Ireland' (the manager is a very well-known ex England player), leading to the observation from a number of quarters that this seemed an attempt to imply that any Irish success was owed essentially to England. (In fact the Irish press also referred to Charlton in this way, which complicates that judgement. Other journalists picked up the habit: both French and German newspapers referred to 'les hommes de Jacky Charlton'/'Die Mannen von Jackie Charlton'.) The British tabloid, *Today* goes further, and explicitly discusses how Irish players play and were often born in Scotland and England. This is used to argue that Britain and Ireland 'are as impossible to separate as Siamese twins' (an idea reflected in the Spanish press which describes the match between Ireland and England as 'a fratricidal duel – *El País*, 13 June). This is an extraordinarily contentious conclusion.

An ironical *Guardian* piece (26 June) on the European summit in Dublin refers to 'violent outbreaks of English nationalism' at such meetings: 'foreigners regard us as the tiny minority who are ruining it for everyone else'. Mrs Thatcher becomes 'the volatile England captain', and Charles Haughey the referee. Commenting on the same summit, *France-Soir* (26 June), in what has proved to be a somewhat prophetic article entitled 'Europe breaks down – the time of the nations returns once more', observes that François Mitterrand and Mrs Thatcher have much less power in Dublin than the barman who pours the last Guinness before the kick-off of the Ireland-Rumania match. Noting the passion of the Irish for football, *France-Soir* concludes:

> Making Europe is no mean feat. Nations exist, states are important, the peoples wish to assert themselves and all this must be taken more and more into account . . . The slowing down of the process of European unity is obviously a result of the fact that the nations are coming back in strength to the fore.

From European unity to national unity: as the host nation of the World Cup, Italy deserves special attention from the European journalists. Totó (Salvatore Schillaci) is presented as the man who reunites Italy. He is the new Garibaldi. When Maradona asked his now infamous question prior to the Italy-Argentina match – 'Why should Naples support Italy when for 364 days every year Italy treats the inhabitants of Naples like country bumpkins?' – Schillaci replied that he had 'reunified Italy'. The Austrian *Kronen Zeitung* (5 July) writes:

More than anything else it is the team in the blue strip which keeps Italy together. Everyone can identify with the Azzurri. And in recent weeks the Sicilian Salvatore Schillaci was able, through his decisive goals, to overcome the abyss between North and South. And now it's all over at a single stroke. The sun has darkened, and the final in Rome, which was to be Italy's triumph, belongs to the foreigners. The nation which was joined in football fragments again into Romans, Neapolitans, Lombards, Tuscans, Friulians, Piedmontese, etc., who bitterly bemoan Italy's plight.

Le Point draws an even more complex parallel:

> Economics, politics, football: everything is seen as linked . . . the end of catenaccio [a heavily defensive Italian style of football] coincides with the beginning of the economic boom . . . Finally, the economy of the Peninsula takes off when the Italian footballers move to the offensive, the ball at their feet.

And *L'Express* (15 June) analyses the history of Italian football in terms of the political history of the country:

> Mussolini was the first to intuit the strike force of Calcio [football]. His vision of the new man included that of the campionissimo . . . The fall of fascism drained the colour from the blue football shirt: from then on suspicion stained the concept of patriotism . . . Ex-spokesman for Bettino Craxi and football historian, Antonio Ghirelli analyses the turn-around in 1982: 'The success of the Italians in Spain was linked to the presidency of Sandro Pertini. A well-known anti-fascist, a victim of Mussolini, he absolved the country from blame. His presence in the stand gave back the colours to our flag.'

These claims are similar to a number of others made, implicating football in political processes. It was widely claimed in Scotland, for example, that had the Scottish team won the World Cup in 1978, the Scots would have voted more decisively for their own parliament in the following year, though it should be admitted that there could not conceivably have been a more improbable route to autonomy. However, by 1992 there was evidence that the Scots were planning to try to qualify again. (For tactical reasons, they began their campaign with a defeat, against Switzerland.)

POSTSCRIPT (1992)

Our broader reflections on Italia '90 are dealt with in a larger context in our general conclusion: particularly the question of how we relate an apparent trend, in some discursive domains, to speak about the *obsolescence* of the nation state, with its apparent *centrality* as a term in the constructions we have been examining in this chapter. We shall limit ourselves here to noting, from the vantage point of Autumn 1992, some relevant developments since these newspaper pieces appeared.

The apparent threat from the developing world to the sporting hegemony of the nations of Europe, North America and the Antipodes has significantly increased. In the world of athletics and elsewhere in sport, Africa has been an ever more potent force. Yet at the same time, since our interest is in sport's conjunction with politics, we might note how detached the positive symbolism of sporting success is from the developing horrors of famine, war and AIDS on the African continent. The celebratory tone some television commentators adopted to welcome the arrival of Africa onto the 'world stage' at Barcelona sounded from certain perspectives like a wrong note. But, certainly, in a number of sports in the intervening period, established ideas about sporting hierarchies have been challenged, as for example Wales felt at first hand during rugby football's World Cup of 1991, when the arrival of Western Samoa was widely treated by the media as another example of the threat to the Old World.

The apparently extraordinary obsession of the British press in 1990 with the two World Wars, whenever relations with Germany were in question on the football field, now seems confirmed as an underlying and rigidly fixed set of attitudes. We comment in the general conclusion on the worsening state of British-German relations in 1992. In the interim, almost everything which has occurred in the domain of politics has confirmed our sense of the United Kingdom as isolated in its own view and in the view of Europe from the rest of the continent, notwithstanding any temporary alliances between the anti-Maastricht forces of Britain, Denmark and France.

And in the interim it may be that British attitudes to Europe have been reaping the saddest of results. We note in Chapter 6 that the generosity of attitude toward British players and fans typical of quite a lot of European coverage is not nearly so visible at Wimbledon in 1991 and 1992, and speculate that this may not result entirely from differing attitudes being applied in differing sporting contexts. The sharpness of some German, French and Italian responses to British criticism during the Maastricht debate may have come as a shock to those in Britain who had failed to realise that their self-appointed occupation of the moral high ground in the UK's relations with Europe was never other than a locally-held delusion.

NOTES

1 We have looked at more than 3000 reports on Italia '90 from the Austrian, English, French, German, Irish, Italian, Scottish, Soviet, Spanish and Swedish presses. It is worth giving some sense of what sorts of press reports these are.

First, there are daily newspapers. These may be subdivided into the quality press and the popular press, a distinction especially crucial in Britain. Newspapers such as the British *Sun* and *Daily Star* have no real equivalent on the continent apart from the German *Bild*, though as we can see the latter lacks some of the licence enjoyed by the former. The Austrian dailies *Kurier* and *Kronen Zeitung* also belong to this category of popular newspapers.

The daily press examined also covers both European and UK quality papers such as *El País* (Spain), *La Stampa* (Italy), *Dagens Nyheter* (Sweden), *The Independent* (GB) and Scottish and Irish qualities such as *The Glasgow Herald* and the *Irish Times*. This category also includes the Soviet dailies *Pravda* and *Izvestija*, and evening papers such as France's *France-Soir* as well as important regional dailies such as *El Diario Vasco* (Spain) and the *Hannoversche Allgemeine Zeitung* (Germany).

As regards this last-named daily, it may be worth noting that Germany is a country in which the regional press dominates, and where there are few newspapers with a truly national readership. A number of the articles appearing in the *Hannoversche Allgemeine Zeitung* were provided by the two main German news agencies, Deutsche Presseagentur (dpa) and Sportinformationsdienst (sid), who regularly service all the main regional newspapers. Indeed, there were a number of duplications between the *Hannoversche Allgemeine Zeitung* and the other regional newspaper studied, the *Frankfurter Rundschau*.

The specialist sporting press has been examined. Italy is an especially strong producer, with *Gazzetta dello Sport*, with over one million sales a day, and the *Corriere dello Sport* and *Tuttosport*. (The *Hannoversche Allgemeine Zeitung* carries a piece portraying the Italians as World Champions in reading, but Umberto Eco says in the German *Stern* (21 June) that *Gazzetta* is read by 'politicians and intellectuals who want to show their closeness to the people', which opens an astonishing vista, however ironically framed, to the British analyst.) The study includes the Spanish daily *As*, the French daily *L'Equipe*, the Soviet daily *Sovetskij Sport* and the German weekly *Kicker*.

We have also looked at weekly news magazines, a category which barely applies to the UK: these include *Le Point* (France), *Spiegel* (Germany), *Cambio 16* (Spain) and others.

The former Soviet press deserves some further specific mention here. In the then Soviet Union, despite the great changes which had taken place in recent years, there was not yet, of course, a 'commercial' national press in the western sense of the word, though this has since appeared in the form of a number of independent newspapers.

As well as the national dailies *Pravda* and *Izvestija*, we looked at the Russian daily *Sovetskaja Rossija* and the weekly *Sovetskaja Kul'tura*. The dailies are normally eight pages long, though on occasions only six or even four. On no occasion did football coverage amount to more than one page and in the majority of cases it was half or quarter of a page and even less. With the exception of the opening ceremony there were no photographs at all, although there were black and white photographs in the sports daily *Sovetskij Sport*. *Sovetskaja Kul'tura* varied between 16 and 32 pages, and on a number of occasions published relatively lengthy articles about the World Cup on its last page. References to the Soviet press should be seen in this light.

2 The Scottish National Party sent formal commiserations to Cameroon when the African side was beaten by England.

3 In the field of politics, the (1992) British President of the Board of Trade's surname (Heseltine) becomes in the *Sun* 'Hezza'.

4 For a German reply, see the cartoon published by the German weekly *Bunte*, 26 July.

5 A tendency also displayed at the outset of the Gulf War, e.g. *Sun* leader in the edition of 16 January 1991 under heading 'Feelthy trick by Jacques' (the name 'Jacques' used here to refer to the French in general) on Mitterrand's last-ditch Gulf peace bid, ends 'There is one thing worse than having the messieurs as your enemy. **That is to have them as your friend**'. The *Star* of 17 January, commenting on the first night of hostilities, carried as its front-page headline 'Where the **** are the French?'

6 Pete Davies relates a conversation with England player Chris Waddle in Bologna before the Belgium game, about how long they've been away from home. Waddle,

referring to Robson: 'He says, what's six weeks away? People were away five years in the war'. Waddle responds: 'But they didn't have to play 4–4–2 in the war, did they?'. (Davies, p. 394.)

7 Such combinations can also be found in discourses on politics. *Le Point* of 19 November described the British politician Michael Heseltine as follows: 'deep down he is a mixture of the passionate Celt and the cold and trenchant nature of the Saxon'.

8 *Sovetskaja Kul'tura* of 14 July published a cartoon showing the German player Matthäus in the form of a tank. That a Soviet newspaper should present a German player in this way strikes us as particularly interesting from the historical point of view.

9 This image is also not limited to linguistic text. The Italian daily *Repubblica* of 4 July (as reported by *L'Equipe* of 5 July) published a cartoon of Vesuvius erupting. Maradona, emerging from the crater, is saying 'Grazie Napoli'.

5

THE WAR OF THE ROSES: DISCOURSES OF ENGLISHNESS IN THE SOVIET SPORTING PRESS

INTRODUCTION

This chapter is based on a study of newspaper reports on the 1990 football World Cup and the 1990 Wimbledon tennis tournament in the following Soviet dailies: *Pravda, Izvestija* and *Sovetskij Sport*. Some additional material was also found in the Soviet cultural weekly *Sovetskaja Kul'tura*. Although the first three of these newspapers continue to exist in the newly configured Commonwealth of Independent States, their status has, of course, changed entirely. In 1990 they were state owned and financed, and were the organs of different elements of the then Soviet state apparatus.

The World Cup was widely reported in all the newspapers mentioned, though coverage was much more extensive in *Sovetskij Sport*, needless to say. Wimbledon, on the other hand, was largely ignored by the main Soviet newspapers – a short article in *Izvestija* of 9 July reporting on the outcome of the men's and women's singles finals being their only gesture in its direction. *Sovetskij Sport*, however, did cover the championship in the form of a fairly lengthy daily article during the fortnight.

The main focus of the chapter will be the discourses of English national identity which appear in the Soviet press, noting in particular how these discourses vary remarkably in texture depending on whether the sporting event under consideration is football or tennis. However, this chapter will also argue that these apparently contradictory discourses are in essence local manifestations (micro-discourses) of a much wider macro-discourse which is fundamentally ideological in nature and which in fact binds them together.

This macro-discourse is the Soviet ideology of sport, which presents sport essentially as a depoliticising agent in contemporary societies, as a harmonising activity which transcends barriers of space and time, and as an arena where the release of emotions is not only legitimate but desirable.

ITALIA'90 – THE ENGLISH ABROAD

DOMINANT METAPHORS

Coverage of Italia'90 in the Soviet press revolved essentially around two metaphors. The first is that of a feast or carnival, used to describe sport, and participation in sporting events, as, in terms of the Soviet ideology, they 'ought' to be. Opposed to this is the metaphor of massed hordes of barbarians who not only refuse to join the feast, but in some sense infiltrate the revellers with a view to subverting the celebrations, and whose ultimate aim is the destruction of the sporting carnival. These twin metaphors combine to form a curiously mediaeval meta-metaphor which we shall see recur below in Soviet coverage of the 1990 Wimbledon tournament (stressing the chivalresque rather than the carnivalesque), and which, as illustrated in considerable detail in Chapter 6, would be a dominant feature of European coverage of the 1991 Wimbledon championship

THE CARNIVAL

On 8 June 1990, the day on which the World Cup began, *Izvestija* carried an article headed 'The celebration begins in Milan'. The Russian term for celebration is 'prazdnik'. It is a key term in all Soviet reporting on the World Cup, as is the related verb 'to celebrate' (prazdnovat') and the adjective 'festive' (prazdnichnij). This family of words sums up the official interpretation of the World Cup to be found in all the major Soviet newspapers throughout the month of the championship. *Izvestija* gives us a first definition of what this 'celebration' involves:

> But nothing can dampen the enthusiasm of the Italian 'tiffosi'[1] or of the many thousands of visitors to Italy who have already filled up the hotels and motels. In hotel foyers, restaurants, bars and cafés passionate discussions rage about who will win the championship, who will be awarded the title of best player in the world.

The fans are allocated a decisive role in this festival of sport: 'Everything will be decided by the skill, will-power and courage of the players, the fairness of the referees, the support of the fans'. The same edition of *Izvestija* returns to this idea in a second article, adding a new ingredient – the value of the World Cup is all the greater for the relative rarity of its occurrence: 'The World Cup is a celebration which fans from all over the world look forward to for four years', it informs us.

It is important to note that, while the disappointment and even grief of those teams who lose at different points in the championship is entirely understandable, defeat in itself does not stop the celebration. This is made very clear in the coverage given by *Pravda* (20 June) to the behaviour of the Swedish team following their exit from the tournament at the end of the group matches (this behaviour is contrasted favourably with that of the Soviet team, whose departure from Italy had been preceded by a squabble over money):

It is possible to take one's leave of the tournament in different ways. The Swedish team, for example, according to the information we received here, following their defeats by Brazil and Scotland invited their wives and girlfriends from Scandinavia to an illuminated party in their training base – they lit ten thousand candles. Was this by any chance a sign of mourning? But why should there be mourning? The football celebration continues.

The idea of a long-awaited event recurs at the end of the championship. On the day of the final *Sovetskij Sport* (8 July) emphasises that the final of the World Cup every four years is awaited eagerly all around the globe. 'Our planet has waited for this event for four long years. Passions raged on all the continents, the fans went mad, the businessmen calculated the profits'.

As can be seen from a number of these quotes, passion is by no means an unacceptable element in the celebration of this festival. On the contrary, it represents all that is good in football. The term 'passion' and its cognates are often to be found in articles praising the action of the fans (and the players). Thus *Sovetskij Sport* of 4 July carries a photograph of flag-waving, drum-beating fans of unidentified origin holding an enormous cuddly-toy mascot. Above the photograph is the title 'You cannot imagine the fan without his trumpet and his drum' (the words for 'fan' and 'drum' rhyme in Russian). The caption reads:

> It is well known that the nerve cells do not regenerate. However, this does not particularly concern the fans who have arrived in Italy for the World Cup. For football is a wonderful invention of humanity and carries within itself exclusively positive emotions.

> A passionate game, passions in the stands. And it is at times no less interesting to observe the excitement in the stands than the events on the green football field.

Indeed, as this last quote illustrates, this passion, which is sometimes referred to in terms of 'fever', is seen as something which is inalienably human. No less a source than *Sovetskaja Kul'tura*, looking back on 14 July when the World Cup was over, offers this description of the final in an article entitled 'In the mirror of football':

> And over two billion inhabitants of the Earth, even though their teams were not playing in the final, stare at their television screen and tremble together in football fever, which no-one will ever invent a vaccine against, for he would be immediately branded an apostate from the human race.

(We may note the veiled religious reference here – it appears in other articles quoted below.)

The most visible expression of this passion is the rejoicing of the fans (particularly the Italian fans) in the streets. *Izvestija* (16 June) describes it as follows:

> Whatever the Italian team does (providing it doesn't lose, of course) is a source of immense joy for the local fans. Once more Rome could not get to sleep until

morning after their unconvincing 1–0 win over the Americans. The beating of drums, the tooting of cars, shouts of joy, crowds in the streets.

This passion and rejoicing is seen by the press as profoundly human in that it speaks to the child in modern man, and allows him to release positive emotions which are otherwise kept in check. This theme recurs insistently throughout Soviet coverage of the World Cup.

On 27 June the journalist of *Sovetskij Sport* starts his article with the questions 'Where are we going? It's a mystery . . . and what will be like when we get there?' He finishes the same article by describing the rejoicing of the Italians over their team's victory against Uruguay:

> The whole of Rome poured out into the streets. In that noisy and in some sense even childlike joy with which the Italians celebrated their latest success we could if we wished hear an answer to those questions with which this article began. Where are we going and what will we be like when we get there? At the very least – we'll be human.

This mixture of childlike behaviour and human values is also to be found in *Sovetskaja Kul'tura*, whose report on 30 June plays down the hooligan element of World Cup fandom and sees a deeper human and cultural worth in the experience:

> All in all, there is very often a lot of exaggeration about the effusiveness of the fans. Needless to say, there are both fanatical elements and hooligans among them. But those who come to the land of the championship from thousands of leagues away don't look at all like fanatics or wreckers. They come with their wives and children, they support their teams as one should with the Brazilian torcida[2], and in the stadia they are noisy like children. But when there is no football, and there is no football until the evening, they stroll around the museums, the get to know the magnificent monuments. Football calls to them with its festive noise, but without being noticed it gives food to the soul, it enriches spiritually.

And indeed such values are not lacking on the pitch either. This gives rise to what at first sight may appear to be a somewhat surprising series of aristocratic metaphors in the Soviet press. Thus *Izvestija* (15 June) refers to football itself as 'Its Majesty the Game', and points out that neither the mean nor the narrow-minded (in footballing terms) can accede to what it calls, in a curiously mixed metaphor, 'the throne of the State of football'. *Sovetskij Sport's* opening article on the day of the final (8 July) is entitled 'Long live the King!' and begins with an explanation of how the phrase 'The King is dead, long live the King!' has come down to us from the Middle Ages. The fusion of these two notions – royalty and tradition – is however less-developed in relation to football than it is in relation to tennis.

And indeed, the fullest construction to the humanising influence of the World Cup is also to be found in *Sovetskij Sport*. In an article entitled 'The first morning without football' published on 10 July, two days after the end of the championship, it laments the passing of the World Cup in elegiac tones. Although this is a longish article, it is worth quoting in full:

We woke up yesterday morning and realised that we had lost something. We had lost part of our lives. It's as though we'd been orphaned.

We realised to our horror that there would be no more sleepless nights or excited mornings. We'll no longer cry and laugh, suffer and be indignant. We will no longer turn the dials of our televisions and radios in a frenzy. We will no longer rush to the telephone and argue and argue till we're hoarse.

Football, Italia'90 left us in the twinkling of an eye. And then we felt all the more keenly how much it had meant to us, to the world – these thirty-one hot summer days.

It brought together in a single impulse billions of people from different corners of the planet, it made them kinder and more charitable. During the games in Italy the shooting stopped in Beirut, diplomatic squabbles stopped since the heads of many states were in the Italian stadia or in front of the TV in their residences. And the Pope, having blessed the 'Foro Italico' in the Eternal City, gave us to understand, so to speak, that football is one of the holy and everlasting acts of man.

The victors – the footballers of West Germany – rejoice. The defeated weep. In the course of 31 days some achieved glory, others were visited by defeat. Well, success in sport cannot be divided out among all. And what about the world? Our tormented world found release from its troubles and problems. It's had enough of tears. 31 peaceful days of football brought people peace, ecstatic emotions.

And now this is the first morning without football. It's sad . . . But the sadness will soon pass. For sport never ends. It lives within us.

This is a key article for an understanding of Soviet discourses on sport. It contains references to what is presented as the inherently human nature of sport ('a part of ourselves'/'it lives within us'), childlikeness ('we'd been orphaned'), strong emotions ('excited'/'cry and laugh'), the depoliticising nature of sport ('diplomatic squabbles ceased'), its humanising influence ('kinder and more charitable'), its power of integration ('different corners of the planet'), even its quasi-religious overtones ('holy act of man').

Selected revellers: Scottish and Irish fans and English players

Before turning our attention to the way in which the English fans are presented in the Soviet press, it is worth while clarifying a few points of potential confusion.

The first of these is that, although the Soviet journalists – like journalists elsewhere throughout Europe – frequently confuse the terms 'English' and 'British', there is no confusion when it comes to differentiating between English fans and those from elsewhere in the British Isles. Scotland, for example, merited scant coverage in the Soviet press, partly because its team did not survive the first round, and partly because it was felt that its football was not particularly interesting (*Izvestija*, 12 June). However, what little coverage its players and supporters earned was positive and sympathetic. Thus *Izvestija* (18 June) comments as follows on the Scottish fans:

However, observers note with pleasure the success of the Scottish team, which beat

Sweden 2–1 in Genoa. The Scottish fans, incidentally, were entirely peaceful and caused no problems for the 'carabinieri'[3] or for their own Secretary of State.

And when Scotland's chances of remaining in the championship were reduced almost to zero when they lost a goal in the final minutes of their match against Brazil, their survival then depending on the results of other teams, *Sovetskij Sport* (22 June) carried on its first page a photograph of a disconsolate Scottish goalkeeper (Jim Leighton) on his knees, with the following caption: 'The grief of the Scots was boundless. And it's impossible to describe Leighton's situation. You see, this was the only time during the match with the Brazilians when he was unable to keep his team out of trouble'. The first paragraph of the report itself continues:

> It's a real shame for the Scots. They have now taken part seven times in the finals of the World Cup, but they have never yet got into the second round of the finals. And there is scarcely any chance of them succeeding now, although there is still a minimal chance left until the final days of the group play-offs. Maybe they'll be lucky after all?

The Irish, even more so, conform with what is expected of genuine participants at the feast, and celebrate in due fashion. In an article entitled 'Penalties and politics', and carrying the additional heading 'Irishmen of all countries unite' (yes, even Soviet journalists had a sense of humour), *Sovetskij Sport* (27 June) reports on the widespread rejoicing in Ireland following their team's victory against Romania:

> . . . on Monday in Ireland large numbers of factories, offices and shops did not work at all. Others closed a few hours before the match to give all those who wanted to the chance to see the match on television. And the owners of the numerous bars resigned themselves to a sleepless and noisy night – the all-Ireland football festival continued until dawn.

Sovetskij Sport of 23 June carries two pictures side by side showing rejoicing fans (presumably Irish, though this is not in fact made explicit) and rejoicing Irish players. The caption reads:

> On the right – Niall Quinn rejoicing surrounded by his teammates. He managed to score the equalising goal against the Dutch and take the Irish team into the last eighteen. A happy day, a happy moment!

> The players rejoice, the fans rejoice. The joy is shared out equally among all.

As required, the Irish retain their positive attitude even in defeat. According to *Sovetskij Sport* of 3 July defeat by Italy has not dented their enjoyment:

> It was not for nothing that thousands of their fellow tribesmen left their island and rushed to Rome to support their team. They can be satisfied with them, even though this match was the Irish team's last match in Italy.

And looking back at the end of the championship, *Sovetskij Sport* (8 July) includes Ireland among those countries where the celebration continued even in defeat: 'There was genuine rejoicing over the performance of their players in Ireland, Columbia, Costa Rica. It was a celebration there'.

The English fans are also not to be confused with the English team. Although there were relatively few references to the team in the Soviet press, those that did appear were positive in outlook. On 28 June *Izvestija* described their game against Belgium as 'a game in honour of football', adding that 'the Belgians and the English played, if you like, a chivalrous game'. The English team was also generously praised for its performance against Cameroon and West Germany, and also for its third-place play-off against Italy, which it lost. And indeed *Pravda* of 9 July, commenting on the English goalkeeper's mistake against Italy, suggests that the English players could give the Soviet players a lesson in sporting behaviour:

> After this goal, which lay on his conscience, Shilton took up his stand in goal again hanging his head. It was a shame for him. His fellow players did not shout at him. This is also a lesson which our footballers should learn – less tension and mutual reproaches, more efforts to recoup the situation, as the English did.

The generosity of spirit shown here by the English players clearly places them among the 'good guys' of the tournament. A similar point is made in relation to the Belgians following their defeat by England. *Izvestija* (28 June) writes, in an article entitled 'Defeat without reproaches':

> Of course, it's painful to lose in the final minutes, but as the Belgian Prime Minister W. Martens pointed out, after watching the match live along with a group of fans in the studio of Belgian Television, 'football is football'.

> The dignity with which the failure of their team has been accepted by the fans is particularly striking. Even immediately after the defeat no bitter reproaches were directed by the press either at the players or the trainer. Even the strongest can suffer defeat, and even the losers are entitled to respect if they battled to the end and remained gentlemen.

The word used in the Russian text is in fact the English word 'gentlemen' transliterated. It represents a vision of Englishness to which not only the Belgians, but also the English players have conformed.

Selected spoilsports: Argentinian and German fans

While the Brazilian fans dance their way through the World Cup – references to dances such as the 'lambada' and the 'torcida' abound – while the Italians and the Irish rejoice, and the colourful Belgian fans, nicknamed the 'red devils', show that even devils can be good fun (*Sovetskij Sport*, 20 June), a number of troublemakers also turn up at the celebrations. Apart from the English, those who merit most attention – and this, incidentally, is only a tiny number compared with the coverage of the English fans – are the Argentinians and Germans, and to a very much lesser extent the Italians. It will be useful to spend a little time looking at these first, since the way they are handled throws considerable light on the specificity of the discourses used in relation to the English fans.

The first reference to the Argentinian fans appears in *Izvestija* on the day the championship started (8 June) in an article entitled '"Brave lads" from Argentina' provided by the paper's special correspondent in Buenos Aires:

> However much the Argentinian police might have tried, however many obstacles the authorities and the airlines and the chairmen of the football clubs might have placed in their way, despite all this 250 'brave lads' (this is the name given to football hooligans in Argentina) armed with drums, ratchets, all kinds of noise-making and not only noise-making devices, headed for Italy as part of a contingent of two thousand representatives of the multi-million-strong army of genuine Argentinian football fans

There are two fundamental elements of this report which need to be high-lighted. The first is that these hooligans are presented as a tiny minority – 250 as compared to several million. Second, they are clearly presented as not belonging to the group of 'genuine Argentinian football fans'. Indeed, the reference to the 'chairmen of the football clubs' shows that the interests of these 'brave lads' are in some sense antagonistic to those of 'real' Argentinian football. The article continues with a detailed description of the disturbances they caused in Buenos Aires, stressing that these elements are seen as an embarrassment in their own country: 'Unfortunately, as the Buenos Aires newspaper "Calrin"[4] points out, these specimens will also represent the Argentinian nation in Italy'.

Commenting that 'Hooliganism, alas, is becoming the inevitable com-panion of football' the reporter notes with regret that these Argentinian rowdies 'look forward impatiently to meeting the sadly infamous football hooligans from England'. The article concludes with a paragraph which combines a number of the key ideas mentioned earlier:

> The World Cup is a celebration which fans from all over the world look forward to for four years. Will it be spoiled by the activities of individuals who have no understanding not only of sporting, but even of human honour?

The Argentinian fans merit no further mention in Soviet coverage of the World Cup until after their team's victorious semi-final against Italy, when the rioting which occurred in Buenos Aires is again covered. The same discourses predominate once more in *Izvestija's* report (6 July), with a genuine 'celebration' being 'spoiled' by the activities of a small number of hooligans. These discourses remain intact despite the fact that two people died:

> The joy of the fans, and in Argentina that is the entire population of the country, knew no bounds: a sea of national flags, Bengal lights, songs, the crackle of firecrackers . . .

> The celebration was spoiled by the activities of the hooligans, who in the hustle and bustle of the general rejoicing began to break into the neighbouring shops . . .

Although the article goes on to report widespread disturbances, it specifically stresses the small numbers responsible: 'It all started when five young lads broke the windows of the "El Trast"[5] department store . . .'

Sporadic references to the German fans occur throughout coverage of the tournament. These are on occasions negative, but are usually subordinated to much longer references to the English fans. In an article entitled 'English threat to Sardinia', and dedicated almost entirely to the English fans, *Izvestija* of 11 June has the following to say of the Germans:

> A difficult situation has also arisen in Milan, where around 800 West German 'tifosi' thronged the city's main square, the Piazza del Duomo. This was in preparation for the match between West Germany and Holland. Shop windows and bar windows were smashed. As a result of clashes with the police 50 'tifosi' were detained. Five police officers and seven West German fans were taken to the Milan hospital.

The paper again goes on to highlight the nature of these fans as outsiders, and as being incompatible with the ideals of football itself. Indeed, they prevent genuine fans from going to the stadia, forcing them to stay at home and watch the matches on TV:

> Needless to say, the increasing tension runs counter to the interests not only of world football, but also of the local authorities, and the entire population of the towns where the matches are taking place. In Italy a spontaneous 'anti-tifosi TV' movement has sprung up. People prefer to hang flags from their balconies, settle down in front of the television. By their 'non-presence' in the stadia they are voicing their protest against the hooligan elements.

The German fans receive a further mention in *Sovetskij Sport* on 20 June. This occurs in an article entitled 'The "match" of the truncheons', which is again dedicated mostly to the English fans:

> The anxiety of the organisers of the World Cup, which was evident prior to the championship in relation to the behaviour of the local and incoming fans, was not without foundation, and the facts recorded in the police records bear eloquent witness to this. The first to demonstrate their far from peaceful intentions were the tourists from West Germany who provoked a massive battle in Milan after the match between their national team and Yugoslavia.

However, such coverage is something of an exception in the Soviet press. There are extremely few other references to the Germans – for example *Izvestija* makes the point on 9 July that 40,000 West German fans attended the final, including a number of East Germans from Dresden and Magdeburg. Even the deaths of a number of fans in the celebrations following their victory in the final are presented more as the result of excessive exuberance by individuals than as a generalised threat to society at large. In view of the fact that four people actually died during these celebrations, their treatment in *Sovetskij Sport* (11 July) is remarkably positive. An article entitled 'Rejoicing with consequences' reports:

Four dead, hundreds wounded – these are the results so far of the wild celebrations of West Germany's victory in the World Cup in Italy. Last night thousands of fans came out on to the streets of West Germany's towns to express their feelings in relation to this joyous event. The general rejoicing went on until morning – the football lovers strolled around the central streets, let off firecrackers and rockets, drove around in their cars tooting their horns all the time.

For some the celebration came to a tragic end . . .

Again, the serious breaches of the peace which followed are attributed to 'small groups in many cities'.

Acts of violence by Italian fans are mentioned exclusively in relation to the incoming English supporters, and will be covered in more depth below. However, it is worth pointing out *Pravda*'s positive reaction to the unusual punishment meted out to an unruly Italian fan by the Italian courts (9 June):

A football hooligan from Genoa was sentenced by the city court before the World Cup to . . . silence. He is 22 year old Claudio Pianura. He had already been detained on several occasions for having taken part in brawls.

And now he has been forced to remain silent in the stadia and not to appear in the stands as one of a group. Well then, a strict but just punishment for an undisciplined 'fan'.

Since noise is an essential element of 'celebrating' in the Soviet press, one can appreciate the deeper significance of this punishment for the Soviet reporter.

THE MASSED HORDES OF ENGLISH FANS

Against this background of general rejoicing and heightened human and cultural values, marred at times by small groups of individuals intent on spoiling everyone else's fun, looms the spectre of mass English hooliganism, one of the most unrelenting themes of Soviet coverage of the World Cup. It is important to note that hooliganism is not seen as a problem caused by a tiny minority of English fans. It is presented predominantly as a problem of English fandom in general, and there is remarkably little differentiation in the Soviet press between the fan (peace-loving or not) and the hooligan. As the tournament continues, this fusion becomes so great that it results in the creation of a new compound term – that of the English 'hooligan-fans' (*Sovetskij Sport*, 11 July).

As we saw already, this started even before the World Cup began (see the article from *Izvestija*, 8 June, quoted earlier). *Pravda*, 9 June, continues in the same vein:

RECORD . . . IN HOOLIGANISM. English football hooligans are a source of fear in the World Cup in Italy. And how! They are 'famous' throughout the entire world. For example, the following information was recently published in England. In last season's matches in all the divisions a grand total of more than six thousand people were arrested for breach of the peace.

According to the English press, Arsenal fans had the highest figures for hooliganism – 735 expelled and 167 arrested.

Three new elements make their appearance here. One is the idea of fear, which will dominate and indeed assume enormous proportions during the World Cup. The second is the notion of hooliganism on a mass scale. The figures mentioned here make the 250 'brave lads' from Argentina pale into insignificance. And the third, also apparent in the article from *Izvestija* mentioned above, is that of infamy on a world scale.

A further element, whose importance will be highlighted later on, is that the source of the information given is the English press itself.

Izvestija returns to the English fans two days later on 11 June in an article entitled 'English threat to Sardinia'. This article shows how, in the eyes of the Soviet journalist, the excessive behaviour of the English fans corrupts the otherwise positive 'passion' of the World Cup:

> The championship has only just started, but passions are becoming inflamed in a geometric progression. The draw has played a dirty trick: in Cagliari on 11 and 16 June the English team will play its matches against Ireland and Holland respectively. The uncooperativeness of the English fans is well known, but it is now going beyond all bounds.

This theme reappears later, with overt contrasts between the behaviour of the English fans and those who comply with the 'rules'. Thus *Sovetskij Sport* (29 June) carries two photographs side by side, one of jubilant Italian fans splashing in a fountain (an activity not normally tolerated by Italian police), the other of English fans, complete with Union Jack, and hiding their faces from the photographers. They are being accompanied by Italian police with truncheons through the airport, and are obviously being expelled from the country. The fairly lengthy caption reads:

> The Italians stay in Italy, the English go home.

> There is no mistake in this statement, since we are not talking about the footballers from these countries, who have got their tickets to the quarter-finals, but their fans.

> If the admirers of the hosts of the championship, still euphoric after their team's outstanding victory against Uruguay, continue their unrestrained merriment in the squares and streets of Rome, some of the English fans have been obliged to leave the 'war torn city'. The photographers were waiting for them in the airport before their flight home.

But not only this. The notion of fear is raised to new levels as straightforward hooliganism gives way to organised terrorism requiring intervention by specialist State defence mechanisms. *Izvestija* of 11 June continues:

> Shortly before the beginning of the World Cup it was made known that certain 'over-zealous' English 'tifosi' were preparing terrorist acts during the games. Precautionary measures have been taken. A detachment of English secret agents has even arrived on the Italian island.

This fear is also supported by *Izvestija*'s photojournalism. One day later it carried a photograph of heavily armed and masked Italian police leaping from a helicopter, with the caption:

> The Italian police have prepared for the World Cup no less carefully than the participating teams. They have worked out measures to ensure security in the stadia, and to neutralise possible terrorist acts

Though the authors of these supposed terrorist attacks are not identified, there can have been no doubt in the reader's mind which particular set of fans were being referred to here.

The battle lines are drawn

The 11 June *Izvestija* article introduces a new element into the presentation of English fans, one which will be developed systematically throughout the remainder of the World Cup – the notion of battle:

> At 10 pm on 8 June in the 'Roma' and 'Orina' bars the first clashes took place between drunken English fans and armed police. Steel helmets saved the heads of the police officers from direct hits by wine bottles and cans. The 'battle', of course, was an uneven one. 14 hooligans ended up behind bars.

Not content with reporting what has actually happened, the article looks forward with eager dread to the possibility of even greater outrages in future:

> But these are only very 'minor incidents', the carabinieri informed us. There is no way of knowing what will happen on 11 June. The newspaper 'Corriere della Sera' gave more details today on how the forces of law and order are getting ready in Cagliari. In the capital of Sardinia extremely urgent works are being carried out on re-equipping the city jail. It is intended to create 6,038 cells equipped with remote control colour television cameras. Now Cagliari should be grateful to Italia '90, stresses the newspaper, for the fact that it can accommodate 70 thousand prisoners . . . almost as many as the city stadium.

The battle continues in *Izvestija* on 18 June, one week later. Commenting on the lacklustre performance of the English team and the anxiety this is causing in England itself, the paper continues:

> However, much greater alarm is aroused by something else – the behaviour of the English fans.

> A battle took place in the streets of Cagliari before the match between England and Holland, provoked by the newly arrived fans. Seven rowdies who attacked the police ended up in hospital. 60 people were arrested. Four of these will appear before a judge and, if found guilty, they face prison sentences of up to seven years.

We might compare this to the sentence of silence imposed on the Italian rowdy earlier. The English fans are no longer simply an embarrassment to their country, they are a source of 'alarm'. They are a canker within British society which is threatening its relationship with other countries, and which arouses negative reactions within Britain itself, even at a diplomatic level. Thus *Sovetskij Sport* of 20 June writes:

> In the coming few days the trial will take place of 14 British citizens who provoked clashes with the police. It should be pointed out that official sources in London have reacted with approval to the actions taken by the Italians to put an end to the hooliganish behaviour of the British fans. The British ambassador in Italy apologised to the inhabitants of Sardinia for the unsporting behaviour of his compatriots, expressing the hope that the 'disgraceful events would not influence the friendly relations between the two peoples'.

The scale of the 'battle' is such that the military metaphors increase in intensity. The fans are presented as having their own command structure and to be operating along overtly political (racist/fascist) lines. According to *Izvestija* of 18 June:

> . . . the English newspapers themselves, after the incident in Cagliari in which 500 fans were involved, report that some kind of organised force is behind their acts of hooliganism. The ringleaders, judging from a number of signs, belong to the neo-nazi 'National Front'.

But not only do they have their own command structure, they are kitted out with the modern paraphernalia of war. In an article entitled 'Hooligans with radio equipment' *Sovetskij Sport* (22 June) informs us that:

> The British Minister of Foreign Affairs, whom the unruly British fans have obliged to come on an official trip to the World Cup, stated that the fans are well organised, that they obey their own 'generals', and that they are equipped with modern means of communication, walkie-talkie radios. According to the Minister, football is only a cover which allows these gangs to carry out their operations.

Thus the behaviour of the English fans results in increasing political intervention in what is, in the Soviet ideology, constructed as an inherently apolitical arena, and football is presented as being used as a cover for subsersive activities. These are elements to which we shall return in our conclusion.

The siege of Turin

While military metaphors in Italia'90 and Wimbledon'91 related overwhelmingly to the Germans (see Chapters 4 and 6), in Soviet coverage of Wimbledon'90 they relate only to the English fans. This sustained military metaphor culminates in the English siege of Turin. In the best dramatic tradition, this event is heralded long before it actually happened, and actually formed something of a 'serial' in the pages of *Sovetskij Sport*.

The serial begins on 30 June with the following report:

> The inhabitants of Turin will follow the matches between West Germany and

Czechoslovakia and between England and Cameroon closely. The thing is that if the first named country of each pair should win, Turin, where their semi-final will take place on 4 July, could become the arena for clashes between English and West German hooligans.

Throughout coverage of this event, references to the 1985 Heysel disaster play a central role. Soviet sympathies are clearly with the Italians. *Sovetskij Sport* continues:

> Moreover, the memory of the Heysel tragedy is still fresh in the minds of the Italian tifosi. There, in 1985, in a match between Liverpool and Juventus 39 Italian fans died. The police are concerned that the arrival of the English in Turin might provide 'their own' hooligans with an excuse for a fight. Slogans sayings 'Death to the English, we have not forgotten Heysel!' have already appeared on the walls of the city stadium. As the head of the local police Antonio Mastrocinque pointed out, the police have worked out a detailed plan for checking the airport and the station, areas which are close to the stadium, and the most 'explosive' parts of the city. A total of 5 thousand police and carabinieri will be on duty.

The story continues on 3 July. By this time it has become clear that the mayoress of Turin is to be one of the protagonists of this serial. An article entitled 'What the Italian newspapers are writing about' carries the following report of the English-Cameroon game:

> On the day of the match it was not only the Neapolitans who came along to the San Paolo stadium who supported Cameroon, in fact almost the whole of footballing Italy was rooting for them. The mayoress of Turin was particularly interested in the game and was hoping that the Cameroon side would win and that it would be it, and not England, which is famous for its aggressive fans, which would be playing in the semi-final in the Turin stadium. To everyone's chagrin these hopes were not destined to come true.

Sovetskij Sport picks up the story again on 4 July in an article entitled 'Turin is ready for the siege':

> A few days ago the mayoress of Turin signora Maria Noya made the proposal to FIFA that the semi-final of the 90 World Cup should be moved to Naples if one of the participants was the English team. The reasons behind the proposal are clear enough. The mayoress of the city fears outbreaks of violence both on the stands and in the streets of Turin, whose football fans have still not forgotten the Heysel stadium tragedy in Belgium when 39 Italians died during a match between Liverpool and Juventus.

> In FIFA the proposal of Signora Noya was met with understanding, but they decided not to 'give in' to the hooligans. 'In the course of the championships we have become convinced that the Italian police is capable of acting effectively under any circumstances. I am sure that the match between West Germany and England will not be an exception', said the representative of FIFA Guido Tognoni.

> The semi-final will take place in Turin as planned, but in any case the mayoress has issued an order banning any football processions after the game in the centre of the city. And, needless to say, not a single drop of alcohol will be on sale in Turin

during the twenty-four hours preceding, and what is more, immediately following the match. During these two days 8 thousand policemen will supervise law and order in the city.

Comparing this report with that of 30 June, we can see that the number of policemen has apparently increased by 3000 in four days.

Though the violence which it had so much predicted failed largely to materialise in Turin (though there were indeed a number of isolated incidents), *Sovetskij Sport* remains undaunted. It chooses instead to report on the wave of violence which did indeed sweep England following the defeat by Germany, using the impetus gained by this report to exaggerate grossly the isolated incidents which occurred in Italy. Thus it informs us on 8 July in an article where absolutes (everything/everyone) predominate:

> England's defeat in the semi-final also gave rise to a great many problems not only in England itself where, in 14 cities, they smashed everything associated with West Germany – from Mercedes to 'Beetles' – but also in the cities of Italy: there they beat up everyone they came across. And then after all that they want to defend football. But this has nothing to do with football.

Such an analysis is in striking contrast to coverage by the European press in general (see Chapter 4), and indeed by the Italian press in particular. Thus, commenting on the England-Cameroon game, Italy's *Gazzetta dello Sport* (2 July) published an article entitled 'Before the game kicked off Naples "looked for" the hooligans without finding them'. In this article it specifically dismantles the 'barbaric horde' imagery of so many newspaper reports. Describing the English fans as 'those young people whose only crime was to be a little bit too "casual" [in English]', it continues:

> You should have seen them, these English lads, sitting in a well-behaved manner at the tables drinking alcohol-free beverages: tins of Coca Cola or orange juice or even milk. Certainly there were things to see. But they were not, thankfully, barbaric hordes attacking who knows what, but lots of little episodes. Like, for example, the improvised game of football beneath the entrance hall of the Politecnico by about twenty brave young men in shorts.

The Austrian daily *Kronen Zeitung* (3 July) agrees: 'There were no problems in Naples with the 10,000 English fans'. Indeed, the general view in the European press was that the English fans were the victims rather than the perpetrators of violence before, during and after the semi-final by the Italian fans. Thus *L'Equipe* (5 July) in France describes how 'some two to three hundred young Italians were leaving no doubt as to their desire to do battle with the supporters from the other side of the Channel', while Austria's *Kurier* (5 July) reports how 'the greatest danger in this city closely guarded by 8000 policemen came from the Italian football rowdies'.

The innocent bystanders

As in all war zones, there are of course innocent victims, 'collateral damage'. A wide range of such victims of the English fans are reported in the Soviet press. The most obvious group (apart from the police) are those who come into closest contact with the fans – the reporters and members of the press. Their nationality is of no importance against the global threat of English hooliganism. *Izvestija* (11 June) reports attacks on Swedish and Italian reporters in Cagliari:

> A number of witnesses to the commotion were also hurt: two Scandinavian correspondents from 'Expressen' and an Italian journalist from 'Nuova Sardinia'.

On 20 June *Sovetskij Sport* reports injuries to a Japanese film crew:

> The police had difficulty in rescuing a group of Japanese television reporters from the hands of British [sic] 'fans'. The Japanese had decided to record the English fans marching through the streets of Cagliari. However, it became clear that they do not like to be photographed. The reporters ended up in hospital, their video cameras smashed to pieces.

Even the mere fact of speaking English is enough to invite trouble. On 8 July *Sovetskij Sport* carried the following report:

> A 21-year old Greek student paid dearly for his knowledge of English when he decided to call his fiancée, who lives in London, from a telephone booth in Milan. Italian fans who were passing decided, when they heard him speaking English, that he was a British fan. The Greek tried to run away from the youths who attacked him and in fact managed to jump on a bus. However, this did not deter his pursuers. They chased the bus in a car, jumped inside and severely beat the unfortunate youth. It took the police, whom the bus driver had called by radio, to prevent any further punishment.

Bearing in mind that the sympathies of the Soviet press lie clearly with the Italians, particularly in relation to the Heysel incident, we might legitimately ask ourselves whether this report is a criticism of the Italians, or of the English who bring misfortune on even the most innocent of bystanders.

On a broader scale, Italy itself is seen as suffering financial damage due to the presence of the English fans. Thus while *Izvestija* had commented on 12 June that 'Italy has always been considered the cradle of civilization, and it is up to each of the 12 cities where the matches are taking place to show their culture, originality and talent', *Sovetskij Sport* (22 June), in an article entitled 'The English bring only losses', reports the subsequent dissatisfaction of Sardinian hoteliers at the effects of the invasion of their island:

> Hotel owners on the island of Sardinia will be nothing but happy when the World Cup is over – compared with the same period last year the hotels are only 50 per cent full. The tourists, frightened off by the 'invasion' of the notorious English fans, have decided to give the island a wide berth.

But of course the real loser, as *Izvestija* of 11 June (quoted above) had already pointed out, is football itself, the ultimate innocent victim, forced into a defensive position which it does not really deserve by those for whom football is merely a cover for other things. As quoted earlier, *Sovetskij Sport* comments bitterly on 8 July: 'And then after all that they want to defend football. But this has nothing to do with football'.

THE VITIATION OF SPORT

And indeed these real or imagined battles come to some extent to supplant the World Cup. They provide a parallel spectacle which is presented as the antithesis and ultimately the vitiation of sport. In Britain we might well view such a presentation as being driven by marketing considerations, as providing a view of fan behaviour which is in fact appealing to a substantial section of the tabloid readership. In 1990, however, Soviet newspapers were entirely financed by the state and were not, therefore, subject to market forces. This presentation of the behaviour of English fans responds not to readership expectations or preferences, but to the needs of maintaining the Soviet ideology of sport.

This process is first adumbrated in *Izvestija's* article of 8 June regarding the Argentinian hooligans:

> The clashes between 'fighting men' upholding the honour of their teams now arouse more interest than the football matches themselves. And indeed it was the best 'prepared' members of the various 'barras',[6] who were selected for the trip to the championship in Italy, and they look forward impatiently to meeting the sadly infamous football hooligans from England.

The verb to 'meet' in Russian is also used (as in English) of two teams who 'meet' in a match. In an article entitled 'The offenders – the English fans' published on 18 June, the same newspaper informs us that:

> The president of the European Football Association UEFA stated that the chances of English clubs being allowed to return to European club matches now seem very slim.

> All of these details dominate the mass media in England, almost pushing to the background purely sporting news about the matches in the championship.

Football has been replaced by what *Sovetskij Sport* (20 June) terms 'The "match" of the truncheons', vocabulary normally reserved for sporting contexts being brought into service in the description of clashes between fans and police:

> Pressurising the hooligans

> In the meantime the English fans have become active. In Cagliari (Sardinia), the day before the England-Holland match, a group of 500 tried to attack the Dutch who were on their way to the stadium. Arming themselves with stones and bottles, the English 'warmed up' by damaging a number of cars. Then, during the 'match'

special police detachments came into play who did not hesitate to use tear gas and truncheons. After only a few minutes the 'match' ended with a victory for the forces of law and order . . .

The metaphor of the 'match' is continued in *Sovetskij Sport* (22 June), where a photograph showing English fans squatting on the ground under the close attention of heavily armed *carabinieri* carries the following caption:

Fans at the end of the century

No, it was not to no avail that the Italian carabinieri prepared so carefully for their meeting with the English fans. These aggressive young people try every method they can to get into the stadium, but, as a rule, they end up in police custody. So far in the 'match' between the forces of law and order and those who are disturbing the peace, it is the hosts of the championship who are in the lead.

The metaphor is a powerful one. The sporting celebration with its childlike rejoicing and noisy release of passions has become a brutal clash in the social arena with strong political overtones.

WIMBLEDON – THE ENGLISH AT HOME

A PLACE OF PILGRIMAGE

While Soviet coverage of Italia '90 opened with grim forecasts of outrages by English fans, coverage of Wimbledon began in a completely different vein. *Sovetskij Sport* of 27 June (three days before the beginning of its serial on the 'Siege of Turin') introduces Wimbledon as follows, in an article entitled 'The "pilgrims" go on strike':

I do not know exactly what feelings the pilgrim experiences when he arrives for the first time on the holy ground of Jerusalem or Mecca, but I think that it can be compared with what a tennis-lover feels when he suddenly turns up in Wimbledon. It takes a while to recover from the shock, to get used to the thought: can this really be true?

It is very true, as it turns out. Tennis in Wimbledon is akin to godliness, worshipped by all and sundry. But it is worshipped quietly, with calm nobility.[7]

On the surface, the contrast could scarcely be more striking: godliness, quiet, calm. There are none the less deeper links between the two descriptions. The calm of Wimbledon is deceptive in one important respect: 'However, this does not mean in any sense that passions do not rage here'. Despite the obvious differences, we are once again within the recognisable discourses of the Soviet ideology of sport.

The references to nobility would recur on a truly massive scale in European coverage of Wimbledon '91 (see Chapter 6). There is, however, a crucial difference. While the Western European metaphor of feudal England is strongly marked by irony and underlines above all the unmodernity and indeed the political failure of British society, there is no hint of such irony in the Soviet construction of Castle Wimbledon. We deal with this difference in the conclusion of Chapter 6.

The aggressive (and predominantly male) 'hooligan-fans' of the World Cup are replaced by genteel 'women-fans' who are prepared to get up early in the morning to be sure of a good seat in the stand. *Sovetskij Sport* of 5 July shows a photograph of three such women sleeping in the stand. Above the photograph is the heading 'The cocks have not yet crowed', and the caption reads:

> Of course, these women could have arrived at the Wimbledon courts at the start of play, but their love of tennis has got them out of their warm beds at dawn. Only when they have 'bagged' their seats in the stand do these women-fans relax and allow themselves a little doze.

The vision of Wimbledon which will be developed over the next two weeks is a fundamentally poetic one. The journalist of *Sovetskij Sport* indicates as much himself when, talking of the prize money available to the contestants, he says in the same article: 'Let's speak a little of the prose of life. In other words, about money'. And this other-worldliness (again linked to the notion of godliness) reappears in other articles. Thus *Sovetskij Sport* of 4 July carried an article entitled 'They stayed in heaven – but only for a little time'. It begins:

> I am sure that each of the 13,107 lucky people who came to Wimbledon on Monday morning with a ticket for the centre court in their pocket must have felt that they were the owners of a pass to a heaven of tennis . . .

and continues:

> But let's hurry now to the centre court, this heaven of tennis which has been promised to us all . . .

> And finally, the last act of this heavenly spectacle on the stage of the centre court

We might, incidentally, compare this heading with a heading in *Sovetskij Sport* of 24 June relating to the World Cup – 'A journey to hell'.

A NEW AGE OF CHIVALRY: CIVILISED VALUES ON DISPLAY

A number of the themes introduced in the opening article of 27 June are developed in later issues of *Sovetskij Sport*. The theme of humanity and nobility of feeling reappears on 29 June, and makes an obvious connection with what has been said already concerning football. The author comments at length on how the Wimbledon crowd is as unstinting in its appreciation of the loser as it is of the winner. This attitude is contrasted with the state of affairs in the Soviet Union (other examples of this occur):

> Above the gates of the centre court, through which the players go out into the court, are engraved the following words by the great English poet Rudyard Kipling:

'Strive to bear both triumph and catastrophe with honour. And behave in the same way towards those whom they have overtaken.'[8]

You will agree how much more human and wise this sounds than the phrase which, though smacking of sadism, is, alas, still in current use here [i.e. the USSR]: 'Let the loser weep . . .'

This is again reminiscent of a not dissimilar lesson which, according to *Pravda* of 9 July, the English footballers could have taught their Soviet counterparts.

But the nobility of spirit displayed by the spectators is also expected of the players. Poor behaviour is unthinkable. John McEnroe, for all his genius, is, this issue of *Sovetskij Sport* informs us, considered by some to be 'a hooligan'. The point is again made forcibly on 1 July in relation to the Swiss player Marc Rosset:

In despair, since nothing was working out for him, Marc hurled the entirely innocent ball somewhere out of sight. For which he received a severe warning from the umpire in his tower. And quite right: no loutish behaviour here, it's not allowed, even members of the royal family come to Wimbledon, not to mention the ordinary ladies and gentlemen.

The Russian text in fact contains the imperative of a verb meaning 'to behave like a hooligan' (*khuliganit'*), and this is a direct command to the player. The praise given to the umpire can be contrasted with the widespread negative coverage of the World Cup referees in the Soviet press[9]. While football referees are unable to keep unsporting behaviour off the pitches, the Wimbledon umpire is successful in banishing it from the courts.

This article also brings in a group of important players – the British royal family.

A BASTION OF ENGLISH TRADITION

The opening article of 27 June introduces yet other elements which are fundamental in Soviet discourses of sport. The title of the article ('The "pilgrims," go on strike') refers to an event described at some length by the journalist. A group of spectators, annoyed that changes in the centre court stand meant they were unable to get a seat there, organised an apparently impromptu sit-down strike outside the gates of Wimbledon. After a short meeting to discuss the matter, the management of the grounds decided to accede to their wishes. The journalist ends this section of his report with the comment: 'After discussing the matter for ten minutes, the local authorities decided to meet their demands. Long live the unshakability of English traditions!'

Wimbledon is transformed by the Soviet journalist into a realm where tradition reigns supreme, which is beyond the reach of the normal course of events. Even the physical surroundings of Wimbledon embody this imperturbable sense of tradition. *Sovetskij Sport* of 1 July dedicates the bulk of an article (entitled 'And they dream of the Wimbledon turf') to the history of the famous lawn, giving a detailed history of when it was first laid, of the various groundsmen who have looked after it, of the height to which the grass is cut at different points of the year.

And indeed, the last paragraphs of the last article on Wimbledon 1991 in *Sovetskij Sport* (11 July) returns us to this theme, highlighting the symbolic value of the turf in the Soviet mythology of Wimbledon:

> When it was all over and the Centre Court had emptied an elderly man with a video camera came out onto it. He was the Wimbledon groundsman, the main lawn specialist, Jim Thorn.
>
> He filmed the wounded, trampled lawn, and probably said into himself: 'Don't worry, be patient, I'll start to heal your wounds tomorrow. You'll rest for a whole year, build up your strength. You've earned it . . .'
>
> And in fact no tennis player, whoever he might be, will set foot on this grass. That's the rule. Imagine, a whole year! See you next Wimbledon.

But the personified grass is not the only player in this particular arena. Key figures in the construction of this extra-temporal haven of dignity and nobility are the British royal family. Thus *Sovetskij Sport* of 7 July writes:

> Yesterday, for the first time in the last ten days, Princess Diana appeared in the royal box of the centre court of the All England Lawn Tennis and Croquet Club. Now, as soon as members of the royal family begin to come to Wimbledon, this is the most certain sign that the tennis tournament is approaching its conclusion and that the most interesting part is beginning.
>
> On this occasion Princess Diana came alone, without her husband Prince Charles. Last week, while playing at polo, he fell awkwardly from his horse and broke his arm. The prince is very sporty in general. As well as polo he does parachuting, pilots planes, does mountain climbing and downhill skiing. He does everything recklessly, on the limits and often beyond the limits of acceptable risk. The whole of England is very worried about him, and someone has even demanded that the prince should be forced to agree to refrain from exposing himself to danger. But can you force him . . .?

A number of links are made in this passage. The royal family and Wimbledon not only have have a similar mission in embodying a sense of tradition, a kind of timeless Englishness (of which 'bravado' is, of course, an essential element) – they also fulfil the important ideological task of *unifying* the country. The fact that Prince Charles is himself a sportsman merely serves to intensify the link between these two missions.

Nothing is allowed to disturb this haven of aristocratic grace and elegance. The conservatism of the presentation is so great that it includes overt sexism and ageism which are in obvious contradiction with official Soviet ideology. None the less, they are presented as positive features. In this sense Wimbledon is presented as superior to the World Cup in that its own logic assures the elimination of incongruous elements even from among the players. As the championship moves into the semi-finals, the journalist of *Sovetskij Sport* writes on 7 July:

I don't know what anyone else thinks, but I for one am glad that we have seen the end of these excessively noisy and excessively self-assured 14-16 year old girls with their masculine movements scurrying around the lawns of Wimbledon. And women's tennis has regained its proper character: elegant, a little enigmatic, full of refinement and charm.

Yes, yesterday entry to the centre court was banned to tennis players younger than 20. Barred by the logic of the play in this tournament itself, when naked physical strength and straightforward unrelenting pressure could not compete with the technical skill and the depth of creative thinking of maturity.

Not even the most portentous events from outside can disturb this calm for long. A bomb alert following the IRA attack on the Carlton Club proves to be part of a 'Day of false alarms' (the title of the article of 3 July), and is indeed treated quite humorously by the journalist:

> This was the first time I had been in this kind of situation. How should I behave: rush headlong out into the street or try despite everything to maintain my dignity and make my way out calmly? In any case, I had a look round. Most of my colleagues from the press box had disappeared like snow on a hot summer's day, and the last of them, like mountain goats, were leaping over the seats towards the exit. And, all things considered, the spectators were not the least bit concerned about their own dignity . . . I can tell you that your correspondent was not the last to cross the finishing line outside the area of the centre court and court number one.

And the imminent collapse of the Soviet economy with its food rationing and deprivation fares no better. The last article on Wimbledon (11 July) is entitled 'And so they've eaten all the strawberries', and begins:

> I wonder what 23 tons of fresh strawberries might look like? A mound? A hill? A mountain? What half a kilo of these berries bought in the market looks like, or even a whole kilo (if it's just after pay day) – that I do know. But 23 tons?

> This is the quantity of the famous strawberries and cream, which have almost become a symbol of the Wimbledon tennis tournament, eaten over the past two weeks by those who have come here. And at the same time they have 'put away' 12 tons of smoked salmon, 190 thousand sandwiches, 129 thousand portions of ice cream, 300 thousand cups of tea or coffee, 75 thousand pints of dark and light beer, 12 thousand bottles of champagne and masses of other things.

> However, having torn himself away from his native soil for a fortnight, your correspondent has rather forgotten the trifling fact that, in view of a series of circumstances, food is not considered an acceptable topic of conversation back home. And that it gives rise to feelings which are no less painful than an attack of appendicitis together with extensive second-degree sunburn. I ask you in God's name to forgive me for this lack of tact. Not another word.[10]

The notion of 'other worldliness' operates here on a number of levels. Not only is Wimbledon itself a haven of plenty, but those visiting it are caught up in its timelessness, 'torn away from their native soil', and no longer subjected to the stresses and deprivations of the real world.

CONCLUSION

THE HETEROGENEITY OF DISCOURSES OF NATIONAL IDENTITY

This study allows us to draw a number of conclusions concerning discourses of national identity in general, the specific discourses of Englishness encountered in the Soviet press, and the relationship between such discourses and ideologies of sport.

Firstly, discourses of national identity are clearly not monolithic. It is obvious from this study that there is no single discourse of Englishness which applies no matter which area is under discussion. Indeed the two discourses arising in relation to Italia'90 and Wimbledon in particular are, in terms of their superficial texture, extremely contradictory.

Similar examples of heterogeneity relating to other countries are not in fact difficult to find (as we demonstrate in Chapters 4 and 6). For example, the discourses of Germanness relating to the theme of work – discipline, reliability, unsmilingness, even dourness – differ strongly from those related to, say, the Munich beer festival. We could think of similar multiple discourses of Italianness depending on whether the theme under discussion was military prowess or fashion design. None the less, we should note that these differing discourses relate to very different aspects of the national life of the country in question.

The English case is to some extent unique: here discourses of national identity which not only differ, but are in fact in many aspects contradictory, arise in relation to two activities from the same social domain – i.e. sport. Discourses of Germanness vary little, for example, between football and tennis. The same could be said of discourses of Frenchness relating to football and rugby. The uniqueness of the English case almost certainly reflects a continuing awareness of (at least) perceived social and class differences in England which have become less acute in other European political cultures.

THE HERMETICISM OF DISCOURSES OF NATIONAL IDENTITY

If discourses of national identity are not monolithic, we can say with some certainty that differing discourses are highly hermetic. There is no detectable cross-penetration between the discourses relating to English football fans and those relating to tennis in the articles studied. Simply no mention of football is made in the reports on Wimbledon (other than the very indirect negative references to hooliganism), just as the negativeness of the discourses relating to football finds no alleviation by reference to those of tennis.

Indeed, the phenomenon is more complex even than that. Discourses of national identity based on a given area of social life tend to draw towards themselves any other topic which comes under discussion in relation to that primary or source area. Thus the boorishness of the English football fan manifests itself not only in relation to his behaviour as a fan, but also as regards his behaviour in relation to broader cultural issues. While fans from other countries are presented as admiring Italian culture, areas where British fans congregate are said to be characterised by empty museums and falling tourist revenues.

This 'imperialistic' hegemony of discourse is pushed to the point of distortion. For example, it was clear that falling tourist revenues was not a problem related uniquely to the presence of English fans in Italy. *Sovetskij Sport* recognises this fact on 5 July when it writes:

Football: one man's meat . . .

Shop owners in Florence had to begin their sales a month earlier than usual – sales of all kinds of goods in June amounted to 30 per cent of their normal level. Hotel owners are also suffering losses – the number of rich tourists, clearly put off by the World Cup, has fallen, and the fans either come for the match from neigbouring countries or wander around without a roof over their head. Restaurant owners are also unhappy – the number of customers has fallen by 10 per cent. The famous museums and theatres are empty . . . All in all, the hopes of the city councils and of the service sector of cashing in on the football celebration have fallen through.

Yet it is only the English fans who attract special mention in this respect. In the same way, but operating in the opposite direction, the civilised nature of Wimbledon makes even the conspicuous over-consumption of its spectators apparently acceptable, despite its painful contrast with the realities of Soviet life.

THE CONSERVATISM OF DISCOURSES OF NATIONAL IDENTITY

Discourses of national identity are known to be conservative – conservative in that they display if not quite immutability, then at the very least a remarkably slow rate of evolution lagging far behind the dynamic pace of change which characterises contemporary societies. Indeed, their very conservatism may be to some extent a defensive response to the increasing uncertainties of modern life. However, as we suggest in our general conclusion, this conservatism may be more perceptive than once we would have acknowledged. The continuing tensions between the former republics of the Soviet Union show that the monolithic construction of Soviet identity was illusory: feelings of national identity in the Baltic republics, the Ukraine and elsewhere were, though officially denied and indeed repressed, powerful forces in Soviet life, and were, in the final analysis, among the most important factors in the ultimate dissolution of the USSR.

In the case of sport, this conservatism is also linked closely to the notion of tradition. In a world where tradition is invented and then presented as being under stern attack, the notion of tradition in sport plays a leading role in the sporting coverage of all European countries. However, tradition must not be seen simply as a personal response to what is undoubtedly a rapidly changing world. It is clear from this study that tradition also fulfils an ideological function.

The prioritisation of tradition takes much the same form in the Soviet case as it takes elsewhere. References to great football matches and great players of the past abound – indeed the players of the past are often sought out by journalists for their comments on the matches and players of the present. Comparisons are made between matches often 20 or 30 years apart as though the changes which have taken place in the teams and the countries in the intervening period are of no significance.

Of course, the Soviet journalists are well aware of the fact that such comparisons are of little value in themselves as comparisons. The journalist of *Izvestija* (11 June) shows this quite clearly in his choice of terminology when he refers to comparisons between the Sweden-Brazil match and the final played by the same two teams in Stockholm over 20 years before: 'Hotheads are comparing this game with the final of the World Championship in Sweden when these two teams met'. But again, awareness of the distortion does not prevent this theme from being pursued vigorously throughout the duration of the World Cup. Their value as comparisons is essentially irrelevant. Their role in providing a sense of continuity and stability of nationhood over time is based on a quite different set of considerations.

In Soviet coverage of the World Cup England is seen as perhaps the major repository of footballing tradition in the world. The English players are constantly referred to as 'the inventors of football', as representing 'the homeland of football', as being the 'fathers of football'. This point is made explicitly by *Izvestija* on 28 June when it reminds its readers in relation to the match between England and Belgium:

> . . . the English reminded us yet again that it is both impermissible and dangerous to look down on them, forgetting that they have the longest footballing culture behind them.

This lends a particular strength to the condemnation of English hooliganism in the Soviet press, since this hooliganism is an attack on the representatives of one of the most important elements in the ideology of sport being presented. This point is also made explicitly by *Izvestija* in its edition of 25 June:

> And how is it that England, the land where football was invented, has been so unexpectedly subjected to the invasion of hooliganism, unfailingly choosing the stadia for its excesses, in order to show off, to go down in history even if it is as a caricature?

As regards the coverage of tennis, we find similar references in *Sovetskij Sport* to great players of the past such as Fred Perry and Helen Wills-Moody. This stretches back to the origins of the tournament itself with a brief history of the 'Great Battle' between Wilfred Baddeley and Joshua Pim in the 1890s (*Sovetskij Sport*, 10 July). The (royal) origin of the major trophies is also explained to us. The detailed history of the Wimbledon turf is part of the same phenomenon, as is the reference to emblematic figures such as members of the British royal family.

Again, awareness of the contradictions involved does not prevent these discourses from being pushed to the point of distortion. For example, the Soviet journalist from *Sovetskij Sport* is perfectly aware of the changes which are taking place in women's tennis. This point is explicitly covered and accepted as correct in an interview with Helena Mandlikova on 29 June:

> All things considered, Mandlikova is right. The tennis played by her generation is on the way out. It is now a tough, athletic game, playing literally for survival, which brings success.

This does nothing to prevent the journalist's self-congratulation when 'those excessively noisy girls' are eliminated in the closing round of the tournament, nor his suggestion (not at all borne out by recent results) that their success will be negated by the 'logic of the game'.

None the less, even bearing in mind the conservatism of discourses of national identity in general, the discourses of Englishness which we find in the Soviet sporting press are strikingly conservative compared with those which emerge in other (in particular Western) European countries. While the French, the Germans, the Italians and even the Spanish eventually warmed somewhat to the English fans, the notion of hooliganism and violence remained uppermost in the Soviet press throughout the World Cup. Such is the extent to which these notions dominate that, when it was announced in *Sovetskij Sport* (11 July) that English teams were to be readmitted to the European championships, this must have come as a surprise to the Soviet reader who had seen nothing in the Soviet newspapers which might have prepared him for this piece of news. It is worth quoting a little of the article in question:

> The inventors of football forgiven
>
> English football clubs have been allowed to return to the 'family' of participants in European championships . . . As is well known, the fathers of football were banned for five years from playing in the European tournaments as a result of the outrages in the stands of European stadia by their hooligan-fans. The most serious of such incidents was the battle in the Brussels Heysel stadium during the final of the European Champions Cup between Liverpool and the Italian champion Juventus. 39 football lovers died in the stands of the stadium. In any case, the disqualification of Liverpool as a result of this incident will remain in force for another three seasons.

The language of this text suggests that, even if UEFA has forgiven the English players, the Soviet journalist has not yet forgiven the English fans.

Likewise, the aristocratic and poetic vision of Wimbledon, though very different in surface texture, is astonishingly conservative in content. History has been essentially banished from the stage. We are in a world with its own logic and its own values which defy interference from the 'real world'.

THE SOVIET JOURNALIST ABROAD

It is possible to account at least in part for the exaggerated conservatism of these reports by the conditions under which the Soviet journalists were working. Indeed, their reports exude a strong sense of isolation, of second-hand experience, of lack of direct contact with what is going on around them. For example, *Sovetskij Sport*, the Soviet Union's most widely read sports daily, was represented both at Wimbledon and at the World Cup by a single journalist. Not only that, in the case of the World Cup he was replaced half-way through by another lone journalist (the change-over is the subject for comment in the editions of 22 and 26 June). The incoming journalist shows a clear sense of disorientation and isolation in his early reports. In an article somewhat metaphorically entitled 'In the prison of time' (26 June) he writes:

> It's a curious scene. In the room, which is crammed with television sets, before the beginning of the transmission of the match between Romania and Ireland . . . people gather who scarcely know each other. In fact, I met neither the Belgian who was sitting to my left, nor the Cameroonian who was drumming with his fingers to my right.

He goes on to describe a rudimentary 'conversation' he has with these two using gestures. And this sense of isolation seems symptomatic of Soviet journalists in general. *Sovetskij Sport* of 1 July carries an interview with FIFA press-representative Guido Tognoni in which the latter complains of the problems caused by the Soviet journalists arriving late in the championship, unlike their 'colleagues from other countries'.

Linguistic problems also seem to be a factor. The only foreign journalist who is quoted directly *at all* in the Soviet press is the editor of the (then West) German sports weekly *Kicker* Karl Heinz Heimann. The reason for this, as explicitly acknowledged by *Sovetskij Sport* (27 June), is that 'he speaks fluent Russian and has been collaborating with our newspaper for a long time'. Three personal interviews are carried in relation to Wimbledon – with Helena Mandlikova, Martina Navratilova and Ivan Lendl, all of Czech origin. Under the circumstances, it is not at all unreasonable to wonder what language the interviews were held in[11]. The curious mistranslation of the quote from Kipling suggests a less than perfect command of English by the journalist.

This lack of first-hand contact with events may explain to some extent the enormous dependence of the Soviet journalists on foreign newspapers as their source of information. A number of the football reports on the English fans come not from Italy, but from the London correspondent, and quote English sources widely. This is by no means a uniquely Soviet phenomenon, needless to say – cross referencing of this kind can be found throughout the national presses of Europe. But the Soviet case, as in so many other areas, is a particularly acute example. In this respect, there is a very real sense in which the crisis of Englishness represented by the English fans in the Soviet press is precisely the crisis of Englishness represented by the English fans in the English press – which may go some way towards explaining its staying power and its lack of forgiveness. (This dependence on the local press is not limited to the British media. It is just as apparent in relation to the discourses of Argentinicity or Italianness which appeared in the Soviet press.)

This lack of real contact may well be the inevitable result of the cultural isolation between East and West which neither *glasnost* nor *perestroika* were able to bridge, and which will only begin to disappear when the links forged between the different countries are much stronger on a social rather than a predominantly political level as they are at present. And of course they are two-way. These Soviet discourses were almost certainly matched by just as conservative discourses of Sovietness on the British side, and their power as a hindrance to real understanding should not be misunderstood.[12] But this isolation is not sufficient to explain the extremes of the Soviet discourses of Englishness in itself.

NATIONAL IDENTITY, IDEOLOGY AND SPORT

Despite the apparent differences between the discourses of Englishness relating to football fans and those relating to tennis, there are none the less, as has been pointed out, a number of strands which bind the two together. They are indeed joined by a common ideology of *sport*. This view of sport is one of an activity which is not only (despite massive evidence to the contrary) essentially *apolitical*, but which also *depoliticises* society, which replaces politics, which succeeds where politics fails. This is very clear in many of the articles relating to the World Cup. It is stated with absolute explicitness in an article on the front page of the 21 June edition of *Sovetskij Sport*:

> The guns grow rusty thanks to football
>
> Football has done what the politicians could not do. When the matches are being played in Italy, the guns fall silent in Beirut. And a long-awaited silence reigns.
>
> Yes, the spectacle of great football attracts like a magnet. And people thousands of kilometers from the epicentre of the World Championship rejoice sincerely together with its direct participants – the heroes of the matches which have just been played.

An article entitled 'Penalties and politics', for example (*Sovetskij Sport*, 27 June), does not suggest in any sense that sport is political. On the contrary, its entire message is that sport depoliticises even politics. This brings positive comment from the Soviet journalist:

> The Heads of State and Government of the EEC, who were meeting at a session of the European Community, rushed through their negotiations in order to watch the penalty shoot-out in the World Cup match between Ireland and Romania.
>
> A minute after the final whistle announcing the Irish victory, Charles Haughey, the Prime Minister of the country, appeared on television. 'The team now needs the support of every man, woman and child in the country', he told his fellow citizens.

These messages are repeated in the final report on Italia '90 in *Sovetskij Sport* (10 July) quoted earlier:

> During the games in Italy the shooting stopped in Beirut, diplomatic squabbles stopped since the heads of many states were in the Italian stadia or in front of the TV in their residences.
> . . .

And what about the world? Our tormented world found release from its troubles and problems. It's had enough of tears. 31 peaceful days of football brought people peace, ecstatic emotions.

While the discourses of Englishness studied above clearly have a degree of autonomy and can indeed be analysed to a substantial extent as discourses of national identity, such an approach can not on its own explain their extreme conservatism. These two apparently contradictory discourses must also be seen as local manifestations, or micro-discourses, of a much wider discourse which is essentially ideological in nature, and this is the Soviet ideology of sport. This ideology presented sport as a unifying activity which brings people together beyond boundaries of place or time.

Such discourses of sport were not unique to the Soviet Union in terms of their general content – they can be found in the press of all European countries and in the public pronouncements of numerous politicians – but the Soviet case was largely unique in the sheer scope and relentless uniformity of this vision. The power of this ideology was such that it overrides even considerations of class and leads to an apparently paradoxical appreciation of aristocratic values and their symbolic representatives. This may seem contra-dictory in a country such as the Soviet Union, for although the Cold War may be over, and the rhetoric of international class war has disappeared, the official credos of communism were still in force during the period under review, as a reading of any of the issues of *Pravda* or *Izvestija* or even *Sovetskij Sport* quoted will show.

The real crime committed by the English fans in the eyes of the Soviet commentators is that they, on the contrary, have *politicised* sport. They make it impossible to cling to the notion of sport as an area of activity where man can indulge in the childlike release of passions and joy which have no place elsewhere in society. They undermine that part of the Soviet ideology of sport which sees it as 'of peculiar utility by reason of its inherent qualities of being easily understood and enjoyed, being apolitical (at least superficially) and permitting emotional release safely'. (Riordan: 1980, 233)[13]

The Soviet journalists were well aware that the heightened atmosphere of the World Cup would give rise to forms of behaviour which would at times spill over into excess. This point is explicitly conceded in *Izvestija*. An article on 17 June dedicated almost entirely to police operations during the World Cup begins as follows:

Late one evening, in the Piazza di Venezia in the very centre of Rome, where precisely 50 years ago Mussolini appeared to announce the entry of Italy into the Second World War, we witnessed three fans starting a quarrel, and only the intervention of the police prevented a brawl. In fairness we should point out that the tifosi were not taken to the nearby police station.

'What can you do?', said one guardian of the peace. 'Passions carry people away, and they are not always able to repress their feelings.'

(In relation to this reference to Mussolini, we may remember the description of the 'fascist' tendencies of the English fans reported earlier.)

But, in terms of the Soviet ideology of sport, the English fans go far beyond what indulgent police treatment can handle and assimilate. Their aggression causes increasing intervention by specialist forces of the state, and brings even the threat of terrorism. They split their own society and the world society of genuine football lovers in two, and cause tension between nation and nation. They are an intrusive element within football, with no real interest in sport for its own sake, and are following covert criminal and/or regressively political aims of their own.

By their behaviour they also nullify the aesthetic and moral aspects of sport, which are also a fundamental element of the Soviet sporting ideology: 'there has been an undeniable consistent aspiration and effort in the USSR to make sport culturally uplifting, aesthetically satisfying and morally reputable'. (Riordan: 1980, 237)

Wimbledon, on the other hand, fulfils all the requirements of the Soviet ideology of sport. It is an atemporal, apolitical haven where good manners and fair play hold sway, where passion is acceptable but never spills over into violence or excess, where tradition is untouched by modernity and the notion of social conflict is nowhere to be found.

In short, the English abroad are seen as undermining essentially the *international* ideological function of sport. The English at home, however, reinforce its *domestic* ideological function.

Reverse discourse

It was pointed out, in relation to the discourses of Africanness which emerged around the Cameroon players during Italia'90 (see Chapter 4, page 76) that such discourses also operate in the reverse direction and simultaneously construct an artifical and pre-packaged European man by implication. The Soviet discourses of English football fandom which we have analysed also operate as reverse discourses on a more directly political (as opposed to sporting) ideological level. The massed hordes of English 'hooligan-fans' retro-construct a Soviet society which presents itself as having integrated its workers (and even given them political power), where there is no subproletariat, where no-one, in short, is excluded. Castle Wimbledon, on the other hand, through its positive coverage explicitly constructs a society of civilised values immune to the vicissitudes of political change, indeed even to economic hardship and terrorism. Ideological transference thus occurs along both polarities.

This process of ideological transference becomes even clearer if we compare Soviet coverage of Wimbledon'90 with its coverage of the 1991 tournament. One year later Wimbledon had become a symbol of everything that was wrong in the Soviet Union. For example, the walls of Wimbledon 'are crowned with barbed wire, which is so well known to the Soviet people, but so unusual in England' (*Sovetskij* Sport, 26 June 1991). Describing how tickets to the tournament are bought and sold on the black market, the journalist writes: ' "Oh God!' the reader will exclaim. 'Everything's just like here!' " Even the queues are part of this process, and evoke negative references to one of the less attractive sides of Soviet life, and to the general theme of shortages, which had been dealt with rather humorously in 1990. The queues, the journalist informs us dourly, 'cannot be compared even with the queues outside our liquor shops'.

Even references to British tradition cause negative memories of life in Moscow to surface. Commenting on the 'the somehow uncomplaining and uncompromising devotion to tradition' of the British, the journalist adds:

> Everything was different from today's Moscow, which is empty, destroyed, deserted, like a large flat whose owners have left in a hurry, leaving the rubbish behind, not wiping away the dust.

In short, the collapse of Soviet ideology has taken with it the idyllic imagery of 1990. Soviet coverage of Wimbledon'91, only weeks before the attempted coup of August which would precipitate the dissolution of the Soviet Union, shows all the signs of a society in political and economic crisis.

NOTES

1 'Tifosi' is the Italian for 'fans'. This word is used throughout the Soviet press to refer to fans not just from Italy, but in fact from any country. It is often (as in the article quoted) misspelled, appearing as 'tiffosi'.
2 The 'torcida' is a Brazilian dance.
3 The '*carabinieri*' are the Italian police.
4 A typographical error. The newspaper is in fact called '*Clarín*'.
5 Another typo. The name of the shop is '*El Traste*'.
6 'Barras' is a Latin American term for 'fans', 'supporters'. Here it seems to refer to the different 'gangs' of hooligans
7 The Spanish sports daily *As* (1 July) begins its article on the Wimbledon tournament as follows: 'Whether it rains, snows, is hot or cold, Wimbledon is still, for the English, whether they are tennis fans or not, what Mecca is for Muslims: a place of obligatory pilgrimage'. In view of the similarity of these two texts, we cannot rule out the possibility that they derive ultimately from a common source. The Spanish version, however, is not integrated into the coherent framework into which the Russian version will be placed.
8 This is a re-translation of the Russian translation of the English original. The Russian translation is, to say the very least, rather free, the English original reading 'if you can meet with triumph and disaster/and treat those two impostors just the same' (from the poem 'If').
9 *Izvestija*, 8 June, 'Are the referees taking bribes?'; 12 June, 'Of leaders, idols and ideals'; 14 June, 'Everyone saw it, except the referee'; 16 June, 'The referees are going home at the same time as us' ('us' is the Soviet football team); 14 July, 'A yellow card for the referees'; *Sovetskij Sport*, 27 June, 'A protest has been lodged'; 10 July, 'The "touch of death" of the referees'.
  Sovetskij Sport of 27 June also carried a cartoon of a referee with a machine gun strapped behind his back. On 29 June it showed two referees with their hands tied behind their backs disembarking from a plane. A figure behind them shouts to a crowd of enraged fans below: 'Here are the referees, the cause of all our troubles'.
  These are only the most obvious references. Others of a more sporadic nature can be found throughout the period under study. The negative coverage of the referees was due at least in part to the fate suffered by the Soviet team. The Swedish referee Erik Fredrikson was widely condemned in the Soviet press for not

awarding a penalty against Maradona when he handled the ball during the USSR-Argentina match.

10 *As* (see note 8) again expresses similar views. Commenting on the stiff price of the strawberries and noting the spectators' apparent willingness to buy them at these prices, it suggests: 'The fact is that the charm of Wimbledon even makes you forget any economic hardships'.

11 Russian was the second language in Czechoslovakia for many years. Czech and Russian are also fairly close – educated speakers of both could probably understand each other without the need for an interpreter.

12 For an analysis of how the Soviet Union is presented on British television, see in particular Brian McNair, (1988).

13 For a detailed history of the theory and practice of sport in the Soviet Union, see also *Sport in Soviet Society*, CUP, 1977, by the same author.

6

WIMBLEDON '91 – THE NATIONAL DIMENSION IN AN INDIVIDUALISED SPORT

INTRODUCTION

This chapter examines coverage of the 1991 Wimbledon tennis championship (with reference to the 1992 competition) in the European and American media, both press and television. The study involves press coverage from eleven European countries: Austria, Belgium, England, France, Germany, Italy, Portugal, Scotland, Spain (where both the Castilian-language press and the Catalan-language press are examined), the Soviet Union and Sweden. To provide a non-European point of comparison, a study of a sample of the American press is also included.

As regards television coverage, the study centres on British terrestrial and satellite coverage, American television (NBC), German television and Catalan television. We return to television, intensively, in the conclusion, most of the chapter being based on the press.

To provide a further point of contrast within the field of tennis itself, a study has also been made of a limited sample of press coverage of the 1991 Roland-Garros tournament in Paris, which precedes Wimbledon by precisely one month, and a small sample of coverage of the 1992 Wimbledon tournament.[1]

GAME

Examination of European press coverage of the early stages of Wimbledon 91 reveals that discourses of national identity *in relation to the players* were very much thinner on the ground than they had been during the corresponding stages of the World Cup finals in 1990. Although this trend was to be reversed fairly dramatically in the later stages of the competition, the initial difference was striking, and requires to be accounted for.

This relative scarcity of discourses of national identity in relation to tennis players relates partly to the nature of Wimbledon itself. As opposed to

An Italian view of 'the new American tennis', featuring Pete Sampras, Michael Chang and Andre Agassi, of Greek, Chinese and Iraqi origin respectively. Questions of national identity can be more complex in an individualised sport. (*Il Tennis Italiano*, August 1991)

nation-based tennis tournaments like the Davis Cup, Wimbledon is an arena where competitors appear essentially as *individuals*, and do not in any *official* sense represent their country of origin. This point was made by the German player Boris Becker when, together with Michael Stich, he won the gold medal in the men's doubles in the 1992 Olympics: 'It's a very special moment for us. You cannot compare it with winning at Wimbledon. There, you are playing for yourself – in the Olympics you play for a land' (*Herald*, 8 August 1992). Perhaps in recognition of this, the abbreviations which once indicated the nationality of the participants have long since disappeared from the Wimbledon score boards.

As further confirmation of this, we might note that the traditional ritual of national representation is entirely absent from Wimbledon (and similar tournaments). There are, for example, no national colours (everyone being subjected to Wimbledon's 'predominantly white' rule), no flags and no national anthems. By way of contrast, the question of national anthems had been an important sub-theme of World Cup reporting, with well publicised interventions by, among others, Luciano Pavarotti and Diego Maradona. And in many countries the various teams were often referred to simply by the colour of the strips.

Wimbledon is, however, very much an international tournament, and it is, by any standards, one of the world's major sporting media events. The 1990 final had been watched by 350 million people in 71 countries, while in 1991 some 5.5 million people watched the women's final and 8.5 million the men's final in Germany alone. By 1992, the total viewing figures had increased to 500 million people in 105 countries.[2]

On such a world stage, the emergence of nationalist interpretations of even the most individualistic of sports (not only tennis) appears to be irresistible. Indeed, the presence of a country's players at Wimbledon can even be something of a national media event. Thus the Portuguese sports newspaper *A Bola* (24 July) celebrated the appearance of the first Portuguese player to take part in Wimbledon since the arrival of the 'open' era with a front-page article and photograph, the article entitled 'Nuno Marques – finally a Portuguese!' (this despite his rather modest position of 108th in the world ranking).

All of the European presses studied either directly or indirectly refer to players from their country as 'representatives' of that country. For example, following the elimination of Javier Sánchez Vicario from the tournament, the Catalan daily *Avui* (30 June) says of his sister Arantxa: 'the elimination of her brother Javier means she is the only Spanish representative in the tournament . . . the only representative of the Spanish state'. When the last two Belgian players were eliminated, *La Libre Belgique* (1 July) wrote: 'Never in the history of modern tennis, that is since the advent of professional tennis, had our country been so well represented on . . . London soil'. Other examples abound.

As was the case in the World Cup, the fate of the nation's tennis players at Wimbledon comes in some way to reflect the fate of the nation as a whole. Thus *El Mundo* (1 July) evokes themes from Spain's imperial past when talking of the Spanish players at Wimbledon. It describes Javier Sánchez Vicario as a 'strange survivor of an "Invincible Armada" destroyed almost without fighting', adding gloomily:

> No-one was surprised. In Wimbledon, the Spaniards go to the slaughterhouse. Imbued with an ancestral fatalism, they disembark on the grass with a sense of sacrifice impregnating their hearts.

When there is more than one player from a country involved, there is even a sense in which journalists from that country attempt to create the idea of a *national team*. Thus, for example, *Corriere della Sera* (24 June) informs its readers that 'there are thirteen of our representatives' at Wimbledon, and, referring to the national colours of Italy's sportsmen, even goes so far as to describe them as 'the dark blue patrol' ('la pattuglia azzurra' – a clear reminiscence of 'la squadra azzurra' of the World Cup). *Matchball* (12 July) also refers to them as the 'azzurri'.

As part of this media attempt to present Wimbledon as a site of national representation, discourses relating to the traditional symbols of nationality inevitably emerge. These include references to national flags, which are of course conspicuous by their absence at Wimbledon. Thus, *La Libre Belgique* (29 June) describes the British player Andrew Castle as 'one of the few efficient carriers of the Union Jack'. The Catalan daily *Sport* (24 June) reports that 'there will be eight Spaniards defending the Spanish flag as from today in Wimbledon', and, in an article entitled 'Agassi waves flag with a bold glory' which combines a number of nationalistic themes, *The Independent* (4 July) writes:

> The outlook for the Fourth of July is reasonably bright for Americans . . . They are guaranteed at least one representative in the men's semi-finals . . . Jim Courier, who meets Michael Stich, from Beckerland, also has an outstanding opportunity to wave the flag.

SETTING

THE REINVENTION OF TRADITION

An obvious difference between Wimbledon and the World Cup is, of course, the setting, the location itself. While the World Cup not only changes its location from one championship to the next, but actually alternates between Europe and South America, Wimbledon has been on its present site since 1922, and the tournament has been in operation, in one form or another, since 1877. This lengthy history, and the presence of large numbers of English spectators, clearly fulfil the conditions necessary for the development of discourses of the national dimension. And indeed, discourses of Englishness revolving around the basic notion of *tradition* form without doubt the largest, the most highly developed and one of the most interesting groups of discourses of national identity to emerge in relation to Wimbledon in both the European and the American press.

THE TEMPLE OF THE WHITE SPORT: THE MODE OF REVERENCE

Discourses of English/British devotion to tradition revolve around a number of clichés. Perhaps the most omnipresent of these is the reference to Wimbledon as some kind of temple. Even the Soviet press participates in this metaphor, referring to the Centre Court as 'the holy of holies of tennis' (*Sovetskij Sport*, 5 July).

In the British press, such references tend to be indirect, with the spectators referred to as 'pilgrims' (*The Glasgow Herald*, 25 June), or evening referred to as 'evensong' (*The Independent*, 27 June), though straightforward references do occasionally occur – thus the *Daily Mail* (23 June), combining both 'temple' and 'tradition' ideas overtly, describes Wimbledon as 'a shrine of tradition'. On a somewhat different level, there is a sense in which the hushed tones of the BBC's Wimbledon commentators reflect the reverential silence of the cathedral.

The French, Belgian and Italian presses clearly prefer the term 'temple'. Thus *La Libre Belgique* of 1 July entitles its Wimbledon report 'A Sunday in the temple of tennis', while *L'Equipe* (29 June) refers to Wimbledon as 'the historic temple of tennis', and adds that the American player Andre Agassi has been 'newly converted to the religion of grass'. The Italian daily *Tuttosport* (25 June) also refers to 'the sacred precincts of Wimbledon, considered as the temple of world tennis'. The German and Austrian presses, on the other hand strongly favour the phrase 'tennis-Mecca', or even 'Mecca of the white sport' (*Hannoversche Allgemeine Zeitung*, 6 July), though references to the 'hallowed lawn' are also quite common.

The Iberian press (the Spanish press, in both its Castilian-language and its Catalan-language manifestations, and the Portuguese press), uses almost exclusively the term 'cathedral' of tennis. Thus the Portuguese sports newspaper *A Bola* (24 June) asks in a title which looks forward to the men's final 'will there be surprises in the "cathedral"?' The Spanish sports daily *El Mundo Deportivo* carried the headline 'La Catedral' over *every single* article published on Wimbledon throughout the entire tournament, as well as numerous references within the articles themselves. The commentator on Canal 33 also referred to the 'cathedral of tennis' during the presentation of trophies at the end of the women's singles final (5 July).

Indeed, it is in Spain that this metaphor reaches its highest point of development. Thus *El Mundo Deportivo* (23 June) tells us that 'The "Cathedral" called to its faithful', adding 'there is no need to ring the bells, the faithful of this particular cathedral never forget their duty.' Wimbledon is described as 'the expiatory temple of world tennis' and the ball boys are referred to as 'altar boys'. *El País* (1 July) describes queueing as 'one of the cruel liturgies of Wimbledon', but explains that it is necessary to gain access to the 'venerated site'.

It is tempting to see this as some kind of reflection of the continuing influence of the Catholic Church in Spain to a degree not found in other western European countries. And indeed an article in *El Mundo Deportivo* (1 July) makes this connection explicitly. The article is entitled 'She beat Lori McNeil easily after fulfilling her Christian duty', and refers to Arantxa Sánchez Vicario's game on 'Middle Sunday':

> Arantxa Sánchez Vicario asked the organizers on Saturday not to programme her for the first game [on Sunday] since she had to fulfil her Christian duty and go to mass on Sundays . . . From the church in the town of Wimbledon she went to the Centre Court. And the 'cathedral' did not close its doors on her on the first Sunday in history on which it opened them.

What is being venerated in this temple is, of course, tradition, a quasi-religious observance of the rules. This theme runs throughout European reporting on Wimbledon. For example, *La Libre Belgique* (26 June) assures us that 'In Wimbledon, as is well known, tradition is stronger than anything', while for the *Hannoversche Allgemeine Zeitung* (21 June – a special tennis edition), Wimbledon is the home of 'traditionalists in the British Isles and throughout the world', and it also refers to 'tradition which is so beloved in the British Isles'.

In extreme versions of this discourse of traditionalism, Wimbledon is presented as almost timeless. Thus *A Bola* (24 June), commenting on the fact that 'the centre court's . . . grass has been carefully tended for 365 days', awaiting the opening game adds:

> This is how it has been for more than a century and this is probably how it will be for another century yet, because the traditions of the All England Lawn Tennis & Croquet Club do not yield to the onward march of time.

However, references to tradition at Wimbledon in the European media are not necessarily positive. In fact, they are frequently linked to notions of conservatism and immobilism which are presented as negative values. Thus *Gazzetta dello Sport* (5 July) refers scathingly to 'the retired generals and the baronets who govern the tournament'. *L'Equipe magazine* (1 July) suggests of the members of the All England Club that 'two thirds are pickled in whisky', and the journalist writing this piece adds: 'I firmly believe that traditions are the very soul of Wimbledon. But that's no reason not to join the twentieth century'.

Wimbledon is presented not only as behind the times, but also, crucially, as out of touch with the rest of Europe. Commenting on the fact that temperature readings on the Centre Court are still given in Fahrenheit, *Gazzetta dello Sport* (7 July) writes:

> Among all the traditions which Wimbledon does not seem in any way inclined to drop is also that of the British unit for measuring temperature. For years newspapers, TV and weather forecasts have espoused the decimal cause of United Europe. But in the All England Tennis Club, where the past always counts for more than the future, no one will ever tell you that 98.8 Fahrenheit is 37.1 degrees.

Wimbledon also becomes a symbol of a country with a class system which is also seen as somehow un-European. Thus *Neue Kronen-Zeitung* (20 June), commenting on the different conditions for the top seeds and the less well-known players (the former rent houses in Wimbledon, the latter have to commute every day from central London), points out that 'even in Wimbledon you find the typically English class society'. But this does not relate only to the players. The Catalan daily *el Periódico* (24 June) sees the conservatism of Wimbledon as a reflection of an outdated class system in a broader sense. In an article entitled 'English society gets dressed up on grass', it writes: 'There you can see . . . almost the entire British aristocracy in one of their few public appearances. Wimbledon is their best display.'

L'Equipe magazine (1 July) pursues the idea of outdated structures and outdated social prejudices. Commenting on the attention to fashion paid at Wimbledon, it writes:

> You might be surprised that the English . . . who are more interested in the softness of their corner divan than in the creases of their Tergal trousers should have set themselves up as the arbiters of elegance at Wimbledon. But in a country where they used to hide those very tantalizing piano legs under covers during the reign of Queen Victoria, it is much more important to defend proprieties than to worry about pastel harmonies.

The notion of 'the puritan British' *El Mundo Deportivo* (4 July) is an important one. And indeed, it was in the area of clothes and proprieties that one of the major media events of the tournament was to be located.

STRAWBERRIES AND CREAM: PRIVILEGE IN ENGLAND

A second major cliché is what *Il Tennis Italiano* (August) calls 'the mythical strawberries and cream'. These, however, are also presented as symbolic of clichéd British traditionalism. Thus *El Mundo Deportivo* (23 June) writes:

> Strawberries and cream, the Duke and Duchess of Kent chatting with the ball boys, the white clothes, Sunday off . . . Wimbledon is more than a competition, it sums up the English love for tradition. If, instead of a young man wearing a white shirt and shorts and holding a racket, it was an elderly man dressed in black, wearing a bowler hat and holding an umbrella who came out on to the centre court, the spectators would not be surprised: this person would be part of a typically British setting.

But, beyond the clichés, even something as apparently trivial as strawberries and cream gives rise to highly developed and complex discourses of Englishness throughout the European media. These strawberries come to represent aristocratic living, which will also become one of the major symbols of what is presented as an outdated British society. Thus *El Mundo Deportivo* (8 July) writes, talking of the German player Michael Stich:

> What neither he nor most of the spectators could see was the large box of strawberries which was going round the Royal Box (about 2 kg) and into which the members of the British nobility were dipping their dainty fingers.

(The terminology is important here. Talking of the women's final, the *Observer* of 7 July suggests that 'in the Royal Box thoughts may have been turning to a cuppa and dainty sandwiches'. See conclusion of this chapter for further comment.)

DOMINANCE AND SUBVERSION: DRESSING IN WHITE

When the rules and conservative values of the club are questioned, complex discourses of stagnation and challenge emerge in the reporting of Wimbledon throughout Europe and America. In the 1991 tournament, these discourses crystallised around the figure of the American player Andre Agassi.

Agassi, well known for his colourful tennis clothes, had not attended the previous two Wimbledon championships because (apparently) of the tournament's 'predominantly white' rule. As the NBC commentator put it (3 July), he was 'the guy who wouldn't play Wimbledon because they wouldn't let him dress like an oil-spill'. Although deciding to take part in the 1991 Wimbledon, Agassi had let it be known that he still did not intend to accept the 'predominantly white' rule, causing unprecedented speculation throughout the sporting press of Europe and America as to whether he would turn up in his usual highly coloured clothes. This led to high levels of expectation among the tennis-going public. As *Corriere della Sera* (24 June) put it:

> An almost morbid curiosity surrounds the dress chosen by the extravagant tennis player from Las Vegas in relation to the rigid rules of Wimbledon which forbid wearing any colour other than white.

Agassi's supposed intention to break the Wimbledon rules was clearly seen as an act of aggression, a challenge to tradition. For example, in an article entitled 'You can change your colour but not your image', *Sovetskij Sport* (29 June) describes his clothes as his 'battle dress', while *La Libre Belgique* (28 June) presents this situation as a challenge to British traditionalism through its royal family. Speaking of the Duchess of Kent, it writes:

> Her ducal mind was no doubt troubled by the question which has been worrying all the English for months: in what colour would Andre Agassi turn up on the Centre Court for his first game after an absence of four years and full many a criticism voiced by him concerning this select club.

(The irony of this interpretation is emphasised by the deliberate use of archaic French, 'full many a criticism' appearing in the text as *moult critiques*.)

Television interest was also intense. On the day of his first appearance (27 June) the BBC interrupted coverage of the Brown-Ivanisevic match to cover the moment when Agassi undressed for play (this programming decision caused some amusement to the Castilian-language Catalan daily *Claro* of 28 June, which expressed incredulity that any event could be so important as to interrupt BBC coverage of British player). In its recorded highlights, the German station RTL Plus introduced its feature on Agassi as follows:

> The fans were very, very excited awaiting the first appearance of Andre Agassi. Will he abide by the rules of the venerable club, will he appear all in white? This was the question which had kept us guessing since Monday.

As he took off his track suit (in a manner which *La Libre Belgique* of 28 June described as being like a 'stripper'), RTL Plus provided a fanfare as background music to what it called 'the moment of truth'.

It is interesting to compare the discourses generated by this event with a description of the 1990 Roland-Garros tournament appearing in *Le Figaro* (1

July). While Wimbledon, whatever the interpretation offered by particular journalists, is characterised throughout by tradition, Roland-Garros is here presented as modern, open-minded, able to cope with even the most outrageous apparel from both players and fans. *Le Figaro* describes the French fans as:

> Noisy, decked out in their gaudy gear, shameless. Formerly, a very long time ago, the spectators contained their emotions. No-one shouted. No-one turned up wearing a vest. That's all been changed. Bands of Red Indians shouting noisily at impassive players. They're wearing beach caps, helmets, berets, braces and even Mickey Mouse masks with ears which applaud. You'd think you were in Disneyland.

Agassi's garish clothes are indeed ridiculed, but the discourses of challenge and contestation are missing. He is described as 'wearing mauve, fluorescent, torn-up clothes . . . Eccentric, Agassi? No, he arrived on the court minus hat and minus feathers. Sober.'

ANDRE AGASSI'S CHALLENGE TO THE BRITISH STATE

In the event Agassi appeared dressed *entirely* in white, an event which acted as a catalyst for the emergence of extended and often conflicting discourses of Englishness as represented by the traditionalism of Wimbledon.

We may note that there were again differences between the metaphors used to refer to Andre Agassi in this context. The British popular press preferred a chivalresque interpretation, referring to him as a 'White Knight' (e.g. *Daily Mirror*, 2 July), an idea also taken up in the USA where coverage of the day's play on 29 June was introduced by the NBC commentator with the question 'And how will they treat the Knight in white, Andre Agassi, who finally answers his Wimbledon invitation?'

The *Financial Times* (29 June) kept to the 'temple' image by describing him as appearing in 'choir-boy white'. The Catalan daily *Claro* (28 June) also keeps to the Spanish 'cathedral' metaphor by presenting him as 'whiter than a bride'. For *Il Tennis Italiano* (August 1991), he was 'like a little boy at his first communion', an image which also appears in *L'Equipe* (29 June) where the caption beside a photograph of Agassi describes him as a 'first communicant'. However, the term which proved far and away the most popular in the French and Belgian presses was 'white angel'. The innocence suggested by such imagery, was, however, entirely illusory.

USA Today (28 June) goes for a pop-music theme by describing him as a 'Bleach Boy' (a term which would surface again during coverage of the 1992 tournament). Both German television (RTL Plus, 27 June) and press (*Hannoversche Allgemeine Zeitung* 6 July) referred to the song by the popular German singer Roy Black, 'Ganz in weiß' ('All in white').

Almost inevitably, there were numerous references to adverts for soap-powders and detergents. RTL Plus in its recorded highlights (28 June) described Agassi as a 'little White Giant', a reference to a well-known German washing powder (Weißer Riese). This same product reappears in the subtitle of an article in the *Hannoversche Allgemeine Zeitung* (28 June). The article also describes Agassi as a 'snow-white giant' ('schneeweißer Riese') and suggests that his clothes 'were as white as the famous advertising slogan of a washing powder firm'. *Gazzetta dello Sport* (5 July) develops the same theme, describing Agassi's appearance as:

> . . . a show which would be the envy of advertising for the best washing machine detergents, that 'whiter than white' appearance.

USA Today (28 June) begins an article entitled 'Agassi surrenders to rules with all-white flag' as follows:

> This bulletin just in from here: Whiter whites! Brighter brights! Zowie! Forget the smashing forehands and artful volleys. There's laundry to discuss.

These references (knights, temples, pop music, advertisements) are neither haphazard nor coincidental. The reference to 'knights' contains the notion of conquest, an idea to which we shall return below. While the temple imagery continues the 'cathedral of tradition' discourse mentioned earlier and suggests at least formal recognition of the sanctity of the site, the references to pop music and advertisements are part of a discourse of Americanness (glitzy, garish, commercial) which would reappear strongly in relation to Agassi in the 1992 Wimbledon tournament, and which suggests, despite apparent compliance, an underlying subversion of tradition.

A number of newspapers saw this event as a straightforward victory for British conservatism. For many European commentators, however, Agassi had subverted the Wimbledon tradition by successfully transforming the venerated site into a stage. Thus *Le monde du tennis* (1 August) saw the event as a 'publicity stunt', for the *Hannoversche Allgemeine Zeitung* (6 July) it was a part of a 'clever advertising campaign', while *L'Equipe* (29 June) saw it as part of an 'immense campaign of seduction' and an 'opération charme'. This notion of 'publicity stunt' may also be part of the subtext of the references to washing powder adverts above.

There is also a strong suggestion that apparent compliance is essentially a mask for underlying conquest. This idea is presented explicitly by *Gazzetta dello Sport* (5 July): 'By bowing to the tradition of Wimbledon he conquered the English'. *La Libre Belgique* (28 June) takes this interpretation even further. Talking of Agassi's opponent the Canadian Grant Connell, it writes:

> Compared to him, Connell, kitted out by the same American firm as the Kid and wearing classic tennis dress though less translucent, looked like a good-for-nothing, an iconoclast. It was touch and go whether the English spectators, led by the Duchess of Kent, would cast the first stone at him for not having made a consider-able effort for the great cause, the virginity of the tennis uniform.

However, further study of these discourses takes us into one of the most important events of Wimbledon 91 for the generation of discourses of Englishness – the question of Middle Sunday.

The first week of play at Wimbledon 1991 was the rainiest on record. This led to a wave of references to rain as a Wimbledon/London/English/British tradition of such dimensions that it could not possibly be itemised here. However, a few quotes will help to give a flavour of this phenomenon. Thus *El Mundo Deportivo* (25 June) reported: 'However, the presence of rain in the tournament is nothing unusual. In fact it is one more component part of the tradition.' *Gazzetta dello Sport* (27 June) added:

> Rain is so much a part of English tradition that the leading bookmakers accept bets on the amount of rain which might fall during any given month or on the number of consecutive days without rain.

But there is more than one tradition involved. So great was the backlog of cancelled games due to the appalling weather conditions during the first week that the Wimbledon officials eventually decided to allow play to take place on the 'Middle Sunday' for the first time in the entire history of the tournament. Such a departure from tradition acted even more than Agassi's clothes as a catalyst for discourses of Englishness with powerful threads of conservatism and class segregation. These were indeed among the most powerful discourses to emerge in coverage of the Wimbledon tournament.

The connection between the two traditions (rain and Middle Sunday) is made explicitly by *The Independent* (27 June) when it writes:

> Even the most sacred of cows was forced to seek shelter yesterday from the rain which had made this Wimbledon the worst on record until a late burst of play at evensong. Whisper it, but play for the first time on the Middle Sunday was broached.

Contradicting interpretations of 'Middle Sunday' are to be found throughout the European press. 'Tradition vanquished, they will play on Sunday', ran the heading of *Gazzetta dello Sport*'s article on 29 June. This 'represents a real setback for tradition', says *El Mundo Deportivo* of the same day. *The New York Times* (30 June) entitled its article on the eve of Middle Sunday 'That crash you here is a tradition falling'. *La Libre Belgique* (also 29 June) sees this defeat of tradition as an open challenge to British conservatism, and again uses the Royal Family in a symbolic role:

> Cocking a snook at the history of the place, at its ancestral tradition, at the princely apparatus and all the fuss and frills, Alan Mills, the referee, has decided to disregard custom and play matches on Sunday.
>
> It will be the first time this has happened since the creation of the tournament in 1877.
>
> What would the ancestors of the Duchess of Kent say? . . .

Matchball (25 July) also refers to the conservatism of those in charge, suggesting also that this decision represents a defeat for them: 'the old fogeys of the All England Club finally gave in, taking a revolutionary decision for that bunker of traditions which is Wimbledon'.

The notion of disturbance, of challenge to an antiquated un-European society is emphasised in many Continental reports. Thus *El Mundo* (1 July) writes:

> Yesterday, for the first time ever, play took place on Sunday during the Wimbledon tournament. And nothing happened. Big Ben did not stop, the Thames did not overflow, Her Gracious Majesty did not abdicate. The rain . . . was the cause of this little great commotion which, after all, has brought Great Britain closer to Europe.
>
> Meteorology overcame tradition. But isn't the rain the greatest and the oldest English tradition?

But the element of Middle Sunday which the journalists home in on most relentlessly is the presence of what they see as a different kind of fan in the stands. This fan breaks with a number of clichés about Wimbledon. Thus *Matchball* (25 July), having carried the subtitle 'The day of the common people' in its main article on Wimbledon, described these fans in another article as 'Ordinary people, people who have little in common with the classic commonplaces regarding the English'. For *Matchball* it is the presence of these fans which is the truly revolutionary element of Middle Sunday: 'At the end of this historic day, however, the extraordinary happening was seeing around the most prestigious courts in the world a young, joyous and at times even unrestrained public'.

The fan presented in this view of Middle Sunday is a working-class fan who, as constructed in these discourses, has never been seen in Wimbledon, or at least in the Centre Court, before. Referring to the low entry prices charged on Middle Sunday, *Matchball* continues:

> This was the key which finally allowed thousands of fans to take the insurmountable gates of Wimbledon off their hinges, people who under normal conditions would never have set foot in the Centre Court in their lives.

The New York Times (30 June) also pursues the idea of a fan never before seen at Wimbledon:

> There are going to be some unfamiliar faces, unfamiliar accents, maybe T-shirts instead of old school ties on the front row at Centre Court. The Duke and Duchess of Kent and the rest of the denizens of the Royal Box are believed to be exempt from the scramble.

These 'young and enthusiastic spectators bring football-stadium songs' to tennis, writes *Matchball* (12 July), while *L'Equipe* (2 July) adds that, as a result, 'the world is upside down.' And this notion of the importing of football fans is put forward by numerous newspapers. In an article entitled 'The "wave" in the cathedral', *La Vanguardia* (1 July) wrote:

It was a different kind of public, young, enthusiastic, passionate and daring, since they got to their feet on several occasions within this hallowed club to do the 'wave', which had been brought into fashion by football fans . . . at times they shouted, as though they were at a football match.

This article was accompanied by a photograph of young fans doing the Mexican wave. *El País* (1 July), introducing a notion of sacrilege, makes very much the same points, emphasising the contrasts between 'youngsters' and 'traditionalists':

Moreover, the spectators were younger than usual yesterday. Enduring a long night outside or an early Sunday rise isn't part of the plans of the 'traditionalists'. Consequently, the atmosphere in the Centre Court, full of sleepy youngsters, was unusually rowdy. They even committed the 'sacrilege' of doing the Mexican wave in the stand, with the enthusiastic participation of Lady Di in the royal box.

Again, there was a photograph of fans doing the wave. *Matchball* (25 July) not only contrasts these fans with the traditional Wimbledon public, but suggests, as many other European reports do (e.g. *La Libre Belgique 1 July*/*Sport Bild*, 10 July), that they are in some way more 'authentic' than those usually to be found at Wimbledon. They were, it claims:

All people who really wanted to be there, all genuine tennis lovers. People who once inside never stopped rejoicing for a second, encouraging the players, singing football stadium songs, doing the 'wave' (even those in the royal box joined in), having fun and causing the players to have fun. The complete opposite of the typical Wimbledon public, stiff and a little snobbish. 'We sold very little strawberries and cream, and the champagne stayed in the refrigerator', said one of the managers of the company which has the contract for the catering services.

The party atmosphere which prevailed is described in a lengthy article to be found in the German sports weekly *Sport Kurier* (3 July):

Remarkable things are taking place now in Wimbledon. We must obviously live with the fact that the much vaunted tradition on which the All England Lawn Tennis & Croquet Club always insists so determinedly is wobbling on its legs this year.

For the first time perfectly ordinary, real tennis fans gained entry to the Centre Court.

Wimbledon was unrecognisable . . . they turned the Centre Court into a veritable bedlam (who would ever have thought that possible?), showed the ladies and gentlemen in the Royal Box how the Mexican wave goes and how to liven up the atmosphere of the honourable temple of the tennis-Mecca.

The 11,000 mostly young visitors never stopped, they were simply happy to be allowed into the Centre Court for once, and sang battle songs which previously we had only known at Wembley Stadium.

Everyone would like . . . another Middle Sunday with the real tennis fans. Tradition or no tradition.

Such discourses are not confined to the foreign press. The *Observer* (7 July), in an article entitled 'When the heat is on for the underprivileged' writes:

> Wimbledon has never been one of the summer's more egalitarian events. This year has seen, if it's possible, a widening of the divide between the pampered and the put-upon.

> [On Middle Sunday] The caterers say the champagne and strawberries were hardly touched as genuine fans, allowed in for just £10 . . . opted for the more working-class fare of fish and chips – to such an extent that the caterers ran out of fish.

> [After being excluded once Middle Sunday was over] The proles hit back on Wednesday when six fans jumped the perimeter fence to gain entry and scurried about among the corporate hospitality tents, with exasperated guards in hot and futile pursuit.

The longest and possibly most highly developed article on this theme was to be found in *Gazzetta dello Sport* (2 July). Entitled 'The revenge of the ordinary spectators', it requires very little comment.

> The first Sunday of play in Wimbledon made room for the people: they took over the terraces of the Centre Court and the entry of the masses gave a genuine flavour to an aristocratic and stuffy tournament.

> However, the abolition of privilege, even if only for a single day, had a revolutionary effect.

> The people took over the terraces of the Centre Court in a joyful tumult reminiscent of the storming of the Bastille . . . and the entry of the masses, although authorised, brought a unique flavour, of real supporters, to a tournament which too often hides behind polite applause a profound lack of interest in tennis.

> Yesterday [Monday], the 'right' people came back to Wimbledon, those who consider a ticket to the Centre Court stand to be like an invitation to a ball at Buckingham Palace . . . a passport to high society, where it's no use knowing the ATP classification, but 'Debrett's', the authoritative 'Who's Who' of the British nobility.

> The 'right' people observe the protocol of the occasion and perpetuate the cliché of strawberries and cream and champagne, as if it was particularly noble to eat strawberries which are always too dear with a little plastic fork from an expanded polystyrene tub and sip low quality 'bubbly' (French 'spumante' in the jargon the VIPs) at Dom Perignon prices.

> The young and non-conformist masses on Sunday gave the strawberries and champagne a miss because they hungered and thirsted only for tennis. Some big wigs at the All England Tennis Club would not be at all opposed to institutionalising in future the 'people's Sunday'. But those given to 'aristocratic pleasures', stung by the fall in takings, are ready to wage war against any return of 'bloody Sunday'.

The notion of a re-establishment of order after a revolutionary event appears elsewhere. The *Madison Capital Times*, (2 July), which also refers to the 'party atmosphere' of Middle Sunday, writes:

Order was restored to Centre Court as the rabble gave way to royalty, the waves and chants disappeared.

Players again bowed or curtseyed to the Duchess of Kent in the Royal Box and the stands were filled with the regular, older, more restrained ticket-holders in blue blazers and fine dresses.

Wimbledon returned to stolid respectability a day after opening its gates to the masses for the first time on the Middle Sunday.

Matchball (25 July) makes the same point, returning to the notion of the timelessness of the traditional Wimbledon: 'The next day Wimbledon had become "serious" again, as it always has been, and as it always will be'.

MIDDLE SUNDAY IN PERSPECTIVE

A number of elements must be borne in mind if the role of Middle Sunday in the construction of images of Englishness is to be fully understood. The first of these concerns the Wimbledon spectators. Tennis is indeed not a mass sport like football, 'in Britain [it] has still to shed its image as a game for the upper classes' (*The Independent*, 5 July 1992), and it does not have a large working class following in the way in which football obviously does in Great Britain. None the less, it is clearly not the case that the stands of the Wimbledon courts are normally peopled exclusively by aristocrats. Neither does television coverage of Middle Sunday suggest that the stands were occupied on that occasion by proletarian masses.

Likewise, although the accent in reports on Middle Sunday was on the youth of the fans, it is also by no means the case that young spectators are not to be found on normal Wimbledon days. This point was made by *El País* (24 June) before the tournament started: 'The teenagers from London are threatening to disturb the peaceful atmosphere of the All England Lawn Tennis and Croquet Club'. *Gazzetta dello Sport* (6 July) mentions the results of an opinion poll which showed that five out of seven teenagers who came to Wimbledon came to see Andre Agassi. Clearly, the teenagers were there.

The queues which formed on the night from Saturday to Sunday were also one of the main features in reporting on Middle Sunday, both in the press and on television. *Matchball* (25 July), for example, talks of 'An apocalyptic queue, a human serpent from the Guinness book of records'. *L'Equipe magazine* (1 July) likewise refers to the badges distributed to those waiting ('I queued at Wimbledon 91'), adding that such a badge 'classifies you as a pure plum-pudding Englishman more surely than an Oxford scarf', and that those waiting were able to 'pretend to have a good time, an activity which the Englishman has raised to the level of an art'. The author offers these reflections as part of his general thesis that 'the real Englishman loves to be frustrated. In fact, in his case it is what comes closest to pure and simple happiness'.

But queues were not confined to this particular day. On 25 June, at the very beginning of the tournament, the Portuguese daily *O Correio da Manhã* had already elaborated on the difficulties of obtaining a ticket and the resulting queues:

> As is well known, getting a ticket for the Wimbledon Tournament is one of the most arduous and difficult tasks facing tennis fans. In fact a long postal process is necessary to obtain a ticket before the tournament starts, otherwise the would-be spectators have to spend hours in the endless queues which form every day around the stadium, most of them ending up going back home.

Similar references can be found throughout the European press. We can safely assume that it was not the 'right people' who had been queueing overnight, and that these were queues of 'ordinary spectators' who had been present at Wimbledon throughout.

In short, Middle Sunday did not represent a storming of the ageing Wimbledon Bastille by youthful proletarian masses who had never before gained entry to these hallowed premises. It clearly *was* different. Since no seats could be booked in advance and entry for anyone involved queueing overnight, the average age of the fans was indeed lower than usual. But the most striking difference was not the absence of royalty (in fact the Princess of Wales was there, and a number of papers make the point that she joined in the Mexican wave), but the unusual availability of seats in the show courts, and above all the lack of a *corporate* presence. Since this day had not been scheduled, no arrangements for corporate visitors had been made. These two factors – relative youth and the absence of corporate 'guests' for whom all expenses were being paid – go most towards explaining the different atmosphere of Middle Sunday.

Bearing this in mind, it can be seen that the discourses of Englishness/Britishness which emerge in relation to Middle Sunday do not derive primarily from Middle Sunday itself. Britain is no more ruled by its aristocracy than Spain or Sweden are by theirs. Such class struggle as exists in this country does not pit proletarian masses against pampered and/or pickled members of the nobility. The discourses which dominate in these reports emanate from a store of such discourses immanent in European political and media culture. They construct a Middle Sunday on the basis of an agenda which is not so much ahistorical as anti-historical.

This point is made at some length in *The Independent* (4 July). In an article entitled 'Fog of quaint clichés', which, though opposing such discourses, nonetheless accepts a number of their key terms, Ken Jones writes:

> Whenever something occurs to put sporting tradition in an unfavourable light, somebody is quick to exclaim, 'Not before time,' or 'You can't live in the past, so let us get on with the future.'

> Thus when Wimbledon uniquely threw open its gates to the proletariat last Sunday some literary toilers from our former Transatlantic colonies were encouraged to explore the limits of xenophobic facetiousness.

> A summary of gleefully transmitted observations supposes the continued existence of a British Empire, quaint victualling priorities and widespread enthusiasm for the unseasonal mowing down of grouse.

In American eyes Wimbledon represents us as a people obsessed with creaking ceremony and obsolete ritual, inherently genuflective in the presence of superiors. As Tom Weir of USA Today put it: 'The world's stuffiest, starchiest and stodgiest sports event finally gave way Sunday to the commoners and found itself having an uncommonly good time'.

It certainly wasn't a day that 'snooty' members of the All England Lawn Tennis and Croquet club had set aside for the hunting (sic) of grouse or punting at Henley. It wasn't, as Mr Weir suggested, 'like calling in every green-haired and pierced-nosed punk rocker in London to read Shakespeare for the Queen.'

It was, by all accounts, a remarkable experience, one fully appreciated by the players, but not a reason for anybody to indulge in wild assumptions, or call up cultural clichés.

We deal with questions about these accounts of Britain in the conclusion of this chapter.

DOMINANCE AND SUBVERSION: ANDRE AGASSI'S CAP

While there was no Middle Sunday in 1992, a miniature version of 'the people versus the aristocracy' would be provided by the case of Andre Agassi's cap (Agassi won the 1992 men's tournament). The issue was raised in the following terms by *Corriere dello Sport* (5 July 1992):

The rigid protocol of the presentation of prizes requires, in fact, the Duke and Duchess of Kent to hand over the golden cup to the winner; it would be reprehensible, it is being pointed out, if the American champion forgot (heaven forbid) to take off his cap.

In the event, Agassi did not take off his cap, though it seemed clear that he forgot to do so in the excitement of winning the final rather than as a deliberate gesture of any kind. While noting this lapse of concentration, the British media in general made little of it. There was a minor note of regret. Bringing the BBC's two-week long coverage of the tournament to an end, Harry Carpenter's final remark was: 'I just wish he'd taken his cap off'.

The *Sun* (6 July 1992), however, chose to place this incident within the theme of 'rebellion', an element of the discourse of Americanness which would again crystallise around Agassi as the tournament proceeded, and reintroduced the notion of anachronistic social relations:

As the Duchess of Kent beckoned Andre forward to collect the old gold pot, the boy from Las Vegas even forgot to remove his cap.

Royalty or not, he wasn't going to tug his forelock.

For *Corriere dello Sport* (6 July 1992), likewise, this incident became the vehicle for again presenting Britain as a stuffy, rigid and outdated society:

As it was easy to foresee, Agassi did not take his cap off during the award ceremony carried out, as protocol requires, by the Duke and Duchess of Kent, thereby causing a minor diplomatic incident.

And, combining this issue with one of the other major talking points of the

By GEOFFREY PARKHOUSE
Political Editor

THE Prime Minister last night rallied his backbenchers with a passionate end-of-term speech which confronted Lady Thatcher's criticism of his European policy — which she re-stated yesterday in the House of Lords.

Mr Major declared: "I don't want us to be a little England, impoverished, devoid of influence, sour in isolation, bereft of hope, languishing on the sidelines of Europe and history."

Britain, he said, could have only one policy, and that is to be at the centre of Europe influencing events and creating a community in the shape we want. "The only way to do that is pitching at the heart of Europe. We do want to be in the middle. We will be in the middle."

He brushed aside the Thatcher criticisms of the Maastricht Treaty negotiated by him last December: "I have to say that if we had been negotiating from the centre throughout the last 20 years, we might have had more influence on the development of the Community than has been the case."

"I'm sending her a warning for grunting"

Mrs Thatcher's unwelcome anti-European comments earn her the Monica Seles treatment from British Prime Minister John Major (*Herald*, 3 July 1992)

tournament Monica Seles's tendency to 'grunt' as she served (the British tabloids christened her 'Moanica', and turned up at the grounds complete with 'gruntometers') – it goes on:

> But the final touch was when, the day before the final, Seles was invited, perhaps so as not to disturb the noble ears of the Duke and Duchess of Kent, to restrain herself. That is, not to grunt and trumpet.

In the macro-discourse of failure aristocracy is a place-holder for rigidity, outdatedness, un-Europeanness, the refusal to be a credible member of the modern society of nations.

If the class structures of British society are presented as anachronistic, in reporting on Wimbledon the fate of British tennis also becomes symbolic of a nation defined by failure. *The Glasgow Herald* (25 June) ironises on the anguish of the English as they ask themselves when 'the nation [will] have another Fred Perry', and on their sense of failure because Britain is not 'in a position to compete with most of the rest of the world'. It talks of 'Brits stumbling around the tennis circuit in an advanced state of rigor mortis'.

Such notions would re-emerge during coverage of the 1992 tournament. Talking of Andre Agassi's manager, Nick Bolletieri, *The Independent* (5 July) would write: 'Nick Bolletieri's critics maintain he produces only one type of player: a huge forehand, a respectable serve and a non-existent volley. And wouldn't Britain be delighted to have just one player so limited? . . . A top British player. The very thought moistens eyes at the All England Club . . . Britain would have been ecstatic even with his cast-offs'.

But such considerations are not confined to the British press. Both *L'Equipe magazine* (1 July) and the Austrian daily *Neue Kronen-Zeitung* (25 June) carry reports on a statement made by a spokesman for the bookmakers William Hill. *L'Equipe magazine* quotes him as saying:

> We have opened bets at 1,000 to 1 for the announcement by the Archbishop of Canterbury of the second reincarnation of Jesus Christ and for an English victory at Wimbledon. We have received two 50 pound bets on Jesus and none on the English players.

This same story was recounted with some glee by the American commentators during NBC's live coverage of the men's final (7 July). This followed shortly after a tennis quiz question asking for the last British singles champion. When the answer was given as Fred Perry, the camera panned to pick out this former player in the stand. Commenting on his age (82) and the fact that he had recently had an operation on his foot, one of the commentators suggested that 'he is still the best British player around, even with a bad foot'.

On 1 July *La Libre Belgique* writes of the short-lived joy experienced by British fans when an unexpected 'hero' – the term also used by the British tabloids – emerged in the form of Nick Brown, the surprise winner over tenth seed Goran Ivanisevic (whom *Today* baptised 'Ivan the Horrible'): 'Britons to their soul, they were also able to go and applaud their new and ephemeral hero, Nick Brown'. *The New York Times* (30 June) makes the connection with the theme of failure even clearer. In an article entitled 'What's that roaring at Wimbledon? A Briton!' (Nick Brown came to Wimbledon each day by motorbike), it writes:

> The British suffer every year when their players are eliminated, usually on the first Monday or Tuesday of Wimbledon, and words like 'failure' leap out of the headlines.

Nick Brown's role would be carried out in the 1992 tournament by Jeremy Bates, who made it to the fourth round of the competition. 'Jeremy Bates made British hearts and expectations soar when he became the first "home town" boy to go through three rounds for 10 years', wrote *The Telegraph* (5 July 1991). *The Glasgow Herald* (now re-named simply *The Herald*) continued in the same vein (22 June 1992):

> Last week he was dubbed a wimp, a bad boy, a man on the brink of quitting the game; yesterday Jeremy Bates became a national hero . . . a little Union Jack was produced as the folk on the Centre Court wondered where the cheers were coming from.

As his progress through the tournament continued, it added on 29 June:

> On marched our Jeremy Bates . . . the sort of chap who sometimes appears to believe that winning is not awfully good form . . . Some of the media are still not his biggest fans. Like Bates, perhaps, many of them are happier coping with disasters rather than triumphs.

This discourse of failure in relation to tennis would again be echoed by the continental press. The Spanish sports daily *As* (3 July 1992) provides a striking example of this, in an article which explicitly links sporting failure with the anachronistic and un-European nature of British society:

> That the English are very strange is beyond all doubt. And not just because they drive on the left, have their own system of weights and measures and cannot buy beer in the supermarket before seven o'clock in the evening, but on countless other accounts. A continental European cannot understand, for example, that they are capable of putting up with all-night queues to get into the All England Club knowing that the chances that it will rain and they'll be left disappointed are particularly high. The question of betting, one of the great national vices, is something else.

> The odds on Jeremy Bates becoming Wimbledon champion were a thousand to one at the start, the same as for the resurrection of Elvis Presley. Subsequently, when the English number one won his first two matches the odds moved to 500–1, the same as would be paid if the existence of the Loch Ness Monster was officially proved. And it's amazing to think that there are people reckless enough to bet on the chance of these things happening.

The connection between sporting failure and the failure of a society as a whole is not lost on British commentators. An attempt to redefine such failure as a result of all that is best about British society can be found in *The Sunday Express* (5 July 1992), which writes:

> Grunting, snorting, spitting and swearing, the stars of Wimbledon once again give us a lesson in what is takes to be a champion.

> It's no use being jolly good sports, like our hapless lady players. It's no use being a gentleman like the brave Jeremy Bates. No sir.

> What we need are scowls as black as midnight, tempers to shrivel the boldest umpire, hours of practice with a handy spittoon and lungs which will enable our players to mimic the high spots of a honeymoon night whenever they hit a ball.

It's called the will to win. And I'm absolutely delighted that so few of our Wimbledon hopefuls begin to measure up.

Indeed, the only answer is the greatness of Wimbledon itself, which allows 'us' to impose 'our' values on those we cannot beat, to absorb and finally neutralise them. This connection is made explicitly by *The Herald* (22 July 1992):

> We Brits do not even like tennis, and we certainly are very bad at it . . . In half a century there will be laudatory obits on any British player who reached the second round of a Grand Slam tournament.

> The Wimbledon gallery, however, are a law unto themselves. Having no home-grown talent to cheer, they select foreigners to be friendly to – provided, of course, they meet certain criteria . . . They must say they love Wimbledon above all other. Boris Becker did so from the start, and was immediately transformed from a Kraut kid into one of us.

And as Andre Agassi won the 1992 Wimbledon championship, *The Times* (6 July 1992) commented: 'The crowd . . . feted the new champion as if Las Vegas had suddenly become part of Britain and Agassi a born-again Londoner'. But in the macro-discourse of failure even Wimbledon, symbol of British greatness, has been subverted by those 'we' hope to persuade of 'our' greatness, and has been made into a symbol of all that is wrong with British society.

BEYOND TENNIS: A MEDIA ENVIRONMENT

So powerful is this macro-discourse of failure that it penetrates even European press reaction to British press coverage of Wimbledon itself. *Matchball* (25 July), for example, dedicated an entire article to this theme, entitled 'The Gossip Open'. This article carried photographs of pages from the *Sun*, the *Daily Mail* and the *Daily Express* and *Bild*, and expressed astonishment at the huge circulation and low prices of what it claims the English themselves describe as 'rubbish dailies'.

In fact the first week of the tournament was dominated by a series of stories some of which are unrelated, or only marginally related to tennis itself (the relative absence of such topics in 1992 would cause one reporter to complain that Wimbledon was 'so quiet this tournament's turning into a sports event': quoted in *The Herald*, 29 June 1992). The most obvious were the reasons for Monica Seles's withdrawal, the law suit currently being brought against Martina Navratilova, Andre Agassi's clothes, the private life of Steffi Graf's father and the effect this was having on her playing.

But it was the coverage of Monica Seles's withdrawal which drew most fire from the European press. Both the *Sun* and *Bild* (quoting a Yugoslav newspaper as their source) suggested that the real reason for her withdrawal was that she was pregnant. This was followed by intense speculation as to who the father might be (it was even suggested by the *Sun* that the culprit was . . . Steffi Graf's father!).

Such reporting was widely condemned in other European countries. *La Libre Belgique* (27 June) reported that 'this withdrawal is, in any case, arousing a lot of indecent fantasies among the specialists of the sensationalist press'. According to the Italian magazine *Matchball* (12 July) it 'gave rise to a series of hypotheses which unleashed a scandal-mongering journalism, the great speciality of the English tabloids'.

The general impression is that the British popular press is unhealthy and hypocritical. Commenting on attacks on the American player John McEnroe, *L'Equipe* (4 July) writes:

> But this fierceness from a certain section of the press has something unhealthy about it. You don't shoot at an ambulance.

> Alas, the English press, which has no match for sometimes digging up news in the dung heap, likes to adopt a high moral tone.

None the less, the condemnation of the British tabloids is unanimous throughout the European press, and is part of a wider discourse not only of 'otherness', but more importantly of 'unacceptableness' and 'failure' in relation to Britain within Europe. Within the discourse this is the downside of a polarised British society. On the one hand pampered aristocrats. On the other, a gutter press pandering to and perpetuating the uncivilised values of a swarming underclass, the same underclass which affronted British society during Italia'90: they are physically absent from Wimbledon, but achieve an all-pervasive presence through the brutalising journalism of which they are presented as being such avid consumers. Only the ebullient and healthy 'proles' of Middle Sunday, with their noisy celebrations and vigorous singing, seem to offer any way out. But Middle Sunday was a one-off: the gates have closed, the British working class is symbolically excluded from participation in British society (a situation not entirely discordant, some might argue, with political developments at least since 1979). Renewal is impossible, and the fossilised world of British society continues to stagnate within.

MATCH

As far as the players were concerned, only two sets of discourses of national identity were to emerge in coverage of Wimbledon which were developed to any significant degree. These relate to the Swedes and the Germans.

THE SWEDES

The major component of discourses of Swedishness is coolness. This discourse has a long history both inside and outside Wimbledon. The great Swedish tennis star of the seventies Björn Borg constantly attracted such media imagery, his name inviting frequent puns based on 'iceberg'. And indeed this imagery is still with him today. The Italian magazine *Matchball* (12 July), reporting on Borg's decision to abandon his proposed comeback, entitles its article 'Ice Borg calls a halt'. And in its coverage of the 1990 Wimbledon tournament, *Sovetskij Sport* (8 July 1990) had also described Stefan Edberg as a 'Swedish iceberg', and describes him as 'taciturn, as befits a Scandinavian'.

Thus the *Daily Record* (24 June) entitles an article on Edberg 'Ice and easy does it'. *Bild* (6 July) sees the men's semi-final between Michael Stich and Edberg as a battle between two ice blocks:

> In a dramatic tie-break in the semi-final an ice cold Stich melted the Swedish ice block Stefan Edberg 4:6, 7:6, 7:6, 7:6 in the oven (32 degrees in the shade).

Speaking of the same match, *The Glasgow Herald* (6 July) said of Edberg: 'It was almost as though the ice-cool temperament was melting away in the afternoon heat'. While the Swedish newspapers themselves acknowledge his 'famous calm' (*Sydsvenskan*, 28 June), they clearly view this notion of 'Nordic coldness' as a foreign generalisation. Indeed, the Swedish press uses quite different and on occasions totally contrasting imagery in relation to Edberg and his style of play. His game against Thierry Champion evoked images of warmth from *Dagens Nyheter* (5 July): 'the title holder's game warmed [the spectators] like the London sun during the first mid-summer day of this year's Wimbledon'.[3]

THE GERMANS

The major pole of discourses of national identity at Wimbledon 91, as also during Italia'90, were the Germans. By providing both finalists in the men's competition as well as the winning finalist in the women's competition, they more than fulfilled all the requirements for the emergence of discourses of national identity and character on a large scale. The components of the discourses of Germanness which emerge clearly match and in some senses surpass those which dominated Italia'90. They centre on notions of efficiency, supremacy and above all aggression with strong military overtones.

The clash of the Teutons

The terms 'Teuton' and 'Teutonic' are used throughout the European press to create a link between the German champions of today and the German heroes of mythology. These references accumulate towards the end of the tournament. Thus *The Glasgow Herald* (6 July) describes Michael Stich and Boris Becker as 'two Teutons' while *Le monde du tennis* (1 August) describes them as 'the Teutonic brotherhood', referring to Becker also as 'the elder of the Teutons'. *El Mundo Deportivo* of 6 July also describes Steffi Graf as 'the Teuton', while the English specialist magazine *Tennis* (July 1991) portrays her as 'sternly Teutonic'. Anticipating the men's final, the *Observer* (7 July) writes 'Now they stand side by side, sharing history's platform and Germany's wondering pride . . . a Teuton final', while *Scotland on Sunday* of the same date describes the women's final as 'a curtain-raiser to today's Battle of the Teutons'.

The longest and most highly developed instance of such discourses is, however, to be found in *Scotland on Sunday*. Anticipating the forthcoming men's singles final on 7 July, it writes:

> If Wagner had been given the opportunity to compose an operatic score around a single tennis match, he might well have taken his inspiration from this afternoon's 105th Wimbledon men's singles final.
>
> Added to the obvious attraction of two mighty Teutonic warriors exchanging blows, it is easy to imagine the Centre Court reverberating to the sound of climactic thunderbolts and lightning, the air heavy with a dark mood of unspeakable menace . . . the prospect of Michael Stich and Boris Becker launching cannonballs at one another from 78 ft has obvious charm.

References to Wagner, both direct and indirect, are also to be found in NBC's live coverage of the men's final (7 July). As Boris Becker shouted out in frustration at his inability to overcome Stich, Dick Enberg opined: 'Boris . . . is crying out to the Gods of Centre Court to rescue him – like Siegfried on his Rhein journey'. A little later the following exchange ensued:

> Jimmy Connors: Here's that Becker self-psyching again.
> Dick Enberg: Wagnerian.

We may recall references to 'Teutons' and 'Wagnerian musicality' in coverage of the World Cup, and note the robustness and staying power of such discourses across different sports, different countries and different times.

The German machine

The three German players who came to dominate the tournament are on occasions referred to in terms of machines, both by their own press and elsewhere. An important element of this metaphor is the notion of efficiency.

Thus, following Boris Becker's rather unconvincing win over Guy Forget in the quarter-finals, the *Hannoversche Allgemeine Zeitung* (4 July) wrote that his 'Wimbledon engine is still not running smoothly', adding that 'In the last set the Becker engine spluttered again'. Steffi Graf is likewise described by *The Glasgow Herald* (5 July) as being 'in perfect working order', the following day's issue of the same paper suggesting that she 'is perhaps [the] only one player at the championships whose game is reminiscent of mechanical efficiency'.

This mechanical efficiency is sometimes compared negatively with a more artistic, 'romantic' approach to tennis. Thus *Scotland on Sunday* (7 July) complains of the all-German final:

> Of course, the contest will hold all Germany in thrall, the rest of the world can only mourn the absence of an Agassi, Leconte or Ivanisevic, let alone the passing of those old romantics, McEnroe, Mecir, Connors and Noah.[4]

The power of these discourses extends well beyond sport. During live coverage of the women's final on Catalonia's Canal 33, an advert for German cleaning equipment appeared twice in commercial breaks. It is described as 'a very efficient weapon for cleaning everything', and was presented as an example of 'German technology'. The connections seem too obvious to be coincidental.[5]

The German artillery

The similarities between a powerful tennis serve and the notion of firing a bullet from a gun, or better still a cannonball, are obvious. As a result, military metaphors are used throughout reporting on Wimbledon in relation to anyone with a particularly powerful serve, man or woman. However, the sheer accumulation of military metaphors in relation to the German players at Wimbledon shows that such discourses in this case have a deeper significance than mere physical similarities.

These discourses accumulate primarily around the figure of Michael Stich. Thus we find references to 'the German's explosive game' (*el Periódico*, 8 July); to his 'deadly forehand cross' (*Dagens Nyheter*, 8 July), his 'fatal' serve (*La Libre Belgique*, 6 July), his 'brutal serve' (*ABC*, 8 July), his 'explosive serves' (*Gazzetta dello Sport*, 7 July), his 'bomb-serves' (*Corriere della Sera*, 5 July), his 'serve missiles' (*Dagens Nyheter* 5 July), his 'violent' serves (*L'Equipe*, 6 July) which 'bombard' his opponent (*El País*, 1 July/*Madison Capital Times*, 8 July), which 'pound' or 'destroy' him (*La Voz de Galicia*, 6 July/8 July), to Becker who is 'pummelled by the bullet-like serves of Stich' (*The Glasgow Herald*, 8 July), who 'bows to his compatriot who has a deadly second serve' (*La Libre Belgique*, 8 July). If we bear in mind that Michael Stich's serve was not in fact the fastest recorded at Wimbledon – this 'honour' going to the Swiss player Marc Rosset who was eliminated by Edberg in the first round – we can see that these discourses are indeed multi-dimensional, and relate only superficially to notions of physical strength.

These military metaphors are developed to an extent which far exceeds their use in relation to any other nationality. Thus Steffi Graf is referred to as 'the battleship Graf' (*Gazzetta dello Sport*, 6 July). She is 'hyper-aggressive' (*Le monde du tennis*, 1 August) and has a 'deadly forehand return' (*Dagens Nyheter*, 7 July) which is a 'killer blow' (*Bild*, 6 July).

For *Dagens Nyheter* (6 July), Stefan Edberg was 'overwhelmed by German strength, power and precision'. *Il Tennis Italiano* (August 1991) talks of 'the military advance of those Germans' (Becker and Stich), and describes Boris Becker as a 'panzer'. *L'Equipe* (6 July) sees the men's final as 'two hours and forty-eight minutes of hand-to-hand combat', a period during which 'brute force now reigns supreme over the "hallowed turf"' (*Hannoversche Allgemeine Zeitung*, 6 July). The NBC commentators suggested as the final was about to begin (7 July) that 'These two men will be sending rocket serves at each other'. According to *el Periódico* (8 July), Becker 'had prepared all his best artillery to regain the title', adding that 'the second set displayed a typical score board for a duel between "gunboats"'. The Spanish daily *ABC* (8 July) opened its report on the match between Becker and Stich with the following metaphor: 'A duel of high precision bombers took place in the Centre Court at Wimbledon'.

German supremacy

According to *Le monde du tennis* (1 August), Wimbledon 'confirms the hegemony of a nation which . . . dominates the international scene'. *Dagens Nyheter* (7 July) refers to 'the German victory celebration', while the *Observer* (7 July) announces that 'in his first final, Stich has declared the 1991 tournament a triumph for Germany'. 'The All England Lawn Tennis Club has never been so marked by the imprint of German supremacy', says *La Libre Belgique* (8 July).

Germany's national anthem is pressed into service. 'Deutchland [sic] Uber Alles', says *Gazzetta dello Sport* (6 July), an identical headline (but with 'Doutschland' correctly spelled) appearing in the Hungarian daily *Pesti Hirlap* (quoted in the *Hannoversche Allgemeine Zeitung*, 9 July). In a similar vein, *La Libre Belgique* (8 July) entitles its report on the men's final 'The All Deutchland [sic] Lawn Tennis Club'.

Imagery from politics and economics appears. 'German summit at Wimbledon' runs the heading of an article in *El Mundo Deportivo* (7 July), while *La Libre Belgique* (6 July), expressing a sentiment to which we shall return later, suggests that 'on Sunday, Michael Stich and Boris Becker . . . will meet in a Wimbledon final which will raise high the flag of economic power which England envies'. It returns to this theme two days later, talking of 'the 100% German final of this economic power'.

There are references to the traditional sign of political and economic supremacy – the imposition of the language of the conquerors: 'In the world of tennis German is the new official language', says *Bild* (6 July), a point also made by the *Daily Express* (6 July): 'German has become the official language of the Wimbledon tournament'. 'Now it's only German in the class', adds *Sydsvenskan* (6 July).

British versions of German militarism

In all the newspapers studied, only two references to the Second World War were found in the presses of continental Europe. One of these comes from a piece on the history of Wimbledon in *La Libre Belgique* (25 June) and is not related to discourses of Germanness as such. Combining the history of the tournament with comments on the dreadful weather of the first week of the tournament, it points out that, rather than rain, 'during the War it was bombs which fell on the centre court'.

The other example is to be found in the Italian newspaper *Corriere dello Sport* (9 July). Commenting on a picture of Michael Stich and Steffi Graf posing at the Championship Dinner, it writes:

> These two young people indeed cut a fine figure. If the times had not changed, fortunately, a couple of this type would certainly have been used by that no doubt crazy old German dictator to reproduce lots of little tennis champions . . .

The following paragraph begins: 'Joking apart, Graf and Stich deserved their respective titles'. But it would be incorrect to believe that the power of such discourses is in any way diminished by their being used in a supposedly humorous fashion. It is those whose interests such discourses serve who have the last laugh in the end.

References to both World Wars are also to be found in NBC's live coverage of the men's final (7 July). 'Do you remember the Red Baron who was an ace in World War I? Well, this guy's an ace right now', suggests Bud Collins at the start of the match, referring to Michael Stich. A little later he adds: 'This place was hit by a German bomb in World War II. Now we've got a couple of bombers'.

However, it is in the British press that the greatest profusion of such metaphors is to be found. While the *Observer* (23 June) had, in an article on Steffi Graf, spoken of 'the cracks that have appeared in her once-impregnable armour', her winning appearance in the final dispelled all doubts about her prowess. 'Steffi leads German advance', ran the headline of *The Times* (7 July), while the *Observer* of the same date noted that in the women's final 'Graf's forehand was an executioner's blow to the Sabatini serve. The South American was outgunned and outrun'.

'The "Red Baron" who had ruled the centre court for so long was shot down', writes the *Daily Mirror* (8 July) of Boris Becker, while the issue of the *Observer* quoted above, commenting that Stich has 'the glider's wingspan and the laser serve', adds 'who will be left standing this afternoon when the gunsmoke clears from the Centre Court?' But the most developed example of such military discourses are to be found in *Scotland on Sunday* (7 July). In an article entitled 'Stich ready for a needle match', it wrote:

> For most, it will be as difficult to watch the first all-German Wimbledon men's final . . . without flinching as it is to heed Basil Fawlty's advice: Don't Mention The War.

> Oh well, here goes. Before Becker won the first of his three titles in 1985, Germany's greatest impact on Wimbledon occurred in October 1941 when the Luftwaffe dropped 16 bombs on the All England Club, ripping a huge hole in the roof of the Centre Court stand. There, least said soonest mended.

> Happily, other sons of the Fatherland have treated the manicured lawns of SW19 with warm affection.

It also refers to the German tennis star of the 30s, Baron Gottfried von Cramm, describing him as 'a committed anti-Nazi'.

As we can see, *Scotland on Sunday* makes reference to the 'Fatherland'. This term is also used by the *Observer* (7 July), suggesting that the Centre Court belonged to the 'Fatherland' during the women's final. Several references to the 'Fatherland' also appear in the *Sun* (8 July).

The British tabloids

The most exaggerated discourses of Germanness are, however, reserved for the British tabloids. They concentrate on notions of violence, aggression, greed and arrogance, pleasure in inflicting pain. On its back page the *Star* of 8 July carries an article on the men's final entitled 'Hans up! This is a . . . STICH UP! Becker blitzed'. This article suggests that 'Becker was not just beaten – he had his nose rubbed in the dirt'. A photograph of Michael Stich alongside the article carries the caption 'All mein'. A further article on the inside back pages, entitled 'Stich as a parrot', is surrounded on all sides by the following exclamations:

All mein says Hun-known hero
Hun-believable
Stich it up your Junker
Triple champ Boris throws in ze towel
Deutschlark
Michael's the new power Kraut
Wunderbar

An article on Stich's former tennis teacher begins 'New Wimbledon champion Michael Stich was last night dubbed a Saur Kraut'. A photograph of Stich with the Wimbledon trophy carries the caption 'Form trooper: Michael Stich lifts the men's singles trophy'. A further article noting that the junior women's title was also won by a German (Barbara Rittner) carries the heading 'Three's a Kraut!'

A centre-page pull-out of Steffi Graf and Michael Stich carries the following text:

It was double Deutsch at Wimbledon yesterday as power Krauts Michael Stich and Steffi Graf stormed to glory.

After dumping Stefan Edberg in the semi-finals, mighty Michael had the final all Stich-ed up with a straight sets win over Boris Becker.

And to complete the his and Herrs set, Steffi overcame Gabriela Sabatini in a thrilling ladies' final.

Perhaps they should call it Vimbledon. . .

A number of these themes also appear in the *Sun* of the same day. Its back-page article is entitled 'FANTA-STICH He tears Becker to blitz', and it tells of Stich's 'devastating straight-set blitz of fellow German Boris Becker'. It continues later 'Fanta-Stich! He blasted down an amazing 15 aces to brush aside the No. 2 seed'. Beside it is a photograph almost identical to that of the *Star* with the caption 'It's a Stich-up'.

Two photographs on the inside back pages carry the captions 'Herr-raising! Hun-believable!' The article, referring to an earlier 'victory for the Fatherland', continues the *Star*'s theme of Stich revelling in Becker's defeat:

Stich gloried and almost gloated in his moment of triumph . . . The salt was already four foot deep in Becker's gaping wounds and yet his 22-year-old fellow country-man rubbed it in even further.

It tells of how Stich 'skewered Becker with a forehand return' at match point, and, in an interpretation of Stich's behaviour during the presentation of the trophy which anyone actually watching the final might feel was highly personal, it assures its readers that when Becker embraced Stich, 'Junior Jackboot put the boot in . . . Stich stuck it up him'.

Later in the same article we are informed that 'the Stich insect had turned into a praying mantis'. Commiserating with Becker for his supposed torture, it asks: 'Could Boris pull it out? No way! It was like looking a Howitzer in the face. He was going to be bombed and he knew it'. The article ends with a lament which the *Sun* knows will be close to its readers' hearts: 'If it was a tragedy for Boris, it was a tragedy for everyone. They even ran out of German lager in the bar . . .'

These reports are, of course, offensive in the extreme, and they have no parallels anywhere else in Europe, but their purpose is not simply, or even primarily, to offend. With their references to 'Form [ie: Storm] trooper', 'Junior Jackboot', to 'Howitzers', with their insistent use of the words 'blitz' and 'Kraut' (the latter military jargon dating back at least as far as the Second World War), with their mock German pronunciations such as 'ze towel', 'Vimbledon'[6] – an essential ingredient of many anti-German jokes, not just in Great Britain, related subconsciously to notions of torture ('ve have vays of making you talk') – they represent an attempt to belittle a clear German victory by interspersing references to it with elements of widespread and deeply rooted popular discourses relating to Germany's greatest failures. (Additionally, and perhaps lamentably, but very importantly, this rather knockabout approach to international relations appears to sell newspapers in Britain.)

These discourses are ultimately political in nature, and, like all such discourses, have a fundamentally ideological purpose. They are connected with the frustrated craving of sections of British society for what they see as dominance, for the return to a time when the Great was still in Great Britain (to quote Mrs Thatcher), and their corresponding hatred of what is presented as blocking this return to greatness – the trade unions, immigrants, foreign competition, even foreigners in general. This hatred naturally extends to the success of others, routinely presented as 'supremacy' or 'domination'.

Everything is referred to periods of history where England/Britain was not only on the winning side, but was also on the side of rectitude and was seen by all to occupy the high moral ground. Germany, basking in sporting success, politically and economically dominant in Europe, arousing, as *La Libre Belgique* (6 July) suggests, the envy of the English, is an inevitable target. And these discourses are not, of course, restricted to sport. In the wake of the 1992 sterling crisis, at a time when British political and media circles were heavily critical of Germany's supposed involvement in the effective devaluation of the pound, the conservative politician Sir Teddy Taylor suggested that 'the Germans are getting too big for their jackboots' (quoted in the *Herald*, 30 September).

Indeed, the macro-discourse of failure attaching to Britain is mirrored by a macro-discourse of success relating to Germany. As British society is allegorised by reference to its feudal past, so Germany is allegorised by reference to a historical period when it looked as if it might indeed overrun Europe militarily. The military discourse no doubt reflects European fears of a

Europe unable this time to offer an effective counterpoint to a politically and economically dominant re-united Germany. The particular contribution of the British press – both tabloids and quality papers – to this discourse is the suggestion that German success has been achieved by brutish and vicious, and therefore morally unacceptable and entirely 'unfair' means. This is the visible expression of Britain's own participation in the macro-discourse of its own failure. In a phrase such as 'Junior Jackboot put the boot in', two powerful macro-discourses coalesce in half a dozen words. In the final analysis, every-thing is reduced to the level of the *Sun*'s subproletarian readership – it's really all about lager in the end, and the Germans couldn't even deliver that.

CONCLUSION

In our conclusion we want to consider three linked questions. Other ques-tions, such as the significance of the treatment of Germany in the press, and questions about the visibility of particular cultures in the structures of European myth, are considered in Chapter 4 and in the General Conclusion.

Here, we focus on the following issues. What do the British media want from Wimbledon? How does the European account of Wimbledon differ from the native product? that is, if such a convenient categorial split presents itself. And how are we supposed to read such accounts? This last question requires to be asked because of the odd ahistorical formulations so frequently deployed by the foreign – and probably the British – media.

In fact, the interpretation of Middle Sunday which dominates in European accounts of this event is the ultimate expression of the construction of an outdated and class-ridden society which, as we have seen earlier, underlies so much of the reporting on Wimbledon: the temple of tradition, the strawber-ries and cream, the predominantly white rule, the presence of aristocracy, even the use of Fahrenheit. By substituting the current class structure of Britain – which of course can really be argued to contain feudal elements – with an imaginary pseudo-feudal structure, this interpretation brings together all the disparate elements of the discourse and fuses them into an almost allegorical representation of a country which is out of touch, stagnating in anachronistic social structures, paralysed by its own lack of modernity, un-European, not part of the twentieth century.

In other words, it is what some British political commentators might see as an accurate picture, though constructed fancifully, and we return to its fanciful nature, in the language of postmodernism theory, toward the end of this conclusion. It is, at any rate, a striking expression of the macro-discourse of failure which attaches to Britain in many domains of European reporting, and of which many British journalists are only too painfully aware.

But in order to answer the questions we have posed, we initially turn our attention to television.

BBC coverage of Wimbledon has become strikingly more dramatised within a putatively 'historic' framework in the last two or three years. The BBC constructs Wimbledon as (1) a historic event, (2) a core part of British

This cartoon appeared in relation to Germany's planned fiftieth anniversary celebrations of the launching of the V2 (the celebrations were later cancelled). (*Herald*, 26 September 1992)

(English) life, (3) a guarantor of certain continuities in the British state, and (4) periodically, an index of British 'character', meaning qualities such as attractive eccentricity and stoicism (for example the qualities of endurance necessary to withstand the vicissitudes of the weather).

At the marketing level, of course, the promise is (5) that tennis is exciting television to compete with any form of television and that (6) the event is inseparable from BBC coverage of the event. In our discussion on satellite and terrestrial television in Chapter 2 we noted the framework of expectations which might operate as to differences between satellite and terrestrial broadcasting, hypothesising that the former might not have the national-ideological burdens of the latter. If Wimbledon is one of a number of pro-televisual events, so to speak, which help Britain to talk to itself and others about itself: or to help maintain the current relations of dominance in British society. then perhaps we should indeed expect Wimbledon's realisation by the BBC to embody these ideological functions at their strongest.

So it probably turned out both in 1991 and 1992. A lot of the feature material on the BBC surrounding the actual tennis does get rather drenched in ideological signification. One compilation of Wimbledon pasts used at the outset of the 1991 tournament has an emotional sequence 'naturalising' the event (almost literally at one point as the camera zooms in on a fox waking up in a suburban garden next to the courts): shots of the site framed against a beautiful sunset are scored by an orchestral version of the Beatles' *Get Back* (unintentionally symbolic of the ideologically retrogressive thrust of the compilation): a commissionnaire respectfully says goodnight to the venerable BBC commentator Dan Maskell as he goes home. The BBC portakabin is filmed against the sunset at the heart of Wimbledon.

Maskell is of course justly famous for speaking in the registers and slangs of earlier epochs: at one point he actually says of a miss by Stich in the 1991 final, 'well the super, brilliant backhand throughout this match just lets him down there just when he needed a real cracker'. This is indeed the language of the England which the foreign press constructs, so who, as he might say himself, is kidding whom?

During Middle Sunday, or during bouts of swearing, or during episodes of otherwise inappropriate behaviour by players, the BBC metaphorically tends to turn its face away. These events do not belong to the appropriate myths. Shots of the Royal Box are more to the point.

On Sky Sport, in fact, Wimbledon coverage for long passages turns out to be spookily similar to that of the BBC. Satellite skyjacks eccentric Gerald Williams for the 1991 commentary. That this is not inevitable given the formal constraints of the game, will be made clear by our comments on NBC reporting, below. Of course Sky does display some American influence in, for example, patterns of cross-trailing, in cutting, though in a very patchy manner: and of course some similarity in the interweaving of the basic sports discourse with commercial ones from sponsors and advertisers. Wimbledon in 1991 was sponsored by *33 Export Premium French Lager*, *Elmlea*, the Delicious Alternative to Cream, and *Head* sportswear. Some assault on historical dignity has to be a consequence, and it is. Moreover, the cutting, for example, from the end of a tennis set to an advertising sequence, certainly illustrates an American influence though it is worth noting as we have in Chapter 2 that there is now a cycle of televisual style whereby terrestrial broadcasters are picking up influences from satellite.

Since we have noted (in Chapter 2) that every ideological dimension of satellite is bound to be terrestrial in origin, it would be surprising were there much difference in ideological approach to Wimbledon. Yet the sonorous 'historicising' (to use Fredric Jameson's word) is largely missing on Sky. Sonorousness is nowhere in sight, at all, on NBC, though there is a possibly different sort of historicising.

Opening sequences make a lot of signifiers of English 'tradition' (London Bridge, town criers, guardsmen) but these signifiers operate entirely within a postmodernist approach wherein they are mixed with adverts for the new US Ford Escort and visually overlaid by the names of sponsors. NBC will play around with the idea of a historic Britain but they are deeply irreverent toward it, as we have already noted. A presentation ceremony disappears for an advertising sequence (so much for American reverence toward British Royalty), and there are innumerable jokes about the British and the weather (Wimbledon is renamed 'Swimbledon'). Naturally we have in mind that there are reasons for the differences in US television output from Britain's which have their roots in cultural differences rather than differences in the television institutions.

The differences are very great, however. American television *sees everything*. Where the British commentators turn away from the swearing, US commentators want to know exactly what is being said. When the Mexican wave hits Centre Court, Bud Collins and his colleagues are delighted (there's a comical, immensely crowded shot of all three commentators in the box grinning at the television audience – what we might call an 'ultimate closed-form NBC three-shot' – which would be inconceivably undignified on British television). A fan appears on top of the scoreboard and the NBC commentator points out that the British don't like this kind of thing – Dick Enberg remarks that during such incidents US fans jeer at the officials, while British fans cheer them.

The BBC is as much part of an economic environment as NBC, but the jokes NBC commentators make, for example, about sponsorship are inconceivable on the BBC, at one point speculating about whether Agassi's (presumed) contract with his dark glasses' manufacturer extends to what they call his 'claque' also (Agassi's entourage are all wearing dark glasses).

Linguistic differences have already been noted.

By comparison with NBC, the BBC's coverage, and to a lesser extent, Sky's coverage, seem to display a selective vision, a regime-accommodating decorum, an ideological conservatism.

(We should note, however, that the BBC displayed much self-control over the Germanness of the 1991 event's final stages. However, right at the end, introducing one of the minor finals with which the event concluded, Harry Carpenter allowed the repressed, briefly, to return: 'and not a German in sight!' he pronounced, demonstrating the revelatory power of a momentary slip.)

If we place these television accounts beside those of the European press, we are in the presence of a substantial question about the postmodernist tendencies of these pastiche-like and frequently ahistorical accounts of England (England rather than Britain) which emerge from the 1991 and 1992 coverage.

Television advertising in the eighties was already demonstrating a view of Europe in which sign/object relationships could be seriously dislocated, for example in advertisements for products such as the Schweppes soft drink *Gini* in which a product made in Britain is advertised as European in the body of the advert – while a 'Made in the UK' caption plays across it. (This is a subversion of meaning in an approach quite different from, for example, British Audi or Volkswagen adverts, in which the *echt* German nature of the products needs to be established.)

Now, to what extent this sort of playing around with signifiers is truly characteristic of the European press coverage of Wimbledon is hard to determine. (We have already implied that any view of the invention of Wimbledon which read it in postmodernist terms would probably want to add the British coverage as well, of course.) And why this question should seem to arise over Wimbledon much more than over – say – the football World Cup is no easier to answer. We might speculate, however, that Wimbledon simply offers a quite different sort of symbolic opening to journalists, and that its early association in the process of the reinvention of tradition marks it off as prime heritage material. Certainly we cannot really imagine that European journalists are to be taken seriously when speaking of the British aristocracy picking at strawberries with their dainty fingers: that is to say, we must assume that these journalists are well aware of this anachronistic and heavily stylised rendition.

So what is it for?

In the conclusion of Chapter 5 we ask a similar question about Soviet journalism before the Union's disintegration, and there we speculate that what we refer to as a 'reverse discourse' operates whereby journalists discuss the Soviet Union while appearing to discuss England.

Almost certainly the Italian, Spanish, German, French and other journalists we have encountered in this chapter are writing about their relationship (and their cultures') with Englishness: almost certainly this involves a hostility to Englishness which takes the forms we have analysed: certainly this hostility is greater in the Wimbledon coverage than in the Italia'90 coverage. And probably this is not only because Wimbledon is a carrier of messages about Englishness in a way that Italia'90 could not be: but also because relations are getting worse, and worse because of what has been happening away from the football pitches and tennis courts, and in the world of politics.

NOTES

1 The newspapers covered are essentially the same as those examined during the Italia'90 study, with the following additions:
Belgium: *La Libre Belgique*, a daily which describes itself as being of 'socio-Christian tendency'.
France: additional material from the specialist magazine *Le monde du tennis*.

Italy: additional material was taken from the other two major sports dailies *Tuttosport* and *Corriere dello Sport*, as well as the specialist magazines *Matchball* and *Il Tennis Italiano*.

Portugal: a small sample of Portuguese newspapers relating mainly to the first week of the tournament was also included. Articles were taken from the dailies *O Diário de Notícias*, *O Correio da Manhã* and *Expresso*, and the sports paper *A Bola*.

Spain: as regards Castilian-language publications, some additional material was taken from the national daily *El Mundo* and the Galician regional daily *La Voz de Galicia*. In the case of Catalonia, *La Vanguardia*, the major Castilian-language daily was examined, as was the more popular *el Periódico* and the tabloid *Claro*. The Castilian-language sports dailies *Sport* and *El Mundo Deportivo* were also included. As regards Catalan-language publications, the two major dailies *Avui* and *El Diari de Barcelona* were also covered in the study.

Sweden: additional material was taken from the evening daily *Aftonbladet*, and from the southern Sweden regional daily *Sydsvenskan*.

UK: additional material from the specialist magazine *Tennis*.

USA: *USA Today*, *The New York Times*, and some additional material from two newspapers from the state of Wisconsin: *The Madison Capital Times* and and *The Wisconsin State Journal*. These last two newspapers make some use of syndicated material.

Television coverage of Wimbledon was extensive throughout Europe (Belgian television carried no coverage, but anyone in Belgium wishing to see Wimbledon could pick it up from the television channels of neighbouring countries, including England). For the purposes of this study we concentrated on the following:

UK: BBC and Sky

Germany: RTL Plus's recorded highlights for the early stages of the tournament (up to 1 July), with some additional material from the recorded highlights also broadcast by the Erstes Program (First Channel) of the Arbeitsgemeinschaft der Rundfunkaustalten Deutschlands (ARD).

Catalonia: live coverage by Canal 33 of selected games from the second week's play, including the women's final.

USA: NBC sports coverage of a number of matches, including the men's final.

As regards the Roland-Garros tournament, coverage was limited mostly to the French press, with some additional material from the Spanish and Italian presses.

Coverage of the 1992 Wimbledon tournament was based mostly on the British press, with additional material from the Spanish, German and Italian presses.

2 Figures for 1990 from *Sovetskij Sport* (29 June), for 1991 from *El Mundo Deportivo* (9 July), the *Hannoversche Allgemeine Zeitung* (8 July) and *Il Tennis Italiano* (August 1991). 1992 figures from *The Times* (6 July)

3 Such imagery is not limited to reporting on Wimbledon. Commenting on the fact that Stefan Edberg had made it to the finals of the American Open, *Dagens Nyheter* (8 September) wrote: 'Stefan Edberg was shining in competition with the September sun over Flushing Meadows when he came to the press conference'.

4 In extended versions of this discourse this lack of 'romanticism' is presented as also obtaining in Germans' private lives. *Corriere dello Sport* of 9 July reports on the fact that Michael Stich and Boris Becker had both broken with their girlfriends (both called Karen) shortly before Wimbledon. It sees this 'very Teutonic story' as part of a broader German characteristic, adding:

> In short, the broken hearts of the unfortunate Karens confirm the tendency of the Germans to prefer sport to love. Precisely. This has been revealed by an opinion poll carried out by the Edias Institute for the monthly magazine 'Sports', published in its July edition. The researchers interviewed 1080 Germans, men

and women, aged 16 to 60. In their answers concerning their favourite activity during the weekend, sport (27% of those interviewed) is ahead of sex (26%).

5 Reviewing the Seat Toledo motor car (the Spanish Seat car company was bought over by Volkswagen in 1986), the *Glasgow Herald* (30 November) wrote: 'VW's Teutonically-efficient influence on SEAT has intensified since the Wolfsburg-based multi-national filled the gap left by Fiat after its 30-year long relationship with Spain's homegrown car industry'.

6 This mock German accent was not limited to the tabloids. The British specialist magazine *Tennis* (July), reporting Steffi Graf's answer to a question relating to the difference in prize money between the men and women players, reproduced it thus: 'Vot is so important about this question?'

7

CENTRALITY AND PERIPHERALITY AT THE BARCELONA OLYMPICS: SPAIN, CATALONIA, SCOTLAND, PORTUGAL

BARCELONA'92 AS A MEDIA EVENT

The 1992 Barcelona Olympics were without any doubt the greatest media event of all time. The opening ceremony was watched by an estimated television audience of 3.5 billion[1], and the closing ceremony by an audience of over 2 billion[2]. The Spanish public service channel TVE2 broadcast coverage of the Olympics – both live and recorded – for 24 hours a day throughout the event. In Catalonia, a special Catalan-language television channel was set up jointly by the Spanish state television company TVE and by Catalan television. Entitled *Canal Olímpic*, it also broadcast non-stop coverage, 24 hours a day. In other European countries average television coverage easily reached double figures. In Japan there were 22 hours of coverage daily. Taking all the events together, 2500 hours of television were transmitted over the 15 days, as opposed to 1800 in Seoul.

The sheer scale of the media operation can be seen from the fact that journalists (television, radio and press) attending the Olympics (over 12,000) outnumbered the athletes taking part (just over 10,500). This was the largest number of journalists ever to gather anywhere for a single event. And, as pointed out by the president of the International Olympic Committee, Juan Antonio Samaranch, in the special Sunday supplement of the Barcelona daily *La Vanguardia* (19 July), in the end many journalists had to be declined accreditation due to the lack of space to accommodate them all, and had to be turned away.

However, the Barcelona Olympics also highlighted unexpected boundaries to the demand for television coverage of sport. In America, NBC's triplecast system, which required viewers to pay a subscription for live coverage of the Games on three channels, resulted in substantial financial losses to the company (estimated at between 100 and 150 million dollars). Viewers preferred to watch recorded highlights free on other channels. While the public appetite for televised sport seems to be extremely large, it is not infinite.

DISCOURSES OF THE NATIONAL DIMENSION IN THE OLYMPICS

A study of coverage of the Olympics in the Iberian media (Spanish and Portuguese) and the British media[3] suggests the emergence of different kinds of discourses of the national dimension from those which had emerged during Italia'90 and Wimbledon'91. We can advance a number of reasons for this.

Knock-out competitions such as the World Cup and Wimbledon have a clear pyramidical structure which inevitably leads to intense media concentration on a diminishing number of participants as the competition continues. In each match or game there is a clear opponent. This entire process culminates, of course, in the final, when all attention focuses on only two participants, be they individuals or teams. There is also, ultimately, a single winner.

The Olympics have no pyramidical structure of this kind. They are in fact extremely diffuse and discontinuous, involving almost 260 different events, with, generally, a number of events running at the same time, whether in the same place (the stadium) or in different sub-sites (football, rowing, tennis etc). With the exception of a very small number of 'blue ribband' events – most notably the 100 and 1500 metre races – the viewer's attention moves constantly from one competition to another. In track-and-field, events such as the long jump will be interspersed with images from races, the shot putt and the like, with perhaps a different nationality leading in each event. Again, although some events do indeed pit one country directly against another (boxing, judo, hockey, tennis etc.), in the swimming and track-and-field events, which are by common consent the most glamorous of the competition, there is no obvious opponent. At any time swimmers or athletes from a number of different countries will line up at the start of the race.

Moreover, despite the traditional rivalry of the medals table, there is no real 'winner' in the Olympics, no climactic reduction to a final 'showdown'. This situation has, if anything, been made more obvious by the collapse of East–West political confrontation, which has undoubtedly taken some of the edge out of their sporting rivalry (though this does still exist, of course). Of the two main representatives of the former Eastern bloc, one, the GDR, had disappeared entirely by the time the Barcelona Olympics began, the other, the 'Unified Team', of the CIS, existed in name only as a sporting whole. Members of the CIS team who won gold medals stood to the national anthems of their own republics. In the case of team events involving members from more than one republic it was the Olympic flag which was raised. The somewhat unreal presence of the CIS was commented on by *La Vanguardia* (19 July):

And if these games call all countries together, for some they will be their farewell. We have to begin by reminding ourselves that the two greatest dominators of the Games, the Soviet Union and the German Democratic Republic, no longer exist. The first has disintegrated into numerous states and its presence in Barcelona will be complex: on the one hand the three Baltic republics, Estonia, Latvia and Lithuania who are returning to the Summer Olympic Games after an enforced absence of half a century; on the other, a united team from the Commonwealth of Independent States made up of eleven ex-Soviet republics and Georgia, something like the remains of the shipwreck of a country which once was in charge in the Olympic rings, and which will, for the last time, bring together those who, united since 1952, once appeared unbeatable.

In Atlanta'96 the CIS will have dissolved into twelve different teams and no-one will remember that Soviet Union which we shall vaguely intuit before our eyes during its Barcelona farewell. The second, the GDR, swallowed up by its capitalist brother, leaves behind, broken into a thousand scandals of genetic manipulation and drugs, the image it once had of the most sport-loving country in the world, a false example in which perhaps too many believed.

Indeed, the increasing commercialism of the Games, and the increasing willingness of some ex-Soviet athletes to participate in it, led, for some observers, to a blurring of the differences between East and West. In an article entitled 'United they stood, divided they went their own ways', Doug Gillon writes in the *Herald* (28 July) of the CIS swimming relay team:

But the CIS swimmers quickly went their separate ways to the podium after having won in a time of 7 min. 11.95 sec. While half of the quartet clasped each other, the other two embraced commercialism, pulling on Adidas tops.

Not even the reunified Germany could provide an obvious potential winner. As the Spanish daily *Diario 16* (21 July) points out:

After the fall of the Berlin wall, now almost three years ago, it seemed inevitable that an all-powerful Germany would re-emerge capable of dominating the Barcelona Olympic Games. The wealth of sporting talent of the ex GDR, combined with the economic wealth of the West, suggested an unbeatable sporting cocktail. But, three years after unification, 'Great Germany' has not become the 'Great Steamroller' which everyone predicted.

This is not to say that moments of heightened visibility did not occur. The American basketball 'dream team' enjoyed high levels of visibility throughout the tournament and attracted discourses of Americanness not dissimilar to those which had emerged in relation to Andre Agassi at Wimbledon a few weeks earlier. The Spanish press referred to them as the 'burger team' (indeed, the hamburger was an important element of American stereotyping, this notion being developed at some length, for example, by the Portuguese daily *A Bola*, 1 August). Rags to riches stories also emerged. The *Herald* (27 July) reports of Charles Barkley: 'You guys wouldn't understand. It's a ghetto thing', he told reporters. 'That's how you get to be better than anyone else in the world. You never let down'. The dream team were also the main symbolic representatives of the increasing commercialism of the Olympic Games.

Visibility can arise both from unexpected failure and from obvious success. When the Americans failed to win anything like the predicted number of medals in swimming, *A Bola* (1 August) announced 'the end of "American Power" [in English]'. On the penultimate day of the Games, however, American athletes picked up 12 medals, including four golds and all the medals in the long jump. This led to headlines such as 'Uncle Sam's Day'

(*Record*, 7 August), 'Yankie Doodle Dandy! The great American dream came true here last night'. (*Daily Record*, 7 August).

It is also not the case that routine stereotyping was entirely absent. On 31 July *El Mundo Deportivo* described the swimmers of the ex-GDR as 'Walkyries' and the Spanish yachtsmen as 'the Spanish Armada'; on 9 August it described the tactics of the Spanish middle-distance runner Fermín Cacho as 'more nordic than Spanish'; on 10 August it described the German boxer Andreas Tews as an 'implacable German' and told how the Brazilians won the volleyball final with 'samba rhythm', an idea also echoed by *A Bola* (10 August). On 6 August *A Bola* had described Charles Barkley as 'chewing gum like any self-respecting American'; on 8 August it tells how the Japanese exhibit 'apparently infinite patience'; and on 10 August it referred to the Korean and the Japanese athletes who won the marathon as both a 'yellow peril' and a 'yellow fever', this last phrase also being used by *El Mundo Deportivo* (10 August).

The particular nature of the Olympics, however, led to discourses of national character and identity being concentrated on (1) the host country Spain (and to a lesser extent Catalonia), and (2) above all on each country's home team. In other words, the British media concentrated heavily on British athletes, the French media on French athletes, the Portuguese media on Portuguese athletes and so on. In terms of television coverage this was greatly facilitated by the fact that each national company could choose those images it wanted, thereby allowing it to concentrate on its own representatives. Many countries also had access to a camera allowing them to provide close-ups of their own competitors. The process was so highly developed that, where regional television stations existed, it was even possible to concentrate on the performance of athletes from that region. Thus the Basque daily *Deia* (18 July) published the Olympic programme of the Basque television station Euskal Telebista announcing that 'everything would be presented from the point of view of the Basque spectator and we will be able to watch the performance of our representatives in the greatest sporting event which is held every four years in the world of sport'.

THE HOSTS

Many well-established stereotypes of Spain would emerge during coverage of the Olympics.[4] Commenting on the presence in Spain of a Japanese television team prior to the Olympics, the Madrid daily *El País* (10 July) reported that 'their work has the twin objectives of preparing the sports coverage and producing reports which allow . . . the Japanese to get to know the reality of Spain'. Referring to the leader of the team, the newspaper continues: 'Shinko affirms that his fellow countrymen have a vision of Spain in which the main elements are "bullfighting and flamenco"'. Japanese viewers would not be the only ones to harbour such stereotypical views of Spain. The opening sequence of the BBC's daily broadcasts from Barcelona began with images of a flamenco dancer, a bullfighter and red carnations, while the Portuguese daily

Expresso suggested that the Spanish public 'reacts to athletics like the spectators at a bullfight'.

Other elements from Spanish history and culture would be drafted into
service. Commenting on the poor performance of the British swimmers, the
Herald (27 July) combined a number of stereotypes of both Britishness and
Spanishness:

> The inquisition was intense and the answer was painful – Britain's best two Olympic
> swimming medal hopes survived the heat, but could not take the fire in the final of
> the 100 metres breast-stroke here this evening . . . but the Nelson touch decreed
> that Britannia could no longer rule the waves.
>
> Water-tortured faces spoke of a British agony as cruel as any devised by medieval
> Jesuits.

Spanish coverage of their athletes concentrated on characteristics long held
by Spaniards to define them as a nation. These are summed up the *El Mundo
Deportivo*'s (2 August) description of the Spanish volleyball team: 'Will to
win, strength, courage and bravery'. In a word, *garra* (roughly 'bite'), certainly one of the commonest words used by the Spanish media in praise of
their own athletes.

There is, of course, in Spain, an awareness of these stereotypical images of
their own country. Thus the *Diario de Burgos* (19 July) writes:

> The Spanish, ancient Iberia, Iberia of the the bull ring, the guitar, love bewitched[5]
> and envy of all the capital sins will for a few weeks be the Olympia of yore.

None the less, there were those in Spain who felt that the Olympic Games
(and other events such as Expo'92) were themselves creating a new discourse
of Spanishness, an account of a dynamic, technologically advanced, high-
consuming country, which was just as unreal as the historic stereotypes, in
that it masked what they saw as the inherently elitist and non-egalitarian
nature of Spanish society. The article of the *Diario de Burgos* of 19 July offers
a particularly striking example of this. It continues:

> The Olympics are a competitive world, lacking in humanity, reluctant to make
> concessions, dedicated of course to records . . . these feasts of competition are not
> designed for the lightweight man . . . The disinherited and the excluded, exhausted
> on the morning of the race, lack the range to win the laurel of applause. Only the
> tallest, the richest, the best-looking, the cleverest, those with the fastest car, the
> apartment closest to the sea, the purest tan who hide the darkest hearts.
>
> When we have forgotten the sanctuary of Olympia-Barcelona, when the curtain
> falls on Expo'92 scorched by the heat of our concerns, perhaps we may be able to
> know the truth . . . who are the real winners of the Olympic Games in a Spain
> where perhaps the chains are greater every day, the power of some greater and
> more cruel, greater the heart only of a few, more empty the hope for tomorrow.

SPAIN AND CATALONIA

NATIONAL AND REGIONAL IDENTITY

The *Diario de Burgos* article also contains the following sentence:

Amidst the mountains of ancient Spain, amidst the folds of the world of Catalonia, hard working and European like no-one else and solitary and personal like no other, the God of Olympus will travel to witness the Games.

The reference to Catalonia is crucial, since the Games would take place in Barcelona, the capital of Catalonia, a region which prides itself on being different from the rest of Spain, and which has its own sense of identity, its own language, its own culture and indeed its own stereotypes (hardworking, dynamic, thrifty). According to *El País* the Japanese television team mentioned earlier would also investigate 'whether the Catalans "are stingy" and whether they will make a profit from the Games'.

The Barcelona Olympics would come to be referred to by many as 'the Catalan Games', and references to a supposedly historical dedication to sport among the citizens of Barcelona and Catalonia would emerge. For example, the *Herald* (27 July) wrote of 'the joy of a city and a nation who have passionately loved sport since a native of the city, Lucius Minicius Natalis, won the chariot race in the 227th Olympiad, in 129AD'.

A detailed explanation of the relationship between Catalonia and the rest of Spain is, of course, well beyond the scope of this chapter. Briefly, however, Catalonia became part of the kingdom of Spain in the fifteenth century during the reign of the Catholic Monarchs Ferdinand and Isabella, though it retained a considerable level of independence until 1714, when it was brought entirely under the control of Madrid. It regained a substantial level of independence during the Second Republic, which it maintained for eight years (1932–39) until the victory of the Francoist forces at the end of the Spanish Civil War. During this period it had its own regional parliament called the *Generalitat*.

Catalonia had been a principal focus of resistance to Franco's nationalist forces during the Civil War. It subsequently suffered considerable repression, including the banning of the indigenous language of the region, Catalan – a language with a long history and its own well-established literature – from all public use, including in spheres such as education and the cinema. Following the death of Franco in 1975 and the transition to a democratic system, the Spanish constitution of 1978 restored the autonomy of the Spanish regions and also recognised Catalan as one of the co-official languages of the new democratic Spain. The new Catalan parliament adopted the name of its predecessor, the *Generalitat*, its president at the time of the Olympic Games being the nationalist-conservative politician Jordi Pujol. These regional parliaments have wide-ranging powers in all areas except Justice, Defence and Foreign Affairs.

Within this general framework, the coming of the Olympic Games to Barcelona was seen as a tremendous victory not just for Spain, but above all for Barcelona and for Catalonia. In a book published during the run-up to the

Olympics, the Catalan writer Margarita Rivière (she in fact comes from Barcelona) gives an idea of the convulsive effect on the city of its nomination as host of the Olympic Games:

> For ten years people in my city have got ready for an Olympic Games which more than 3,500 million people will follow on television, which have led to the State undertaking an effort in terms of the infrastructure which would have been unthinkable without this excuse, which have put the politicians on a war footing, which have provided the local media with practically all their stories during these ten years, which have brought about private and public investment of over one billion pesetas, as a result of which the city is expected to leap to *world fame*, which have caused new professions to appear, which will bring together more than thirty-five Heads of State during the inauguration. What no ideology has been able to achieve, whether left or right, what religious events such as the 1951 Eucharistic Congress in Barcelona could not achieve, all this has been achieved by an organisation such as the International Olympic Committee which turns into cash-on-the-nail profits its passion for competition as a way of life.
>
> On 17 October 1986, the day on which Barcelona was proclaimed the Olympic City, hundreds of thousands of people poured onto the streets of the capital waving flags, blowing horns, singing and dancing. Nothing as important as this had ever happened in the history of the city. The Games were more important than winning an election or achieving democracy, they enabled the transformation of the city into a planetary shop window; and everyone was aware of the fact that it is only in this way that you bear witness to your existence.[6]

Barcelona's leap to 'world fame' was plain for all to see. But the notion of increased Catalan visibility during the Games would arouse strong reactions elsewhere in Spain, where this new Catalan prominence was seen as a threat to the unity of Spain.

A CONFLICT IN THE MAKING

A number of incidents in the weeks leading up to the opening of the Olympic Games were to set the scene for the Catalonia-Spain conflict which would emerge vigorously in the Spanish media as the opening ceremony of 29 July drew closer. The most important of these are outlined briefly below.

An apparently trivial incident which occurred during the arrival of the Olympic torch in Catalonia (in the town of Empúries) was to focus media attention on the question of the 'Catalanicity of the Games' and what was (and indeed had been for some time) perceived in some circles as the danger of their consequent 'despanification': a young man appeared before the television screens of the nation carrying a placard which said, in English (a feature to be much ridiculed later) 'Freedom for Catalonia'. Similar incidents occurred as the torch passed through other parts of Catalonia.

As the day of the opening ceremony approached, the centre-periphery debate would crystallize around the questions of which symbols were to dominate the opening ceremony. Would it be the Spanish flag or the Catalan flag, the Spanish national anthem or the Catalan national anthem (Els Segadors)? A further crucial issue would be that of the language of the Games

– which would be spoken, would it be Catalan or Castilian? The Generalitat urged the use of the Catalan version in each case.[7]

The controversy, however, was to reach its peak with the publication by the *Generalitat* of a two-page advertisement in a number of leading American and European dailies and weekly magazines. The first page showed simply a dot with the question: 'In which country would you place this point'; the second page, showing a physical map of Europe with only Catalonia shaded black (not the rest of Spain) answered 'in Catalonia, of course'. The second page goes on to describe Catalonia as 'a country in Spain', and continues with a list of artists and opera singers presented as representing Catalan culture. It ends by describing Catalonia as 'a country which secured the Olympic Games for its capital, Barcelona'.

Finally, on the Tuesday immediately before the start of the Games, the Spanish Minister of the Economy, Carlos Solchaga, announced a package of economic measures calling for significant 'belt tightening' all round. Though apparently unrelated to the Games, this issue would be an important element in a number of the reactions to emerge as the conflict unfolded.

In order to follow completely the conflict analysed below, it is also important to bear in mind that in 1992, as well as Barcelona hosting the Olympic Games, the city of Seville, situated in the region of Andalusia, once one of the most depressed regions of Spain, was also the host of Expo'92. The World Fair is known in Spanish as the *Exposición Universal*, and the question of 'universalism' would be an important element of the conflict.

CATEGORIES OF DISCOURSE

These various events, and in particular the advertisement, were to provoke a deluge of reactions from many different sources. The three fundamental discourses to emerge can be categorised generally as follows:

A unitary discourse: for this discourse the Spanish regions, however diverse, are merely different component parts of Spain. What is important is the historic unity of the Spanish nation, which is superordinate to any region, whatever its history.

A differential discourse: this discourse is to some extent a derivative of the unitary discourse. It accepts the notion of Spain as a single political unit, but stresses the historic domination of the centre (Madrid) at the expense of the periphery. It also contains the notion of the emergence of a new geographical order which it opposes to the historical continuity of the unitary discourse. This discourse has both an associative capability (which stresses solidarity with other peripheral regions) and a dissociative capability (which stresses differences with the centre), either of which can be invoked in accordance with the circumstances, and it is to some extent the most flexible of the three.

A disjunctive discourse: in the debate in question, this relates only to Catalonia. According to this discourse, Catalonia is an autonomous reality, and exists without the need for any reference to Spain. The notion of 'Europeanism' is an important element of this discourse in that it provides a point of reference which is superordinate to the nation-state (in this case Spain).

The ensuing debate would be structured almost exclusively around different expressions of these three discourses.

Disjunctive discourse

Though it was the emergence of the unitary discourse which was to trigger the conflict concerning the nature of the Spanish state and Catalonia's position within it, it is interesting to note that the expression of this discourse made relatively little use of linguistic resources (although these were not entirely absent). Its main vehicles were a slogan, flags, and a map of Europe with its accompanying text.

Leaving aside the semantics of both the Castilian and Catalan word for 'country' (*el país* in both languages), which is rather more complex than its English translation (no Spaniards, for example, have ever had any problems in referring to the Basque Country as *el País Vasco*), there can be little doubt that in particular the advertisement placed by the *Generalitat* in the major organs of the European and American press was designed to stress not simply Catalonia's autonomy within Spain, but indeed its existence without the need for reference to Spain. The map of Spain included in the advertisement was described by one observer as a 'dumb map of Spain'. It is also worth noting that the *Generalitat's* greatest efforts in promoting the unitary discourse were made in promoting it outside Spain.

Differential discourse

The journey of the Olympic torch through each of Spain's seventeen Autonomous Communities would provide one of the main vehicles for the development of the differential discourse. This discourse would be sustained most forcefully by Pasqual Maragall, socialist mayor of Barcelona and Chairman of the COOB'92 (Barcelona Olympics Organising Committee). As the torch passed through the Canary Islands, he addressed the islanders in the following terms:

> The physical and cultural distance which separates you and us from the centre of Spain is, in one sense, further than that which separates Tenerife and Barcelona . . . We are joined in feeling. We should never confuse Spain with the centre. Either we are all Spain equally or no-one is. (quoted in *El Mundo Deportivo*, 15 July).

The journalist recounting this speech adds that 'The inhabitants of the Canary Islands thanked Barcelona for remembering in the journey [of the Olympic torch] this land which is so often forgotten by other groups'. Maragall's attitude is, therefore, presented as one of solidarity with other less fortunate regions of Spain.

As the Games drew close, and the form of the disjunctive account used by the *Generalitat* shifted from the linguistic field to the heraldic/symbolic, by mounting a campaign for the the citizens of Barcelona to use the Catalan flag during the Olympic Games, Pasqual Maragall distanced himself immediately from such a campaign by invoking what we would define as the associative version of the differential discourse. *El Mundo Deportivo* (19 July) reported:

> The mayor of Barcelona, Pasqual Maragall, yesterday defended those citizens who want to carry the Spanish flag, saying that it is 'a common symbol of the peoples of democratic Spain which must be respected', and he pointed out that the Olympic Games are not 'our property'.
>
> Maragall made these statements . . . in an attempt to settle once and for all the controversies over the greater or lesser use of Catalan symbols during the Olympic Games.

Pasqual Maragall was equally quick to distance himself from the advertising campaign. In a long interview in *La Vanguardia* (19 July) he explained his reaction to this advertisement as follows:

> I don't think much of it. . . . As a citizen I would criticize taxes being used on this kind of publicity. They seem to be more interested in advertising the government of Catalonia than Catalonia itself. A country which advertises itself too much is not attractive.

His answer was to stress the new importance of Barcelona as an important city on the periphery of Spain:

> Barcelona has forcefully affirmed its desire to be one of the great cities of democratic and plural Spain, the new Spain which has emerged from the periphery . . . In the coming days we have to show that we are capable of demonstrating that the Barcelona city model exists and that we can export it, at a time when there is a real desire to solve urban problems.

This would also be his message during the closing ceremony of the Olympic Games.

Unitary discourse

The incident of Empúries has been outlined above. The disjunctive discourse manifested here in slogan form was not without social resonance in Catalonia. None the less, it is clear that a significant sector of Catalan opinion, on the other hand, found the Empúries and other such incidents embarrassing. Writing in the Sunday magazine of *La Vanguardia* (19 July), Eugenio Madueño summed up the crisis sparked off by this incident by presenting it from the view of the members of the Brotherhood of the Torch, a group of people responsible for the journey of the Olympic flame through Spain. For this group, he writes:

> The popular success and the displays of Catalanicity which greeted the torch in its early stages as it passed through Catalonia were a cause of both joy and concern. Joy because of the enormous enthusiasm of the people who came out into the streets in much greater numbers than had been expected; and concern because they

feared that the Games would be seen as Catalan and therefore not considered as their own by other Spaniards.

The question of 'ownership' of the Games would be a major element of the ensuing debate. The author goes on to suggest that such 'excesses were encouraged by yet more independence tirades kept going by those organisations which are supported by conservative nationalism', a clear reference to Catalonia's ruling conservative nationalist party *Convergència Democràtica de Catalunya*. The term 'excesses' is also a term which would recur.

Despite Maragall's clear recognition of the 'common symbols of the peoples of democratic Spain' in relation to the Spanish flag, opinion elsewhere reacted violently to what was presented as 'Catalan exclusivity' in relation to the Games and the unitary discourse came to the fore. For example, the conservative Madrid daily *ABC* (21 July) published an article entitled 'Nationalist excesses' claiming to speak for the State and for Spain as a whole. In this article Lorenzo Contreras writes:

> So far rampant nationalism has politicised the Olympic torch. But the time is about to come when it politicises the whole of Catalonia, with overtones of exclusivity, with the corresponding effacing of the symbols of Spain.

> No-one denies that Catalonia is different. But let's not forget that Spain is full of differences, from Galicia and Aragon to Castile itself and Andalusia. To consider difference as a bottomless pit is beyond all doubt a supreme error.

There is no clearer example of the unitary discourse. It counters Pasqual Maragall's message of solidarity with the other regions of Spain with an implicit attempt to recruit these other regions against Catalonia. And indeed, this would be an argument used by others claiming to speak on behalf of other Autonomous Communities.

An example of this is an article entitled 'Catalanes' which appeared in the Cantabrian newspaper *Alerta* on 21 July. In it, Juan Luis Fernández writes:

> It would be very regrettable if the political result of the Games, that great event of world-wide fraternity, was a separation between Catalonia and the rest of Spain. It would be very sad and a victory by the most obtuse. Seville knows how to live the universal universally. Will backward Andalusia overtake progressive Catalonia in its ability to act without complexes and berets? Because securing the Games has been done by the State, and the national public purse has contributed copious funds to the Olympiad (in fact, the bulk). The support of the whole of Spain to Catalonia must not now be turned round into an autonomous achievement by the nationalists, since this would be a lack of respect to the facts, and also to our feelings.

And so, in a continuation of this essentially paternalistic variation of the discourse, Catalonia is accused of ingratitude, of behaving badly, and is challenged to act in a more grown-up fashion like Andalusia (which, as Fernández points out, is one of the historically underdeveloped regions of Spain).

The *Generalitat's* advertisement raised the fundamental question of the relationship between Catalonia and Spain. Reactions from elsewhere in Spain were extremely varied in tone and style, but uniform in their underlying message.

Official reactions were aloof and along the lines that there was no real conflict. A good example of what we might see as a legalistic variation of the unitary discourse is to be found in an interview with Miguel Rodríguez Piñero, newly-appointed president of Spain's Constitutional Tribunal, also published in *La Vanguardia* (19 July). When asked what he thought were the specific traits of Catalonia, he answered:

> The Spanish Constitution talks of nationalities and regions. Catalonia is a nationality. But that Catalan nationality has always been historically linked to an all-embracing whole, a higher political community, the Kingdom of Spain. In other words, if Spain were to lose Catalonia it would be less Spain. I don't see the difference between Spain and Catalonia, except that Spain without Catalonia would not be Spain any more, it would be something else. The personality and identity of Catalonia is as strong as its forming part of the essence of Spain, of Spanish culture. I do not share the view that there is any tension between the Spanish and the Catalan. There has been a historic coexistence. Catalonia's cultural integrity, leaving aside historical developments, has been maintained. The historic outcome is that that culture has been so rich that it has been maintained despite the difficulties.

A party-political expression of the unitary discourse would be made by the leader of Spain's main opposition party, José María Aznar. In it he mentions the *Generalitat* specifically, and lists some of the components of 'Spain': 'it is a mistake for the *Generalitat* to try to monopolise and appropriate the Olympic Games . . . All us Spaniards paid for the Olympic Games, those from Almería, Valladolid, Albacete, Madrid and Barcelona, and, therefore, they belong to all of us' (quoted in *Alerta*, 21 July). His use of the first person plural, his willingness to name his opponent clearly and specify illustrative components of Spain, are, in a sense, a signal of his willingness to provide impetus to the popularisation of the unitary approach, within the framework of this specific issue. The reference to the cost of the Games – an issue with which it is easy to secure public identification – would be a major element of the account.

In addition to these legalistic and political expressions, the unitary view is given journalistic expression by Emilio Romero, writing in the *Diario de Burgos* (19 July). His article, entitled 'Barcelona is Catalonia and Spain' contains the same outright condemnation of the *Generalitat*, but invokes historical and other arguments which present the actions of the *Generalitat* as an attempt upon Spanish greatness. It begins:

> This article will be a warning to and a criticism of the Catalan leadership – the *Generalitat* – for its advertising campaign in the international press concerning the Olympic Games. I am unstinting in my admiration for Catalonia . . . but, of course, I see Catalonia as one of the admirable regions of Spain, and I go no further. Spain as the all-embracing point of reference, with all its regions integrated, has been a reality for several centuries, and it is together that we played a leading role on

various occasions in Europe, a great leading role in America and even other continents, as Spaniards.

In the world we are known as Spain, and we know that we are an old people which has the three ages, the Ancient, the Medieval and the Modern, with specific characteristics which would later be integrated . . . because they were in a common geography.

This is an undisguised appeal to the Spain which is 'una, grande, libre' ('one, great, free'). It also combines the paternalism of other articles as Catalonia is invited to abandon its tantrum and return to its usual sensible approach. Separation is retrograde and carries the implied risk of Balkanisation. He continues:

The intelligent Catalonia of tradition has a better future inside Spain, as has always been the case, than setting itself up as a country in the fashion of certain contemporary nationalisms which have no similarity with our historic process, but which are going through, and will continue to go through difficult times. The Spain which was built five hundred years ago was built by all its peoples . . . the Spanish Nation chose Barcelona.

The Madrid daily *ABC* (21 July) allows itself a much more scathing reference to the issue of Balkanisation (or, in this case, Baltification, with its concomitant ideas of insignificance on the world stage), and also introduces direct personal attack as the range of the discourse increases: the Olympic Games are, it suggests, 'the Olympiad of Catalonia, Latvia and Lithuania of saint Jordi Pujol and the new Catalonio Juan Antonio Samaranch'.

The Madrid daily *Diario 16* (21 July) continues the personal attack and lowers the register in which the discourse is expressed even further, to that of the street. It also presents Catalonia as a cheat and a thief. Claiming to speak on behalf of Seville, host city of Expo'92, Antonio Burgos writes:

They ask us Sevillians to justify the cost of that bridge they built for us, and which they owed us since 1939, and of that motorway which Franco ought to have built.

Catalonia was already a land which had been favoured by all the previous regimes [sic], while the Old South cannot break out of its backwardness and its unemployment.

And to crown it all, they make Seville kneel in homage to Spain, while Catalonia is rewarded by strengthening its position as a nation which has gone to the head of the queue to steal from Europe in the same way as it stole from Madrid before. Can't they understand that from Andalusia, on this Tuesday of economic measures, we are looking at this panorama in indignation?

And today, when Solchaga tells us how bad things are everyone will know that it is due to the money which was thrown away in Seville, and not the money which was invested in Barcelona, you can see the nuance between *thrown away* and *invested*, can't you? Once again we are jumping through the hoops. This time, Olympic hoops.

SPAIN *VS* CATALONIA

Were there winners and losers in this debate? The unitary approach was promoted in the Spanish media with a scope and a vigour not evident within other discourses. It is sobering to consider that, while the *Generalitat's* advertising campaign cost a reported six million dollars (*El País*, 21 July), the much greater propagation and exposure achieved by the unitary discourse in Spain was largely paid for by Spanish newspaper readers. Indeed, this entire incident provides a clear example of how hegemonic ideas relating to the nature of the structures of the state can be energetically disseminated throughout a society with relatively little need for official representatives of those ideas to take part in the process (though of course this formulation of the reproduction of ideology varies according to how the relationship between the Spanish media and State are accounted for).

There can also be no doubt that the television presentation of the Olympic Games represented a crushing victory for those advocating a unitary conception of Spain. Spaniards (and indeed viewers from other countries) were treated to numerous shots of the Spanish King Juan Carlos embracing Spanish medal winners irrespective of which Spanish region they came from (the Portuguese daily *Expresso* of 8 August reported enviously how 'his presence has become a real good luck charm for the athletes'), and indeed on occasions his wife and daughters would reward the victors with kisses on the cheeks. The sound of the Spanish national anthem resounded through Spanish living rooms everywhere as Spain went on to win 13 gold medals in the Games.

This was indeed one of those relatively rare occasions on which international viewers become privy to the ideological workings of television on a national scale, a phenomenon which occurs only during the transmission of international events, and mostly international sporting events.

As foreigners we may lack the shared cultural baggage necessary to read or even at times to identify the process of signification in the way in which Spaniards (in this case) would, perhaps more subconsciously than consciously, identify it, but it is not difficult to think of parallels in our cultural and political experience. A shot of the Princess of Wales during Wimbledon will be seen all over the world, but its meaning for the international audience will be different from its significance in Britain.

The Spanish organisers were well aware of the power of such images. When the (Catalan) athlete Daniel Plaza won the 20 kilometre walking race on Friday 31 July, he was not awarded his gold medal that day as would normally have been the case, much to the disgruntlement and even disgust of the crowd, many of whom left in protest. Instead, the organisers rescheduled the medal ceremony to take place the following day in the short period between the women's and the men's 100 metre final, the moment enjoying the highest viewing figures of the entire Olympic Games. Not only the whole of Spain, but in some sense 'the world' was shown scenes of a Spanish victor standing to the Spanish flag and listening to the Spanish national anthem, deliriously fêted by a massive crowd waving both Spanish and Catalan flags. This blatant manipulation of the Olympic timetable was, if anything, an even greater ideological coup than the *Generalitat's* advertising campaign, and was, again, paid for by television stations around the world.

The *differential discourse*, as we have defined it, was manifested almost solely by Pasqual Maragall, and was not in evidence elsewhere in Spain, though there were exceptions. None the less, the enormous coverage given to Barcelona during the Games, and Maragall's own very high profile in the opening and closing ceremonies, will no doubt have contributed to the strengthening of Barcelona's claims in the centre-periphery debate.

The *disjunctive discourse* was not characteristic of media comment in the other regions of Spain, as one might expect, but also in Catalonia itself, where Catalans in general applauded the victories of all the Spanish medallists and refused to be drawn into a campaign to politicise the Game[8]. During the final of the Olympic football tournament in the Nou Camp in Barcelona, the overwhelmingly Catalan audience, described by *El Mundo Deportivo* (9 August) as '95,000 spectators . . . with Spanish flags', supported the Spanish team unstintingly (see *Cambio 16*, 17 August). The same issue of this newspaper reports that after the match groups of fans were heard shouting 'Pujol is deceiving us. Catalonia is Spain' (the slogan rhymes in Spanish: 'Pujol nos engaña. Cataluña es España'). Despite this, the attempt to establish Catalonia as a region in its own right no doubt enjoyed some success outside Spain.

The general outcome of the controversy is summed up by the Portuguese daily *Record* (11 August) when it describes the Olympics as 'a spectacular success for a country which emerged strengthened in its unity, despite Catalonia taking advantage of the situation to broadcast to the world the reasons for its own individuality and showing evidence of a unique, Mediterranean culture as part of all those cultures which go to make up the very rich Spanish universe'.

TWO SMALL NATIONS: THE CASE OF SCOTLAND AND PORTUGAL

THE SCOTS

Scottish pride

Scotland sent three World and European champions to Barcelona, all, of course, as part of the British team. These were Tom McKean (800 metres), Yvonne Murray (3000 metres) and Liz McColgan (10,000 metres). These three, together with Tom Hanlon, a steeplechase runner, were generally seen as certainties to bring home medals, and very probably some gold medals.

These hopes filled Scottish newspapers with expressions of characteristically swollen Scottish ambitions ahead of the event. 'For a nation of only five million, Scots can exercise a disproportionate influence', wrote the *Herald* on 25 July. However, Tom McKean failed to reach the final of his event, and Yvonne Murray came eighth in the final of hers.

The resulting coverage was dismally unhappy 'Double Olympic shocker: TARTAN TORMENT!' Yvonne, Tom sent crashing', bemoaned the *Daily Record* (3 August) on its back sports page, while a yet larger headline dominating the same edition's front page screamed 'I COULDN'T GIVE IT ANY MORE: Games Agony of Gold Medal Hope Yvonne'. 'OLYMPIC CHUMP!' was the Scottish edition of the *Sun's* characteristic verdict on Tom McKean (3 August), while the Scottish quality papers were more restrained: 'Murray Stranded As She Fails To Make Final Break', was the technicist comment of the *Herald* (3 August).

The English qualities were civilized, but instantly prone, like those in Scotland, to get straight into considerations beyond the sporting. Under the sympathetic headline 'McKean And Murray Suffer Day Of Misery', the *Independent* (3 August) referred to the scene of a famous defeat of the Scots by the English in 1513:

> Barcelona held as much charm as Flodden Field for Scotland yesterday as, in the smothering heat of the Montjuic stadium, their hopes of success, in the form of Yvonne Murray and Tom McKean, were stifled.

None the less the hopes and ambitions remained. As the steeplechase and the 10,000 metre race approached, the Glasgow *Evening Times* (5 August) announced: 'SCOTTISH PRIDE: McColgan and Hanlon can fly flag', having failed to learn from earlier predictions that Yvonne Murray would win gold in the 3000 metres instead of placing eighth. 'I'M THE TARTAN BANKER: silver's is no good to me' were the sentiments likewise incautiously attributed to Liz McColgan in the *Daily Record* (5 August). When Tom Hanlon came sixth in the steeplechase, leaving Liz McColgan as the only medal hope, the *Daily Record* (7 August) added: 'Scotland will say a prayer tonight for Liz McColgan – our one and only hope of a golden Tartan fling at the Olympics . . . the deceptively frail and fragile McColgan carries the full load of the Tartan banner'. 'Liz set for golden moment' said the *Herald* (8 August). In the event, she came fifth.

'McColgan finally runs out of steam' was the way the *Scotsman* (8 August) dealt with the athlete's fifth place in its sports section, while its front page was more dramatic: 'Olympic dream ends in agony for McColgan'. 'LIZ'S FINAL AGONY' said the Scottish *Daily Express*, while the *Daily Record*, Scotland's top-selling tabloid, showed how the linguistic influence of the *Sun* has spread north; 'GUTTED', it proclaimed on its front page.

(This stylistic influence is well seen in the increasing variability of some writing in the Scottish qualities. For example, the *Herald* of 5 August contained the following fairly literary piece: 'Liz McColgan used to work in a Tayside jute mill, helping to weave sacks for the wholesale trade. Now she is weaving again, but here she is creating the cocoon of introspection and concentration from which she hopes to emerge with 10,000 metres gold on Friday'. Later, the same journalist would vary his register considerably, describing the 4x100 relay runners who appeared to oversleep on the morning of the race as 'dozy relay men', in a mild nod in the direction of tabloid-speak.)

However, not all Scottish reporting treated its failed Olympic representatives with magnanimity. Evoking long-standing Scottish regional antagonisms, the *List* (issue 181, 14–20 August) writes:

> McColgan's defeat has been greeted as something a national calamity, but let's accentuate the positive. Her profoundly irritating helium-dosed Tayside tones are unlikely to get much air-time in the near future as the one-paced plodder from Arbroath joins Tom 'Bunched In' McKean and Yvonne 'Where did They All Go?' Murray in the ranks of Scottish flops. Perhaps the media types who chose to deify Liz will take a long hard look at her conqueror, the Ethiopian Derartu Tulu, a truly stylish athlete who took the 10,000 metres gold and made the race look like a breezy 1500m. I'll take grace, speed and assurance over grim Presbyterian work-rate any day.

A *Herald* feature writer is yet more dismissive. Referring to a traditional site of the Scottish Highland Games, he declares: 'Forget Barcelona: bring on Braemar' (8 August) advocating a return to amateurism in a bout of Little Scotlandism. This piece was written only weeks before a drugs scandal hit the Highland Games scene.

The abysmal performance at the Games of Scotland's three World and European champions had been preceded in the spring by the Scots' unexpected loss of energy at the ballot box, when not only did Tory support in Scotland, against every single prediction (except the Tories'), go up when it was supposed to collapse, but the spectacular rise in the nationalist vote predicted by the opinion polls failed entirely to materialise, resulting in a *loss* of seats by the nationalists. The Olympics were a sad reminder to the three out of every four Scots with ambitions for increased political autonomy of how hollow these ambitions were. The abject tone of some of the Scottish coverage of the Games belongs to an episode in Scottish political culture, not just in Scottish sport.

The British question

It is a commonplace of Scottish conversation that the metropolitan-based British media ascribe a British identity to Scottish public figures when they are associated with positive activities, and a Scottish identity when they display negative values. According to this commonplace, for example, Liz McColgan's triumph in the earlier World Cup would have been a great day for *British* athletics, whereas her inglorious performance in Barcelona would be a tragedy for *Scottish* athletics. (It is often observed that, in a related fashion, wayward English football supporters will become 'British' supporters, whereas in the old pioneering days of Scottish football hooliganism, the culprits were plainly Scottish).[9]

Taking sports coverage overall, there is more than a grain of truth in this line of judgement, but as far as BBC TV coverage of the Olympics was concerned – and this has recently been true of TV athletics coverage in general – this complaint probably does not have much substance. In fact,

BBC TV's coverage tended to refer to the gold-medal triumphs of English athletes such as Linford Christie, Sally Gunnell and company as successes for *British*, rather than English athletics, while referring with apparent (but possibly only apparent) generosity to the dual Scottish/British identity of the Scots in the team. And there was no hint of any discursive reconstruction of the unfortunate McKean, Murray and McColgan, after their failures, in such a way as to subtract their Britishness from them. None the less the lack of consistent behaviour is revealing. The duality of reference to Scots remains a rather bizarre index of Scotland's uncomfortable stateless nation position

We would want to note, then, in the first instance, that discursive domains such as sub-domains of sports discourse (in this case athletics) develop their own vocabulary of national recognition and mutual awareness. Because, side by side with this heavy use of the 'British' qualifier in Olympic coverage by English commentators can be found linguistic behaviour in other domains in which the term 'English' is used almost automatically in the sense of 'British'. In everyday speech in England, 'England' is often used exclusively to refer both to the UK and to England, as in 'the Prime Minister of England' or 'the Queen of England'.

Of course, since an activity such as international sport by its nature requires greater nomenclatural precision about the British/English distinction, especially in relation to the minority of sports occasions in which, such as in the Olympics, a 'British' team functions, this greater refinement is only to be expected. But there is more to it than that.

Since ideals of fairness and community are bound up with the self-definition of athletics and of its coverage, and, more calculatedly, with its marketing as a television product, its discourses of national character will inevitably be different from those of football, for example, which is often now marketed on some quite sharp competitiveness, including a lot of edge between, specifically, Scotland and England. This sense of athletic community even extends to warm and celebratory pieces on foreign athletes such as Carl Lewis. In this respect, athletics plainly makes its own sorts of demands on journalists.

However, whereas the Scottish media traditionally display little sympathy with English football clubs and even less for the English national side, a tendency echoed in other sports like rugby union, it is notable that, in their coverage of the Olympics, they also appear to celebrate the victory of English/British athletes, and bemoan their failure, with no less commitment than the English papers. They do so, however, only in terms of the 'British' nationality of the English athletes, never in terms of their 'English' nationality: as we suggest later, there may be a sense in which this is a precondition for Scottish approval of English achievements in events where a British team is in operation.

Thus, while the *Daily Record* (4 August) observes of Yvonne Murray that 'Scotland was firmly behind her, so the disappointment of her flop was all the greater', two inches below this article another piece begins: 'Britain's red-hot 200 metre trio are ready to declare war on the Yanks'. This piece of British patriotism in Scotland's best-selling newspaper is, of course, about three Englishmen. 'BRITS BLITZED: Redmond badge of courage' continues the same newspaper in highly sympathetic vein on the failure of English athletes in the 110 metres hurdles and 400 metres, referring in particular to the runner Derek Redmond, who pulled a hamstring and had to be helped over the finishing line by his father. Likewise the quality newspapers: 'Sad night as medal hopefuls fail the test' is the *Herald*'s view (4 August) of the same events, as it goes on to describe how 'British hopes . . . took a dive'. 'Proud Gunnell still glowing over clean sweep to victory', says the *Scotsman* (7 August).

We might schematise the referential system, therefore, as follows: during the Barcelona Olympics English commentators refer to English athletes uniquely as British, and to Scottish athletes as both British and Scottish. Scottish commentators, on the other hand, also refer to English athletes uniquely as British, but to Scottish athletes uniquely as Scottish. Thus while Scottish identity is maintained by both sides, English nationality has apparently disappeared. Though perhaps this disappearance is indeed only apparent, since it may well be the case that for English commentators Britishness and Englishness are identical.

The apparent agreement on the British nationality of the English athletes may, however, also be illusory. As pointed out in Chapter 3, the ascription of Britishness to non-English nationals is not untypical of an (in fact quite consistent) English approach to the participation in international events of sportsmen not only from other parts of the United Kingdom, but indeed from other parts of the British Isles: it was noted that in the 1988 European Nations Football Championship even the Irish could, under certain conditions, be presented as adoptive Britons by English commentators. This phenomenon no doubt stems from a (perhaps ultimately imperialist, though in its own terms not unsympathetic) English belief that the superordinate British political nationality applying to all inhabitants of the United Kingdom is by and large accepted or even welcomed by its non-English inhabitants as a means of access to and sharing in 'British greatness', despite any random indications to the contrary (a view not dissimilar to that expressed by a number of Spanish commentators in relation to Catalonia).

On the Scottish side, however, in view of the traditional hostility of the Scottish media to English successes in other sports, and the universal unwillingness to recognise the Englishness of the athletes in question, the ascription of Britishness to the English athletes seems opportunistic rather than ideological: it may well be a mechanism which allows temporary Scottish participation in English triumphs in the glaring absence of Scottish success. This point is pursued further below.

This ascribed duality in athletics coverage is worth dwelling upon: there is no reason why Linford Christie or Sally Gunnell should not be 'English' if Tom McKean is generally 'Scottish', but it is generally felt, it would seem, by commentators in this domain, that to be Scottish and British constitutes dual identity which must be described plurally, while to describe someone as English and British is merely tautological. Certainly, in this context, being Scottish is apparently an exceptional case of Britishness, or perhaps even an exception to being British, or an exception to echt-Britishness, or known (or believed) to involve some rejection of Britishness.

From hope to despair

Portugal, Spain's much smaller Atlantic neighbour, sent a team of over 100 athletes to the Barcelona Olympics. This was the largest Portuguese team ever to participate. Portugal is a country with a relatively modest Olympic record, but with some notable successes: Carlos Lopes won gold in the men's marathon in Los Angeles in 1984, Rosa Mota also won gold in the women's marathon in Seoul in 1988, and various silver medals had been won at different times in running and shooting. With them this largest team of all time took the heightened hopes of a country for renewed success in athletics, shooting and in particular roller hockey, which, since Portugal was the current World and European champion, achieved huge coverage in the Portuguese press during the Olympics, despite the fact that it was only an exhibition event. 'Medals on the horizon' ran the title of *Gol's* article looking forward to the Olympics (24 July).

Portugal's Olympics got off to a bad start on a number of fronts. Even before the Games began their reigning Olympic marathon champion Rosa Mota announced that she would not be travelling to Barcelona, and on the morning of the opening ceremony the cyclist Ana Barros was knocked down by a car and injured while training in Barcelona, and had to withdraw. To make matters worse, neither the Portuguese President nor the Prime Minister attended the opening ceremony: though justified by circumstances, this was an absence which was judged to be a serious political error by the Portuguese media.

From that point on things simply got worse. Writing in the *Gazeta dos Desportos* on 5 August Luís Avelãs expressed the dilemma of many Portuguese when he said:

> I'm beginning to get worried! I no longer know what to say when people ask me how many medals Portugal is going to win during these Games. During the first week it was easy to avoid these uncomfortable questions by answering that, in theory, five or six medals was not beyond us. The days passed and these longed for symbols of power, strength and courage did not appear.

One day later the tone of *A Bola* had become even more aggressive. Carlos Miranda writes with overt irritation:

> Facing up to the realities, it is obvious that the Olympic Games, this year, for the Portuguese, are, if you'll allow me to say so, unworthy of well-bred people, which we all pride ourselves on being . . . the Olympic Games are 'mierda'.[10] I'll say it in Spanish because it gives more local colour.

Portuguese athletes not only failed to make it to the finals of their various events (with a few exceptions), a number of them were also disqualified or even failed to complete races which they had begun. The most notorious cases were the women's 10,000 metres, where two of the three Portuguese competitors retired at different points in the race, and the men's marathon, where all

While Britain begs for Deutschmarks (*Herald*, 30 September 1992), Portugal begs for Olympic medals. Notice: 'I have over 100 athletes to keep'. Bubble: 'Spare a medal for a poor man' (*A Bola*, 1 August 1992)

three Portuguese competitors dropped out one after another. These withdrawals in particular were perceived as humiliating by broad sectors of the Portuguese media.

At the end of the Games Portugal had recorded its worst Olympic performance since 1976, and had not won a single medal of any description, not even in roller hockey.

Initially, the general tone of the reports was muted. As the Portuguese swimmers failed to make it to the finals, *A Bola* (1 August) wrote: 'We had a lot of hopes. Dreams as well. They were dissolved in the water'. However, even though this same issue of this newspaper saw the initially promising performance of the marksmen as a 'breeze of hope in a week which had been an emotional desert for the Portuguese', the failure of the Portuguese athletes quickly took on a significance which involved Portugal's image of itself and implicated its government in the failure. Writing in this same issue, Carlos Miranda, mentioning the 'pseudo-hopes, manufactured by our will, by our imagination', commented:

> We suffer the fate of all poor countries in not having a top-level sport and living off the greats who emerge from time to time.

> But even so, the average level of our sportsmen will always be low. We are not a sporting country, or anything like it. You only have to look at how the State supports sport in the schools to reach a very simple conclusion.

In an article which refers explicitly to 25 April 1974, the day on which the Portuguese dictatorship was overthrown, the failure of Portuguese sport becomes merely the final point in centuries of historical failure, which not even democracy has been able to overcome. Pointing out that any government's priorities must be food, housing and education, Homero Serpa, also writing in *A Bola* (1 August) comments:

> I want to stress that I am not criticising the present Government, since this would be to forget, unjustly, more than eight centuries of history, in fact I think that the Government is still addressing the priorities I mentioned earlier despite the marked improvement in living conditions brought by the 25th of April, reflected in the push it gave the country and dragged it out of the quagmire of immobilism in which it was stuck.

By 8 August *A Bola's* view had become less generous: 'In the meantime the country is ashamed and suspects that, in the end, nothing has been learned in these years of democracy'. At the very end of the Olympics, the *Gazeta dos Desportos* (12 August) would also highlight the necessary support of the State to avoid a repetition of this situation:

> These Olympic Games were depressing for all of us. We want athletes. But athletes with a capital A. It is, therefore, up to the State to apply itself to the task of reformulating the current rules.

The hopes pinned on Portuguese athletics to save the day would soon prove illusory. In another article in *A Bola* (1 August) Carlos Miranda commented:

> The Gods of Olympus are decidedly not with us . . . We thought that, after the first

few days, things would change. Nothing could have been further from the truth. A week later the tide has not turned.

We thought that things would get better when athletics joined the fray . . . In short, we hoped that athletics would wash our face . . .

But as Caesar asked, some years ago, as our readers will surely remember, 'You too, my son Brutus?' [sic], so I now ask: 'You too, my old friend athletics?'

'Face saving' became important. On 8 August *A Bola* would still be writing that 'there are still events to take place in which, by a miracle of miracles, we might save face'. As the situation deteriorated from the sporting point of view, Portugal came to be presented in its press not just as a poor country, but as a Third or even Fourth World country: Thus *A Bola* of 6 August suggests that:

In view of the meagreness of the result, there will be those who will take the view that the presence of the bulky Portuguese team had something heart-breakingly . . . fourth-worldish, because countries from the so-called Third World achieved results of an incomparably higher level to those achieved by our representatives.

This theme is continued by Joaquim Semeano writing in *Record* (11 August):

In short, Portugal seems to have a sport which is worthy of a Third World country. In any case, most of the so-called 'Third World countries' present in these Olympic Games either won medals (and this was the case for not a few of them . . .) or achieved results which were substantially better than those achieved by the Portuguese. It is difficult to imagine how a country which describes itself as in an accelerated process of development, which prides itself on its presence among the greats of Europe, can, in such an important competition as the Olympic Games, give such a pale image of its sport.

For *Expresso* (8 August) these results were a lack of Portugal isolation in world athletics.

Up until the last three days, all the Portuguese athletes who dreamt of medals ended up being examples of a lack of realism and an absence of knowledge of the competitive levels achieved abroad. Our evaluation of the possibilities of the Portuguese was hasty and leaders of the COP were rash enough to suggest that it was 'the best Portuguese team ever' when, on the contrary, it was simply the largest.

Even when the 4x400 relay team made it to the final on the last day, for *Expresso* (8 August) this simply 'disguises the mediocrity' of the Portuguese effort, while *A Bola* of the same date again pursues the Third World angle:

But it has to come as something of a blow to our 'Triumphant Democracy', or whatever it is, that teams without traditions, without schooling, without anything, as in the cases of Sierra Leone and Senegal, came ahead of us.

In the final analysis, Portugal came 18th among the 21 teams who got through, coming home in front of Saint Vincent and the Grenadines, Papua New Guinea and Zaire. It was, in truth, a great historic event.

Portugal felt in a position of ridicule within its 'geographic/economic space' since, 'we were also, according to the statistics, the only EEC country without medals' (*Gazeta dos Desportos*, 12 August).

In the end, the failure of the Barcelona Olympics and the longing for the great athletes of the past (specifically Carlos Lopes and Rosa Mota) becomes yet another expression of Portuguese *saudosismo* a 'longing for the past' which is often presented (by the Portuguese themselves) as an integral part of the Portuguese character and culture stretching back into the mists of history. As the closing ceremony took place, Vítor Serpa mused in *A Bola* (10 August):

Not very far away was a bitterly disappointed people, with nothing really to celebrate: the Portuguese.

I should be happy at the end of the Games. Happy at having seen the spectacular apotheosis which Barcelona provided as a dessert for the games. But everything reminds me of that destiny or curse, that Portuguese ill luck, that fate of our lives, which forces us to long for the past. It was King Sebastian,[11] it was the epic of the Discoveries, it was Henry the Navigator, the valiant father of our kingdom, now it's Lopes and Rosa.

The final touch is a savagely sarcastic article in *Record* (11 August) describing how the misfortunes of the Portuguese athletes were actually the result of kidnaps and covert actions by terrorist organisations and the secret services of their various opponents, from ETA to the Mossad. Only such an interpretation, it is argued, could make sense of such a catastrophic performance.

When it was all over, when Portugal had drunk its 'bitter chalice to the last drop' (*A Bola*, 10 August), the *Gazeta dos Desportos* (12 August) preceded its A to Z summary of the Games with the heading 'Portugal at the tail-end of the world'.

Two important sub-themes: the death of amateurism, and the Spanish ascendancy

There were two important sub-themes in Portuguese analyses of their own team's performance. The first is the notion that the original Olympic spirit as proposed by baron de Coubertin – 'it is not important to win, it is important to take part' – and as exemplified by their own team has now become hopelessly romantic and unrealistic. While *Gol* (24 July), pinning its hopes on the middle- and long-distance runners, suggested that 'in the other disciplines it is already a victory to be present', this attitude was quickly abandoned amidst accusations that many members of the Portuguese team had gone to Barcelona principally as 'tourists' and had indeed made life difficult for the 'serious' athletes. Thus *A Bola* (1 August) writes sarcastically: 'For almost all the Portuguese athletes the spirit of Barcelona is the spirit of Coubertin – it is important to compete', the clear suggestion being that they are uninterested in winning.

The same idea reappears in its issue of 8 August: 'Do we have the Olympic spirit or don't we? Coubertin would be proud of us and would repeat with us: "The important thing is not winning, but taking part"', writes Carlos Miranda. He suggests that Portugal has to 'put an end to a style of athletics which in other times we would have called "Coubertainian", and now, with our senses concentrated on the dollar sign, we will have to conclude that it is an athletics of the minnows, of minima, of misery'. *Expresso* of the same day agrees that in 'this giant competition . . . the Portuguese never got beyond being extras'. The *Record* of 11 August finally turned the entire idea on its head by announcing in a large middle-page headline: 'Barcelona-92: a great Olympic Games in which the Portuguese "did not take part"'. Taking part has become synonymous with winning, or at least competing on a realistic level.

Two days later Carlos Miranda ventures the view that the Olympics will soon become an event for sporting elites, and that Portugal has already missed this High Speed Train. He concludes: 'Our Olympic era has come to an end, and we are taking our leave very sadly. We Portuguese. Just as communism came to an end, marxism, even democracy itself. We are living in new times, the times of "Big Boss" [in English]'.

A second sub-theme is Portugal's painful realisation that Spain, whom it once considered to be on the same level as itself, has now left it far behind, winning 22 medals, 13 of them golds (the Spanish daily *El Mundo Deportivo* of 9 August had suggested that 'in less than 15 days sporting Spain had gone from pre-history to the year 2000'.) *A Bola* (6 August) reports how the Portuguese journalists 'naturally spoke about the opposite situation which people are experiencing in Spain, which has been one of the great surprises of the Games, having already achieved more than ten gold medals'. *Expresso* of 8 August agrees: 'Spain had arrived at the end of the Olympic cycle as one of the sporting powers of the future' and *A Bola* returns to the same theme on the same day: 'Not so long ago Spain and Portugal were at the same stage . . . as far as the prospects of winning medals was concerned. Because the Games were in Barcelona, because the organising countries have certain preoccupations, the Spaniards intensified, and how, the preparation of their main athletes'. Reporting on the closing ceremony, Vítor Serpa of *A Bola* (10 August) returns to the same theme: 'After everything we've seen no-one can doubt that Spain has moved ahead of us, 20 years on . . .'

These acknowledgements of Spain's success are remarkably generous and contain no note of bitterness or even envy. It would be difficult to imagine such an uncomplicated recognition of English successes in the Scottish press – because, of course, English success in the Olympics is glossed as British.

Perhaps only nations existing in their own right have the confidence to pay tribute to the progress of others, no matter how great their own level of failure.

Portugal has roughly twice the population of Scotland, though they are both, by European standards, small nations. Beyond that, however, similarities would be difficult to find. The standard of living in Scotland is substantially higher than that enjoyed by Portugal, the general infrastructure is much better, as is the sporting infrastructure in particular (for example there were numerous complaints in the Portuguese press that there is not a single 50-metre pool in the entire country).

None the less, it is clear from the analyses above that the failure of the Portuguese competitors at the Olympic Games unleashed a vastly more serious crisis of confidence in Portugal than the failure of the Scottish competitors did in Scotland. While disappointment and disillusion were obvious in the Scottish press, there were no calls for a change in government policy, no anguished sensation that Scotland had been reduced to the level of a Third World country, no feeling of looking ridiculous compared to a much more successful neighbour, no search for explanations in the mists of Scottish history.

How is this difference between the Scottish and the Portuguese reaction to be explained? The fact of the matter is that the Scottish media were able to take refuge from the failure of the Scottish athletes by identifying with the wider performance of the British team: this point is made absolutely clear in a number of the quotations given earlier. The British performance may not have been vintage, but it did contain a number of notable successes, 20 medals were won (including five golds) and Britain figured in the top quarter of the medal table. Such an option was simply not available to the Portuguese. A Portuguese failure is uniquely a Portuguese failure. The result is glaring exposure with nowhere to hide. This sense of exposure may be largely subjective, of course, since Portugal is not, by and large, considered important enough on a world scale for other countries to care unduly about its sporting performance, but for the domestic audience it is absolute. (Naturally, there are large historical differences in the constitution of Scottish and Portuguese identity which we cannot explore here.)

In the footballing arena, where no British identity is available to Scots, it is entirely unthinkable that a collapse by the Scottish football team of the same magnitude as the collapse of its Olympic competitors could be shrugged off quite so painlessly. In fact, Scotland's defeat by Costa Rica in their opening match in the 1990 World Cup gave rise to discourses of Third Worldism strongly reminiscent of those which emerged in the Portuguese press (see Chapter 4). Moreover, the references to great moments from Portugal's history mentioned above are touchingly similar to the Scottish tendency to reach into the past, either for better times or equally bad times, against which to adjust collective self-identity in the present when it is clearly a *Scottish* identity which is involved. In Scotland this tendency operates within sport – Scottish contemporary football, for example, is invariably compared to the great days of victory in Europe when Celtic and Rangers were teams to be feared – as well as from sport to political and military history. Scottish sport is forever poised between the exaltation of Bannockburn and the despair of Flodden.

This issue raises a number of questions about the 'dual nationality' of groups such as the Scots. While many Scots object to being labelled British, it seems clear that an alternative nationality is not always disadvantageous. This may also explain why the notion of Britishness is nurtured by the Scottish media during events such as the Olympics, when it is shunned at other times. If Scotland were ever to achieve real political independence, no easy hiding place from eventual failures in whatever field would then be available. (But the psychology of Scottishness is another matter altogether.)

EUROPE *VS* THE DEVELOPING WORLD

It will have been evident that a number of the quotations from the Portuguese press contain, by implication, a view of a ranking of nations in which European countries (Portugal included) assume a certain level of superiority over so-called 'Third World' countries. Part of the anguish surfacing in the Portuguese media comes from a feeling of having failed to meet European standards, those of its own 'geographic/economic space', and of having been relegated to what it sees as peripheral status.

A number of Portuguese commentators observed bitterly that Surinam and Mongolia had won medals, while Portugal had failed to win any. The Portuguese official Carlos Móia called the comparisons with these two countries 'more or less cynical hypocrisy' and attempted to reframe the issue in purely sporting terms: 'My question is this. Who has won or is going to win medals in athletics . . . The United States, the CIS, Germany, Great Britain, Kenya, Morocco and . . . the odd country where a miracle takes place' (quoted in *A Bola*, 6 August). Despite this, the geopolitical value judgements lying behind these comparisons are clear.

This view of some kind of 'natural' European superiority is not limited to the Portuguese media. *El Mundo Deportivo* (1 August) reports how, when the Spanish volleyball team was beaten 83–63 by Angola, such was the general anguish of both players and spectators that athletes from other countries thought that 'someone had died'. The general feeling was that 'the Angolans have humiliated us'. 'Twenty points of shame' ran the title of one of several articles on the game. The shame was not just in losing, but in losing to 'an African team'. The author of this article continues: 'losing by 20 points to Angola is more comic than tragic. Playing badly against a team like Angola can be explained away. But there is no excuse for losing'. In a later article in the same issue a Spanish official comments: 'We were on such a high that the fall has been very hard, particularly against an African team. They've taken us down a peg in one go.' While the American basketball team is the 'dream

This rather ambiguous cartoon appeared shortly after Angola's victory over Spain in the Olympic basketball tournament. The team of monkeys is clearly identified as the 'Spanish team' ('selección española'). The figure with his back to the reader addresses the Spanish coach Antonio Díaz Miguel as follows: 'I think you've gone a bit too far in revolutionising the team'. The coach replies: 'Well, with this lot and a bit of luck I could last another 27 years'. *El Mundo Deportivo* 9 August 1992

team', *El Mundo Deportivo* recounts how one fan 'baptized us the "shit team" [in English]. And not without reason.'

The most interesting case of an assumed view of natural importance on the world stage is, however, to be found in British television, in particular in the commentary which accompanied a number of the Olympic events. This view does not take the form of overtly judgemental comments such as those found in the Spanish and Portuguese presses: on the contrary, it appears as the result of a set of assumptions which are historically embedded in at least certain areas of English/British culture. These assumptions are by and large invisible to a British audience, but leap to the fore with striking clarity when the behaviour of British commentators is compared with that of commentators in other countries.

It is, from this point of view, extremely revealing to compare the commentary of the women's 3000 and 5000 metre races on both Spanish and British TV. The Spanish commentary is extremely laconic. There are long pauses. When the commentator speaks, he provides technical information about the race: who is occupying which place, how the placing has changed, at the end who has crossed the finishing line in which order. The British commentary, on the other hand, allows itself a wide range of observations on a whole series of political issues on a world level. For example, when Derartu Tulu of Ethiopia won the 5000 metre race and then did a lap of honour with Elana Meyer of South Africa, the British commentary was as follows:

> What a sight this is. The Olympic Games have brought South Africa back into Africa, because you couldn't imagine this happening some months ago. With the promise of apartheid being thrown out the South Africans are back and here we've got an Ethiopian competing against a white South African and the Ethiopian winning and the white South African in second place and at the moment they're going round the track together celebrating. Apartheid, the splits between black and white Africans in the rest of Africa forgotten for a moment as Tulu celebrates the gold medal and Elana Meyer joins her to celebrate silver. Well, perhaps the promised changes in South Africa will produce a new face in international sport.

There is simply nothing to match this in the Spanish commentary. Likewise in the 3000 metres race, won by the Algerian runner Hassiba Boulmerka: while the Spanish commentary restricts itself to the progress and eventual outcome of the race, the British commentators expand at great length on the role and position of women in Islamic societies, on how Boulmerka had in fact run this race for them, and how the fact that she had run in shorts had led to her being ostracised in her own country.

How can such striking differences be accounted for? We should like to suggest that the answer lies at least partly in the fact that there is a strong current in British media and political culture in which the sense survives that Britain, despite the numerous crises it has suffered and indeed continues to suffer, still occupies a central position on the world stage: if Britain is by common consent no longer a superpower, it still sees itself as one of the most important countries in the community of nations – victor in the Falklands War, a leading player (at least in its own eyes) in the Gulf War, a member of G7, a country with still recent memories of an imperialist past. For a nation with such a view of its own importance, it is in a certain sense its duty to formulate opinions on prominent geopolitical issues and offer them for public consumption. And perhaps this has important functions of distracting attention from internal difficulties, not least those of failures in the running of a British multi-cultural society.

Spain, on the other hand, nurtures no ambitions of this scale, or, at least, if it does nurture them, it has not yet, despite its own sense of its growing European importance since the arrival of democracy, managed to believe that it can realistically achieve them: they have not become part of the popular culture of the country. Spain still sees itself to some extent in the wings of the world stage, or at least in a less central position. There is no reason for it to express views of this kind, since they would not correspond to its evaluation of its own importance as a commentator on a global level.

CONCLUSION

A major element of the official rhetoric of Olympism is the notion of the family: indeed, the inhabitants of the Olympic Village were referred to

MESA - MADERO

La tregua

Sport and politics: the Basque terrorist organisation ETA invites the Spanish Prime Minister Felipe González to jump through the olympic hoops in return for a 'truce'. The PM, here presented in the form of the Olympic mascot Cobi, declines (*Diario de Burgos*, 19 July 1992)

routinely as the Olympic Family throughout the competition. But the Olympic Family is seen, of course, essentially as a family of nations.

Much was made of the fact that the Barcelona Olympics were the first 'post cold war, post apartheid' Games, and that for the first time in many years there were no boycotts or bannings: the South Africans were there, the North Koreans were there, the Cubans were there. Even the rump of war-torn Yugoslavia had representatives at the Games competing under the title IOP – Independent Olympic Participant – and standing to the Olympic flag. Politics were seen as 'outside' this cosy family home. As one Spanish commentator put it: 'Now that the Berlin wall has been demolished, the rampart has been rebuilt. In Barcelona. Politics and sport will once again be separated' (*La Vanguardia*, 19 June).

It has long been clear that the distance between the reality and the rhetoric of Olympism is great. Indeed, they are to some extent 'parallel universes' which meet only briefly and symbolically in the spectacle and ritual of the opening and closing ceremonies. These fleeting moments of imposing 'global' – it isn't really global – ritual are of course deeply impressive as drama. The lighting and dousing of the Olympic flame must, because of the vastness of their audiences, constitute a significant moment in media history, though, as we argue in the General Conclusion, almost certainly not in political history.

But the Olympics are the site of both intra-national and international struggle as fierce as that occurring in any other international sporting arena: perhaps even more fierce, since, unlike other tournaments, contrast and comparison operate on the grandest of scales, everyone's visibility is potentially great, the potential for the reconstitution of myth and ideology is considerable.

The relationship between this symbolic domain and the actual sporting events is complex. Suffice it to say here that the Olympics constitute a particularly elaborated symbolic system. Its complexities and contradictions include aspects which it has not been our intention to analyse here (such as the tensions between the rhetoric of amateurism and the realities of commercialism): but certainly one of its central contradictions lies in the tensions between the rhetoric of internationalism and the realities of national concern.

The Olympics are primarily a media event in which the hosts aspire to world-wide prominence; where established nations come to reassert their dominance, even if only in their own eyes; where aspiring nations must not only be seen, but be seen to do well, or face a crisis of self-esteem; where those deemed insignificant may well have their insignificance confirmed by being ignored by those deemed to count; where engulfed nations of one kind or another strive to project their identity, even if only for internal consumption. In no other arena does the fusion of sport, politics and media turn into such a vast signifying structure, and perhaps it is the largest media-political event available, sport notwithstanding.

But this 'global' audience is as fragmentary as the Olympic Family. It is the statistical aggregate of countless parochial audiences who read events in a variety of unexamined ways. Global television becomes the locus of what is none the less still the politically and culturally provincial.

We further discuss the rhetoric of media globalism in the General Conclusion: here let us simply note that we are struck much more by the elaboration of the concerns of the local in the mediation of Barcelona '92 than we are by any putative construction of 'global' community.

And so it will continue. In Barcelona the populations of no less than 172 countries took part in this periodic retraining course in national awareness. In Atlanta in 1996 the Spaniards (Catalans included) will attempt to maintain their new-found prominence, the Scots will hope to see their nation symbolically resurgent, and the Portuguese will be back hoping to rediscover their sense of European importance. No doubt in turn Atlanta will be the biggest media event of all time, too. Meanwhile in the world of *realpolitik*, fragmentation and conflict will continue unabated, for the rhetoric of the familial at the Olympics is just that, rhetoric.

NOTES

1 This figure was actually a *forecast*, and had been in the public domain long before the opening ceremony actually took place. It was not replaced subsequently by any estimation of *actual* viewing figures. There is a clear sense in which this figure was part of the advertising campaign for the Olympics themselves.
2 Viewing figures for the closing ceremony are taken from *Gazeta dos Desportos* (12 August).

3 This chapter is based on an analysis of Olympic and pre-Olympic coverage in the Spanish, Portuguese, Scottish, and to a lesser extent English presses.
   In the case of the Spanish press the Madrid dailies *ABC, El País, Ya* and *Diario 16* were studied, as well as important regional dailies such as *Alerta* and *El Diario Montañés* (Cantabria), *Deia* (the Basque Country), *El Diario de Burgos* (the city of Burgos in Castilla y León), *El Diario de Navarra* (Navarre) and the Castilian-language Catalan daily *La Vanguardia*. Coverage of the Games themselves was taken mostly from the sports daily *El Mundo Deportivo*.
   In the case of Portugal the daily *Expresso* was studied as well as the sports newspapers *Gol* (weekly), *A Bola* (four issues weekly), *A Gazeta dos Desportos* and *Record* (dailies).
   In Scotland the analysis centered mainly on the quality dailies the *Herald* (Glasgow) and the *Scotsman* (Edinburgh), the popular daily *The Daily Record* (Glasgow) and *The Evening Times* (Glasgow), as well as the Scottish editions of the *Sun* and the *Express*.
   TV coverage by both the BBC and Spanish state television TVE was also included.
4 Not all references to things Spanish were in exemplary taste. For example, in an article entitled 'The lisp-along Olympics' published in the *Herald* (3 August), Jack McLean writes: 'The Olympicth Gameth, I don't like, even in, ethpecially in, Barthelona. For the Olympicth hath, by its very ethenth, a lithp. In short, to end the tiresome notational rendition of the Spanish speech defect, there is a serious flaw in the Olympics'. Needless to say, the aspect of Spanish pronunciation being referred to is no more a 'speech defect' than a Scottish 'r'.
5 In Spanish, *el amor brujo* the title of a very famous ballet (at least in Spain) by the Spanish composer Manuel de Falla, believed by many Spaniards to in some sense sum up 'the Spanish soul'.
6 *Lo cursi y el poder de la moda* (*The Vulgar and the Power of Fashion*), Espasa-Calpe, Madrid, 1992, page 223. This book won the Mañana essay prize for 1992.
7 The linking of language with other symbols of nationality (coat of arms and flag) is nothing new in the relationship between Catalonia and Spain. In a book entitled *La persecució política de la llengua catalana* (*The Political Persecution of the Catalan Language*), Edicions 62, Barcelona, 1985, the Catalan writer Francesc Ferrer i Gironès describes how, in a parliamentary debate on Catalan in 1916, an MP for Barcelona of Andalusian origin announced that 'there is only one official language, just as there is only one coat of arms, just as there is only one Nation, just as there is only one flag'. (p. 250) This book achieved a wide readership in Catalonia, going through five editions in its first year of publication.
8 *La Vanguardia* of 19 July carried the results of an opinion poll in Catalonia showing that almost 78 per cent of Catalans were opposed to the politicisation of the Games, and that over 65 per cent felt that the symbols of Catalonia were sufficiently or more than sufficiently represented.
9 When English supporters went on the rampage in Malmö during the 1992 European Championship in Sweden, the then British Minister David Mellor referred in the House of Commons to the behaviour of 'British' fans abroad. Swedish television covered the Malmö events in a short news broadcast just before the Sweden-Denmark match on 14 June, and again during half time forty-five minutes later. In the first news broadcast the Swedish newsreader also referred to 'British' fans. By half time, however, the references to British fans had been replaced by references to 'English' fans.
10 'mierda' is the Spanish for 'shit'. The Portuguese term is 'merda', so that no Portuguese reader would have been in any doubt about the reference being made.

11 In Portuguese 'Dom Sebastião', also known as 'O Desejado' ('The Longed For')
and 'O Príncipe Encoberto' ('The Hidden Prince'), King Sebastian disappeared
without trace during a battle against the Moors at Alcazarquivir in Morocco in
1578. Legend has it that he is not really dead but is hiding on a mysterious island
and may return at any time. 'Sebastianism' is a long-standing undercurrent in
Portuguese culture.

General conclusion: Sport, Europe and collective identity

In the new Europe, almost anything can happen, including the re-emergence, in west as well as east, of the old Europe.

A very few weeks after the Barcelona Olympics had quite successfully presented a generally uplifting view of the potentialities in the new Europe to contrast with the bleak events in the Balkans, the old Europe also bubbled up out of the western hemisphere of its collective unconscious, tribal as ever. The triggers, though not in any sense the causes, were the currency market developments leading to Black Wednesday, and the French referendum on Maastricht.

More than one element of the relationship between media output, media institution, state and political culture was highlighted by these developments, suggesting the size and complexity of the discursive and ideological framework in which the previous chapters have to be placed for analysis.

'The French and us have had a rough old history', says the *Daily Star* (18 September 1992) in a sudden unexpected bout of camaraderie two days after Black Wednesday (when the currency dealers destroyed British economic policy) and two days before the French referendum on Maastricht (when the French narrowly saved the symbolic fabric of the EC with their 'petit oui').

'Over the years we've occupied each other and beaten hell out of each other', continues the *Star*. 'But twice this century we have stood bayonet to bayonet against a common enemy', continues a front page leader pleading with the French to vote no. The leader is reprinted in French on page two, next to the Page Three Leggy Lovely, under the heading 'Courage, Mes Amis'. A cartoon Eiffel Tower divides the front page leader, titled 'NON: only France can free us from the shackles of Maastricht' from the banner headline 'WALK AWAY RENÉ'. This is as far away from the *Sun*'s earlier advice to 'Hop off you Frogs' as the British tabloids are likely to get unless they ever come under French ownership.

The sudden sense of common cause against the Germans was in the air: the

In an interview given to the *Spectator* (published on 14 July 1990), the then British Government Minister Nicholas Ridley suggested that Germany was out 'to take over the whole of Europe'. Here the cartoonist Garland, in a cartoon which appeared on the front cover of the same issue of the *Spectator*, depicts Mr Ridley expressing lingering British fears of a re-emergent Third Reich in the form of the newly-reunited Germany. Various references to Hitler made in the course of this interview were one of the factors in Mr Ridley's subsequent resignation.

previous night had seen ITN's main ten o'clock news run a story with wartime footage of German troops in Paris (in relation to the prehistory of Maastricht), and on the very day of the *Star*'s rediscovery of Anglo-French bonhomie there were harsh words between the British and German chancellors on the question of blame (even of definition) for the sterling/ERM crisis.

A cool period began in British-German relations. The German Chancellor, now no longer visible in one of his previous media versions, the avuncular, rational arch-European, reappeared as Helmut the Huge – as a *Guardian* piece had put it during Maastricht – leader of our Wartime Enemy and reincarnation of the Teutonic threat.[1] A photograph appears in the *Herald* (21 September 1992) of a powerful and thoughtful-looking Kohl swallowing a large mouthful of beer from an opulent stein over the caption 'here for the beer': the photograph is in the middle of the foreign news page but since there is in fact no story on the page concerning either Kohl or Germany, it gives a curious effect of an irruption by Germany not just onto the international scene but out of the British unconscious.[2]

When UEFA's Control and Disciplinary Committee ordered a replay of the Stuttgart-Leeds first round European Cup tie at the beginning of October 1992, apparently favouring the German side despite its having broken the 'foreign players' rule in the second leg of the tie, German lobbying was seen by the British press as having secured an unjust reward. The coupling in the real domain of ideology of sport and politics was well illustrated by the *Herald*'s comment (5 October 1992) that 'the real truth is that the Bundesliga has completed the double initiated by the Bundesbank'.

In the tabloids, of course, the enmity toward Germany was overt and brutal, and the anti-German racism spread well beyond the tabloids (and well beyond the media). The apparent arbitrariness of loyalties, aggregating and dividing and reassembling, could be seen in the hostility directed one moment at the French and the next at the Germans, and then inward at the Conservative government, or at the British Chancellor, and the Prime Minister.

It was as clear an instance as could be found of the way in which many seeming acts of journalistic interpretation are merely moves within a discourse dictated by immediate needs – to reassure and be reassured, to condemn, to exonerate, to jockey for sales, and position, and ratings, and for favour with influential politicians: or else are demonstrations of subjecthood under ideological restraint. At moments like these the relativists and textualists among contemporary academic commentators make a good case, so much does discourse seem to have freed itself from political reality. In *America*, Baudrillard remarks that 'governing today means giving acceptable signs of credibility': 'political weaknesses or stupidity', he notes, 'are of no importance'.[3]

The media formulation of the events in the money markets and at the French referendum hustings might well have been judged to place events in the domain of the hyperreal. Six or 7 years after Baudrillard had referred to the way in which Reagan's cancer had become part of the advertising 'look' of government, Mitterrand's cancer was alleged to have become a component of the Maastricht referendum.[4]

Nearly all the discussion of the French Maastricht debate in the British media was discussion about the *presentation* of the case by the Yes and No camps. Most of the British media discussion took place conceptually within the paradigms of publicity and advertising. European politics were barely in sight.

But since the conflicts in the former Yugoslavia raged on and the starving were still dying in Somalia and the Bank of England had really used up billions of pounds worth of British currency reserves, presumably it would have been idiotic to conclude that the answer to the question 'what is really happening in Europe?' was that the question was jejune. In fact, what was happening in the British media was not a postmodern concern with signification, it was rather a prevarication for ideological reasons.

A depressing congruence in some of the media interpretations suggested, at best, a quality of conservatism and ethnocentrism as a recurrent feature of

British media responses to the world outside, and, at worst, a debilitating participation by journalists and editors in the reproduction of state-serving (and Conservative party-serving) ideologies.[5]

We have noted the power which the national element in collective identity has for sports journalists. We have observed how again and again the will to construct a historically continuous account of other peoples' national character prevails against the contrary indications of everyday experience. We have noted, further, and in particular detail in the case of the United Kingdom, the way in which sports journalists are also agents of some significance in the relations of dominance between state and (in the British instance) subjects, and the manner in which the former tendency to present national traits as 'given' may serve the interests of the latter.

Just such rhetorical activity was characteristic of the media reinventions of Europe in the political domain itself during this inflamed period in the summer and autumn of 1992, suggesting, among other indications, that the use of these rhetorical forms in sport are only an instance of a much larger field of production.

The turn, in the September 1992 currency crisis coverage, from local, specific, criticism of British fiscal policy, to an atavistic explanation in terms of the villainy of historic enemies was simultaneously disturbing and ludicrous. Disturbing because of a strange albeit uneven similarity of response right across the spectrum from *Sun* journalists to television news reporters: ludicrous, of course, because of the contortions necessitated by having to turn Frogs into our dear old historical partners (and back into Frogs again, of course, at the next need for conflict).

The particular emotional load carried by the idea of Germanness within British discourse will be evident from more than one of the case-studies above. The anti-German quality of much television and press reporting of the currency crisis suggested further, as we have done above, how the anti-German tendencies of sports reporting have to be seen as elements in a larger discourse. The correlative of the 'military machine' football metaphor in the domain of politics is, in the early 1990s, the formulation of a 'return to German character' in the interpretation of the anti-immigrant riots of the sort most publicised in Rostock in mid-1992. In both instances, the return is to conceptions of historical continuity in the most striking defiance of local and specific evidence, and, in general, in the face of the need for what within academic parlance would be an 'actionist' account. But while some things stay the same, like German character in the British press, it was none the less plain that the media account of Europe would never really settle for a moment.

Writing even very recently[6] it was possible to conclude that the assertiveness in sports journalism over the importance of the national dimension had to be explained as a conservative or in some sense obtrusively unfashionable approach to the topic at a time when regionalism, super-regionalism and globalisation seemed to suggest more persuasive clusters of explanations for what was happening and about to happen in the geopolitical realm. That was not very long ago, but writing now at the onset of autumn 1992, the visibility of the 'national dimension' is much greater in the world beyond sport: and what was written in 1990 about obsolescence in the context of the European nation-state seems, in the second half of the year of Maastricht, to have been written in a less complicated and less alarming Europe, hard to read as it was even at the time.

Subjective reckoning or not as this may be, anyone writing on these national themes has the sense of constantly being outmanouevred by political events. In September 1992 the British press was full of stories whose politico-emotional drive was that of a retreat back into the national matrix, a recoil from Rostock and Sarajevo, an irresistible urge to see the French ditch Maastricht and a desire to prove that they had done so even after what the *Sun* termed the 'wee oui'.

In the summer of 1992 it became fashionable for political journalists to say, on the basis chiefly on the Danish 'No' vote in their Maastricht referendum and on rumours of French unease, that a gap had grown up between popular opinions of European integration and the negotiations of politicians (BBC *Newsnight* referred to the latter, in an indiscreet outburst in a programme at the beginning of September, as 'diplomatic cavortings'). Perhaps, likewise, there has also been a gap between changes in the development of the nation state in the late twentieth century, and academic writing about its fate.

Certainly in the realms of analytical discourse on national identity there has been a strong current expressing a sense of the obsolescence of the nation-state, especially in the European context, with both region and super-region widely regarded as more satisfactory socio-political, economic and symbolic forms or units.[7] (We may note in passing that extending the boundaries of such a discussion to cover the rest of the world has to be accomplished with a wary eye upon the dangers of eurocentrism.)

The relationship between globalising and localising forces which characterises postmodern geographies has been interpreted in a variety of ways in academic circles. A number of commentators, emphasising that which is positive in the imagined postmodern condition, have celebrated the return to forms of (restructured) local significance and meaning characteristic of the development of a new spatial ordering of work and capital distribution, and the apparent resurgence of regional identities and locally-framed material and cultural demands. Super-regionalism, namely, close relationships between areas such as Metz in France and Saarbrücken in Germany, is likewise optimistically conceived as a rational reframing of identities, needs, interdependences and allegiances.

Other commentators have concentrated on the (generally held to be negative) effects of a less complicatedly-conceived form of globalisation, which is seen, broadly speaking, as having homogenising cultural effects. The most sophisticated commentaries attempt to acknowledge the possible material reality of both these tendencies, but within these plural accounts emphases again differ.[8]

We should not, of course, expect symmetry among discourses from (say) academic sources and those of sport, politics, television fiction and elsewhere. But if sports journalists, at the time of these globalisationist trends, initially seemed to negotiate with their readers within a particularly conservative sort of discursive relationship to the idea of national identity, perhaps its characteristics of tribalism were uncomfortably closer to the real truth about that element of collective identity which is the national.

Observers of the sports world may initially be inclined to comfort themselves with the thought that displays of misunderstanding and hostility therein between one nationality and another are a local and therefore only marginally indicative phenomenon. But perhaps we have reluctantly to conclude that international sports events are diagnostically just as useful for a wider understanding of mutual attitudes and beliefs as they superficially appear.

SPORTS JOURNALISM AS A DISCOURSE IN ITSELF

First of all, then, is this form notably conservative? We have demonstrated differences in the extent to which this is true, but by and large it does seem reasonable to note the static conceptions of national character and the national dimension of identity which inform much sports coverage. Some adjustments appear to have been taking place as a result of a reconceptualisation of 'Eastern Europe' and the 'emergence', so-called, of Africa, but elsewhere we are offered an ossified account whose cracks, while revealing the tensions and absurdities consequent upon an ahistorical account, fail to interest its exponents.

Nor should we be surprised.

We have spent a significant amount of time detailing not only the ideological connectedness of the language of sports journalism but also its economic determinants. Perhaps the latter on their own would be enough to account for fixed accounts of the national dimension, for their economic utility has been substantially evidenced.

We have seen differences, of greater or lesser significance, from sport to sport in the ideological and political nature of coverage: differences between and among different forms of media coverage: and, within each form, differences from one instance to another, depending on a series of variables affecting subsectors such as the popular press or satellite television: and differences from one country to another, in relationship with the foregoing variables. All of these variations can be approached, however, within a larger framework demonstrating some elements of uniformity.

Further analysis of implications in the specific field of the mass media would need to be informed by a number of related considerations. For example, there are questions about the nature of *popular culture* in relation to the framing of these topics of national identity and nationhood which we have been unable to explore further here. We are aware however of some intriguing questions about *agency* – other than those we have already raised – connecting the relationship between the functioning within popular culture of these discourses, and the role of specific groups, including élite groups, in the formation of national myths and ideologies.

And as suggested above in connection with comments about the British popular press, but undoubtedly more widely applicable, there is also an important relationship here with questions of gender which in this context we have been able only to indicate in passing. Additionally, it is tempting to see the sorts of formulations of nationhood and identity which we have been discussing in relation to explanations more specific than a mere inertia of sporting discourse. These might include the possibility of a reaction to the disintegration of national certainties, brought about by the consciousness of modes of regional, super-regional and supranational identity of the sort referred to above.

Different nations produce journalistic discourses which display specific concerns within this nexus of relationships. For example, the Italian press was conscious of the imagined Italianising effect of the World Cup upon regional (e.g. Tuscan, Lombardian) self-identification. Likewise, during Barcelona, regionalism was a topic to the fore in the Spanish press because of the Spain/Catalonia relationship. In Scotland, sports journalism, except in its rarely justified moments of triumphalism, often sounds like a keening at the long wake for Scottish aspirations to statehood.

But another strand in most of the national presses reasserts nationhood, arguably, against 'external' challenges. This seems plausible given apparent threats to nationhood of the sort posed by europeanisation and globalisation: or given the question posed to the sense of uniform national character by the presence of what are ideologically constructed as large numbers of non-autochthonous citizens, or in some countries, by the presence of so-called 'guest workers' (in both these latter instances, a 'threat' both from within and without).

More parochially: the discourse of national organization, national character and national identity which characterises media coverage of international sporting events is paralleled by a discourse of regionalism or localism in the coverage of national sport, whereby, let us say, a club runner from one of Britain's (post) industrial areas becomes the 'gritty' or 'tough' northerner or Scot who wins a local road-race.

At the other end of the spectrum is a defensiveness or hostility, both sometimes reformulated as condescension masquerading as amiability, toward the 'emergence' – that is, the belated arrival in European consciousness – of participants in sports events from outside the European and American zones of domination.

Finally, here, we should note that sport presents a special category for debates about the integrative, homogenising or imperialistic tendencies of the mass media, especially television. (We say more about this in the next section.) There have been celebrations of the integrative power of World Cup and Olympic competitions, but much of this sort of interpretation is incautious. The notion that the world in some sense comes together in what would probably tend to be termed the 'celebration' of such events has limited theoretical appeal, as will by now be obvious.

Based, in part, on the remarkably durable concept of the so-called 'global village', which sometimes surfaces even in otherwise sophisticated accounts of the effects of the audio-visual industries, but also operating as rather dangerous ideology, this notion of 'togetherness', which we have seen claimed as operating at national level, where the idea is suspect enough, is yet more certainly illusory when applied to the world as a whole. Increasingly this sort of framing of international sport can only be offensive in a world characterised by oppression, war and famine.

And in fact sports journalism, albeit very unevenly, is as likely to produce a turning inward toward national concerns, and a buttressing of a sense of difference, as it is to operate ideologically on behalf of a harmonious world, even, as we have seen, at that mythic habitat of the familial, the Olympics. Perhaps this bolstering of the national is even preferable to the pretence that the civilities of village life could ever operate on a global scale.

Lacking evidence to suggest that the metaphor of village life is applicable to the world-spaces created by the audio-visual industries, and in the presence of so many indications of continued, in some domains even expanded, distance and atomisation, we should not exaggerate the political and cultural significance of a moment of worldwide admiration for Totó Schillaci or Carl Lewis, for Steffi Graf or Derartu Tulu, no matter how wonderful it may have been at the time.

SPORT AND COLLECTIVE IDENTITY

The foregoing chapters have in the main concerned themselves with one element of the ongoing process of reconstruction of national identity, namely the symbolic work of the mass media, and with only one aspect of that.

Needless to say, we don't really know how different segments of any one society read these texts, we don't know what levels of consensus operate among *Dagens Nyheter* readers, or within the ranks of *Sun* readers, or *Frankfurter Rundschau* or *El Pais* purchasers about the claims of journalists, even about the effects of overall, recurring patterns of discourse into which individual contributions are subsumed.

Newspapers with large or small circulations alike are read by readerships with varied, in some cases very varied, demographic characteristics. An eighteen year old working class reader in Basildon and a forty-five year old lower middle class reader in Dundee may produce extremely different readings of a *Sun* report about English football hooligans, or for that matter about many other subjects. And how these readings might impact on a field such as political behaviour is still to an uncomfortably great extent a matter for speculation. What we have been attempting to do is to suggest the potential, and especially the ideological potential, of a variety of mass media formulations of the national dimension.

In the final part of his *Media, State and Nation*, Philip Schlesinger (1991b) explores deficiencies in 'media imperialism' approaches to cultural development, a common element of which is the assumption that the transnational spread of the media (mainly television) has some globalising or homogenising effect on local cultures. He further identifies some problems in what he refers to as the 'new revisionism' of a series of audience studies in the 1980s which tended to downplay the operation of the media on relations of dominance, instead stressing the importance of local interpretative mechanisms and arguably overemphasising the micropolitical domain as the site of the symbolic operation of media products. Schlesinger goes on to argue the need for an actionist perspective in which identity is seen 'as a continually constituted and reconstructed category' (p. 173) whose collective dimension is enabled by a process of sustained agency within 'a determinate set of social relations': and within definite spatio-temporal conditions: specific conjunctures of which characterise collective identity at the national level.

We cannot know (to take our specific field of analysis) how the operation of discourses of the national dimension in the domain of sport exactly contribute toward the constitution and reconstruction of this evidently central component of collective identity. But we have attempted to demonstrate, in what appears to be an unusually revelatory field of discursive production, how evidence of beliefs, opinions and attitudes, elements alike in the processes of auto- and hetero-typification, emerge as components in the development of European self-awareness and in the reproduction of some of the ideological patterns within which European consciousness is developing.

Trying to arrive at some overall evaluation of the evidence, in simple positive or negative terms, would be contrary to our theoretical assumptions. Specific conclusions have already been suggested. But one clear meaning arising out of any overview of this research probably establishes itself as central.

Any attempts to transcend or subvert or fragment or recode that element of social memory and continually reconstituted collective identity, whose self-recognition is nourished by the symbolic repertoire of the national dimension, take on a great battle against inertia: whether that battle is conducted in the symbolic or the geopolitical domain.

That inertia may be ultimately defined and located according to the theoretical inclinations of the inquirer: in the perceptual categories of language, in the intersections of language and power, in limitations of the socially conceivable idea of the collective, or in other formulations all of which are beyond the scope of our inquiry here. More probably there is no 'ultimate location', but rather a production which is the result of the interaction of complex symbolic and social elements over space and time.

In simpler terms, our overwhelming sense is not only of the continuing centrality of this 'national' element in contemporary ways of making sense of the world, but more persuasively, *of its operational strength in a wide range of specific instances*, its tendency to become prevalent when in contention with other interpretative or rhetorical constituents of this process.

And, as the 1990s unfold, the persistence of this form of understanding (or misunderstanding) will have particular impact upon relations between Britain and Germany, and, probably, between Germany and the rest of Europe: and, along a different axis, between Britain and all of Europe. Other national or quasi-national boundary lines across which our evidence may be placed in order to suggest additional indications are Spain/Catalonia and Scotland/England, though of course in the end it is the boundary between explanations of the world which invoke the national dimension, and those which do not, which have been problematised in this book.

ENDPIECE

The day before the Maastricht vote in France, the *Independent* newspaper (19 September 1992) carried a technically very accomplished photograph, occupying more than the top third of the page. It was of, in the distance, Cap Gris

Nez, with the English channel in the middle, and in the foreground, 22 miles nearer than the French coast but getting closer for travellers, Folkestone. 'Beneath the seabed', said the caption, 'work continues on the Channel tunnel, due to open in autumn next year'.

A related piece in a series on Channel ports in the Weekend section is titled 'Britain lets down the drawbridge'. There is an illustrated feature on 'Your first drive through the tunnel', featuring a smiling British family travelling to France in a series of nine drawings. In Calais 'motorists will simply drive off the train and on to the motorway'. (The French truckers' blockade, during which the British *Daily Express* had wondered why the French hadn't been able to block the roads to the Germans in 1940, is now a distant memory two and a half months old.) We may note the effect here – operating, as it were, beyond discourse – of a material world of change underlying that of linguistic exchange. The trans-Pyrenean motorway and the Channel Tunnel remind us that 'communications' in its broad sense has manifestations other than the discourse of the mass media, and just as relentless.

And the reconstitution of Europe in the mass media will meanwhile take another turn every 24 hours or so. Sports journalism has a justly famed elasticity in its ability to reconstitute its symbols.

The same edition of the *Independent* features a recovery from Olympic disaster for Scotland's heroine: 'McColgan fit as a favourite' is the headline, the sorrows of Barcelona now behind her (anaemia and a viral infection were the villains, as it turned out), and the world half-marathon title just ahead. This piece is at least clear about the element of invention in media presentations of sport: 'the world champion who will attempt to add a world half-marathon title tomorrow to the 10,000 metres gold medal she won last year should not, she wants it to be known, be mistaken for the sorry figure who finished fifth in this year's Olympic 10,000m.' (She won. 'McColgan irons out her problems', said the *Herald*, 21 September 1992).

Recognition of Britain's categorial distinctness from the rest of Europe is arguably now becoming established within the more reflective regions of popular culture. The *Herald*'s perceptive Murray Ritchie writes about the invasion in September 1992 of the fans of Scottish club sides in the European competitions. Hibernian and Rangers fans have been bringing back memories of the pioneering days of Scottish football hooliganism in the early 1970s. Ritchie reminisces about the lowest moment of this British tradition:

> When Liverpool fans invaded Brussels en route to committing murder and mayhem at the Heysel, they urinated on the chocolate displays and rampaged through the restaurants stealing food and terrifying the customers.

> How can you explain such behaviour to the people here in a culture where taxi drivers or waiters or check-out assistants routinely speak a minimum of three languages and public drunkenness is notable by its absence? (*Herald*, 5 October 1992).

The embarrassing cultural failings of the British in European social life may become yet more problematic as the nineties unfold.

Meanwhile, in the world of European football, a small, impoverished Scottish team from postindustrial Lanarkshire – 'languishing', as journalists might put it, tenth out of twelve in the Scottish Premier League – was doing its best.

What would probably be called 'brave little' Airdrionians (from the recently consolidated Scottish component of the United Kingdom), unluckily 1-0 down against Sparta Prague (from the recently disintegrating Czechoslovakia), were pondering their best response in their away leg of the Cup Winners' Cup.[9]

In the Europe of the nineties, there's everything to play for.

NOTES

1 'Helmut the Huge and friends run grey Britain into the mud', *Guardian*, 10 December 91

2 After a fatal chemicals explosion in a Yorkshire factory on 21 September, the BBC main news broadcasts of the day gave prominence to a witness's description of the sound as being *'just like a Hurricane bomber passing over'*.

3 Jean Baudrillard, *America*, Verso edition p.109

4 What was striking was not so much the scandalised reaction of some to Jean Marie Le Pen's suggestion that Mitterrand had timed his prostate operation to maximise the sympathy vote, as, rather, the easy acceptability of the idea by everyone else. Cancer, suffering, human sympathy, joined the complex and detailed map of European political integration in their subordination to a fascination with the world of signs. Even a cancer operation is read as a rhetorical operation.

5 The television critic of the *Observer* summed up the journalistic performance thus:

> In (Baroness Thatcher's) absence one was left . . . wondering why it was that television anchorpersons were not crucifying the authors of the currency debacle. The only ones who even approached the requisite level of derision were Jeremy Paxman of *Newsnight* and Peter Jay, economic editor of the BBC . . . But these two were the exceptions who proved the rule. Elsewhere, the debauchers of the currency were given an astonishingly easy ride. (John Naughton, *Observer* 20 September 92)

6 Blain and O'Donnell (1991)

7 On the question of nationalism, see for example Tom Nairn, *The Modern Janus – the new age of nations*, London, 1990: as opposed to E. J. Hobsbawm, *Nations and Nationalism since 1780*, Cambridge, 1990.

8 Chapters 9, 10 and 11 of David Harvey's *Condition of Postmodernity* (Oxford 1990) provide a readable account of the theoretical background in economics and geography. See also Schlesinger (1991) Part III for (among many other considerations) a survey of writing on spatial aspects of identity, also Robins (1989).

9 Airdrie lost 2-1. It was probably a word processing error, rather than a failure in British solidarity, which during the parallel European Cup competition caused a *Herald* correspondent (10 October 1992) to refer after the occasion of Leeds United's replay victory over Stuttgart to 'the celebration party for Leeds' tiny but vociferous fans [sic]'. Or perhaps constant references to 'the diminutive Gordon Strachan' simply took root too deeply.

BIBLIOGRAPHY

Allison, L. (ed.) (1986) *The Politics of Sport*, Manchester University Press, Manchester.

Anderson, B. (1983) *Imagined Communities: Reflections on the Origins and Spread of Nationalism*, Verso Books, London.

Ang, I. (1990) 'Culture and Communication: Towards an Ethnographic Critique of Media Consumption in the Transnational media System'. *European Journal of Communication*, 5: 239–60.

Barnett, S. (1990) *Games and Sets: The changing face of sport on television*, BFI., London.

— (1992) TV World Special Report, 'Sports: The price of admittance', *TV World*, April.

Baudrillard, J. (1989) *America*, Verso, London and New York.

Bens, E. D., Kelly, M., and Bakke, M. (1992) 'Television Content: Dallasification of Culture?' in Suine, K., and Truetzschler, W. (eds.) *Dynamics of Media politics: Broadcast and Electronic Media in Western Europe*, Sage, London.

Birrell, S. and Loy, J. (1979) 'Media Sport: Hot and Cool'. *International Review of Sports Sociology*, vol. 14 no. 1.

Blain, N. & O'Donnell, H. (1991) 'Italia 90 en la prensa europea: historias de la vida nacional', Barrera C. and Jimeno M.A. (eds), *La información como relato*, Pamplona.

Boyle, R. (1992) 'From Our Gaelic Fields: Radio, sport and nation building in post-partition Ireland', *Media, Culture and Society*, October, vol. 14, 623–636.

— (1990) 'Nation Shall Speak Peace Unto Nation: Television, Sport and Nationhood', Unpublished MA research thesis, Dublin City University.

Burns, G. (1986) *Pocket Money: Bad-Boys, Business-Heads and Boom-time Snooker*, Heinemann, London.

Buscombe, E. (ed.) (1975) *Football on Television*, BFI Monograph no. 4, London.

Cardiff, D. and Scannell, P. (1987) 'Broadcasting and National Unity', in Curran, J. et al (eds.) *Impact and Influences: Essays on Media Power in the Twentieth Century*, Methuen, London, New York.

Chaney, D. (1986) 'The Symbolic Form of Ritual in Mass Communication', in Golding, P. et al (eds.), *Communicating Politics*, Leicester University Press, Leicester.

Chippindale, P. and Franks, S. (1991) *Dished: The Rise and Fall of British Satellite Broadcasting*, Simon and Schuster, London.

Clarke, A. and Clarke, J. (1982) 'Highlights and Action Replays: Ideology, sport and the media', in Hargreaves, Jen. (ed.) *Sport, Culture and Ideology*, Routledge and

Kegan Paul, London.
Clarke, J. Critcher, C. (1985) *The Devil Makes Work: Leisure in Capitalist Britain*, MacMillan, London.
Colley, I. and Davies, G. (1982) Kissed by History: Football as TV Drama, in Sporting Fictions, Centre for Contemporary Cultural Studies, Birmingham.
Collins, R. (1989) 'The Language of advantage: satellite television in Western Europe', *Media, Culture and Society*, vol. 11, July.
— (1990) *Satellite Television in Western Europe*, Academia Research Monographs, John Libbey, London and Paris.
Dahlén, P. (1991) *Sport/TV – anteckningar kring ett försummat forskningfält*, Stockholm University.
— (1992) *Notes on Swedish Television Sport and 'Imagined Community'*, paper presented at the Workshop on Communication, Media and Identity, Grenoble, September 1992.
Dayan, D. and Katz, E. (1987) 'Performing Media Events', in Curran, J. et al (eds.) *Impacts and Influences: Essays in Media Power in the Twentieth Century*, Methuen, London.
Davies, P. (1990) *All Played Out: The full story of Italia 90*, Heinemann, London.
Deeley, P. (1987) Sport and TV, *Sportsweek*, no. 20, 29 January 87.
Donnelly, P. (1988) 'Sport as a site for Popular "Resistance"', in Gruneau, R. B. (ed.) *Popular Culture and Political Practices*, Garamond Press, Toronto.
Dyson, K. and Humphreys, P. (eds.) (1990) *The Political Economy of Communications: International and European Dimensions*, Routledge, London.
Forsyth, R. (1990) *The Only Game: The Scots and World Football*, Mainstream Publishing, Edinburgh.
Geraghty, C., Simpson, P., Whannel, G. (1986) 'Tunnel Vision: Television's World Cup', in Tomlinson, A. and Whannel, G. (eds.) *Off The Ball: The Football World Cup*, Pluto, London.
Goldlust, J. (1987) *Playing For Keeps: Sport, the Media and Society*, Longman Cheshire, Melbourne.
Hargreaves, J. (1986) *Sport, Power and Culture: A social and historical analysis of sports in Britain*, Polity Press, Cambridge.
Harvey, D. (1990) *The Condition of Postmodernity*, Blackwell, Oxford.
Hauser, T. (1988) *The Black Lights: Inside the World of Professional Boxing*, Pan Books, London.
Hebdige D. (1988) *Hiding in the Light*, Comedia, London
Hill, J. (1989) *Out of his Skin: The John Barnes phenomenon*, Faber and Faber, London.
Hoberman, J. M. (1984) *Sport and Political Ideology*, Heinemann, London.
Hobsbawm, E.J. (1990) *Nations and Nationalism since 1780*, Cambridge University Press, Cambridge.
Holt, R. (1990a) *Sport and the British*, Oxford University Press, Oxford. (original hardback 1989)
— (ed.) (1990b) *Sport and the working class in Britain*, Manchester University Press, Manchester.
Jarvie, G. (1991) *Highland Games: The making of the myth*, Edinburgh University Press, Edinburgh.
Jones, S. G. (1992) *Sport, politics and the working class*, Manchester University Press, Manchester. (original hardback 1988)
Keleher, R. (1989) Getting to Grips with a Question of Sport, in *Marketing Week*, 7 April 89.
Laclau, E. and Mouffe, C. (1985) *Hegemony and Socialist Strategy*, Verso, London.
Lever, J. (1983) *Soccer Madness*, University of Chicago Press, Chicago.

Lyotard, J.F. (1988) *The Differend: Phrases in Dispute* Manchester University Press, Manchester.

Mandle, W. F. (1987) *The Gaelic Athletic Association and Irish Nationalist Politics 1884–1924*, Gill and Macmillan, Dublin.

Mason, T. (1988) *Sport in Britain*, Faber and Faber, London.

McNair, B. (1988) *Images of the Enemy*, Routledge, London.

Morris, B.S. and Nydahl, J. (1985) 'Sports Spectacle as Drama: Image, Language and Technology', *Journal of Popular Culture*, vol 18:4, Spring.

Morse, M. (1983) 'Sport on Television: Replay and Display', in Kaplan, E.A. (ed) *Regarding television: Critical Approaches – an anthology*, American Film Institute.

Murdock, G. (1989) 'Tearing Down the Wall', *New Statesman and Society*, 25 August 89.

Mulgan, G. (1989) 'A thousand beams of light', *Marxism Today*, April.

Nairn T. (1981) *The Break-up of Britain*, 2nd edition, NLB/Verso, London.

— (1988) *The Enchanted Glass*, Radius, London.

— (1990) *The Modern Janus – the new age of nations*, Radius, London.

Negrine, R. and Papathanassopoulos, S. (1991) 'The Internationalisation of Television', *European Journal of Communication*, vol. 6.

Norris, C. (1990) *What's Wrong with Postmodernism*, Harvester Wheatsheaf, Hemel Hempstead

— (1992) *Uncritical Theory: Postmodernism, Intellectuals and the Gulf War*, Lawrence and Wishart, London.

Nowell-Smith, G. (1981) 'Television-Football-The World', in Bennett, T., Boyd-Bowman, S. et al (eds.) *Popular Television and Film*, BFI, London.

Poel, H. van der, (1991) 'Media policy in Europe: compromising between nationalism and mass markets', *Leisure Studies*, 10 (3), September.

Poster M. (1988) *Jean Baudrillard: selected writings*, Polity, Cambridge.

Rader, B.G. (1984) *In Its Own Image: How Television has Transformed Sport*, The Free Press, New York.

Real, M. R. (1977) *Mass-Mediated Culture*, Prentice-Hall, New Jersey.

Riordan, J. (1977) *Sport in Soviet Society*, Cambridge University Press, Cambridge.

— (1980) 'Sport in Soviet Society: Fetish or Free Play', in Brine, J., Perrie, M. and Sutton, A. (eds.), *Home, School and Leisure in the Soviet Union*, George Allen and Unwin, London.

Robins, K. (1989) 'Reimagined Communities? European Image Spaces, Beyond Fordism', *Cultural Studies*, 3 (2), May.

Rothenbuhler, E.W. (1988) The Living Room Celebration of the Olympic Games, *Journal of Communication*, Autumn.

Rowe, D. (1991) '"That Misery of Stringer's Cliches": Sports Writing', *Cultural Studies*, 5 (1), January.

Rowland, W. and Tracey, M. (1988) 'The Breakdown of Public Service Broadcasting', *Intermedia*, vol.16 No. 4–6, Autumn 1989.

Scannell, P. (1989) 'Public Service Broadcasting and Modern Public Life', *Media, Culture and Society*, vol. 11 no. 2, April.

Schlesinger, P. (1987) 'On National Identity: some conceptions and misconceptions criticized', *Social Science Information*, 26, no. 2.

— (1991a), 'Media, the political order and national identity', *Media, Culture and Society*, 13: 297–308.

— (1991b), *Media, State and Nation: political violence and collective identities*, Sage, London.

Shaw, D. (1985) 'The Politics of "Futbol"', *History Today*, August.

Sugden, J., Bairner, A. (1993) *Sport, Sectarianism and Society in a Divided Ireland*, Leicester University Press, Leicester.

Thompson, J. B. (1990) *Ideology and Modern Culture*, Polity Press, Cambridge.

Toibin, C. (1992) 'It was ugly for a few moments it could have gone either way . . .', *Esquire*, May.

Tomlinson, A., Whannel, G. (eds.) (1986) *Five Ring Circus: Money, Power and Politics at the Olympic Games*, Pluto Press, London.

Tudor, A., (1975) 'The Panels', in Buscombe, E. (ed.) *Football on Television*, BFI Monograph, no.4 London.

Tunstall, J., Palmer, M. (1991) *Media Moguls*, Routledge, London.

Wagg, S. (1991) 'Playing the past: the media and the England football team', in, Williams, J., and Wagg, S. (eds.) *British Football and Social Change: Getting into Europe*, Leicester University Press, Leicester.

— (1984) *The Football World: A Contemporary Social History*, Harvester, Brighton.

Walvin, J. (1986) *Football and the decline of Britain*, Macmillan, London.

Whannel, G. (1983) *Blowing the Whistle: the politics of sport*, Pluto Press, London.

— (1984) Fields in Vision: Sport and Representation, *Screen*, 25 No. 3.

— (1992) *Fields in Vision: Television Sport and Cultural Transformation*, Routledge, London.

Williams, J., Wagg, S. (1991) *British Football and Social Change: Getting into Europe*, Leicester University Press, Leicester.

Williams, R. (1977) *Marxism and Literature*, Oxford University Press, Oxford.

Wilson, J. (1988) *Politics and Leisure*, Unwin Hyman, London.

INDEX